ALTERNATIVE APPROACHES
to the STUDY
of SEXUAL BEHAVIOR

ALTERNATIVE APPROACHES
to the STUDY
of SEXUAL BEHAVIOR

Edited by

Donn Byrne
Kathryn Kelley

*State University of New York
at Albany*

LEA LAWRENCE ERLBAUM ASSOCIATES, PUBLISHERS
1986   Hillsdale, New Jersey   London

Lawrence Erlbaum Associates, Inc., Publishers
365 Broadway
Hillsdale, New Jersey 07642

Library of Congress Cataloging-in-Publication Data
Main entry under title:

Alternative approaches to the study of sexual behavior.

 Bibliography: p.
 Includes index.
 1. Sex — Research — Addresses, essays, lectures.
2. Sex (Psychology) — Research — Addresses, essays,
lectures. I. Byrne, Donn Erwin. II. Kelley, Kathryn.
HQ60.A47 1986   155.3   85-27528
ISBN 0-89859-677-7

Printed in the United States of America
10 9 8 7 6 5 4 3 2 1

Contents

List of Contributors

J. Gayle Beck
University of Houston

Donn Byrne
State University of New York at Albany

William A. Fisher
University of Western Ontario

Gordon G. Gallup, Jr.
State University of New York at Albany

Edgar Gregersen
Queens College, City University of New York

Kathryn Kelley
State University of New York at Albany

Kathleen McKinney
Oklahoma State University

Raymond C. Rosen
Rutgers Medical School U.M.D.N.J.

Dolf Zillmann
Indiana University

1 Introduction: The Study of Sexual Behavior As a Multidisciplinary Venture

Donn Byrne
State University of New York at Albany

Over the centuries, science has evolved as a process combining simple curiosity, the satisfaction provided by being able to make accurate predictions about events, and the power that resides in the ability to manipulate and control any aspect of our universe. Altogether, the assumptions and procedures of scientific activity have proved to be the most successful of all human enterprises in terms of providing understanding, prediction, and control.

It is tempting to describe scientific activity as an objective and selfless search for truth. Successful scientists often express a less grandiose view of their endeavors, however. Edward Teller has suggested that research "is a game, is play, led by curiosity, by taste, style, judgment, intangibles," and Albert Einstein proposed that the goal of science is "to keep the scientist amused" (Byrne, 1971). Scientists are humans first, and individuals involved in even the most glorious of quests may also be motivated by such mundane factors as greed, desire for fame, and envy of fellow scientists. Watson's (1968) description of the race for the discovery of the structure of DNA is an insider's view of the way in which this intellectual game may also be seen as a hard-driving competitive undertaking with resultant honors and sinecures that are every bit as alluring as an Olympic medal, political office, or monetary gain.

Individual scientists are also guided, held back, enlightened, and/or misled by what they have learned as citizens influenced by cultural beliefs, societal norms, religious dogma, political ideology, familial bonds, and so forth. Newton thought of the calculus as a way to demonstrate God's existence in that He obviously must have produced an orderly world. Some of Darwin's greatest difficulties involved an internal struggle to reconcile the empirical evidence he examined first-hand with what his religion taught about creation, the age of the

1

earth, the Flood, and the unchanging nature of geography, flora, and fauna. Galileo was forced by the Church to recant his correct, though heretical, views about the way in which the solar system functioned. Lysenko's incorrect belief about the transmission of acquired characteristics across generations was much more compatible with Marxist theory than was any potentially elitist view of the power of genes and chromosomes. Throughout history, the ideas and behaviors of scientists have been affected by multiple nonscientific factors, and the reaction of others to the fruits of science have been even more strongly affected by such factors.

If these general truths apply to the study of astronomy, biology, genetics, and even to the creation of mathematical tools, they have also been strikingly evident in the study of sexuality. Sex is sufficiently powerful, personal, and private that each of us is, by definition, a front-row observer of at least some of the phenomena in question. In addition, sexual behavior has been the focus of more religious and legal prescription and proscription than most other human functions. The emotional difficulties attendant on all aspects of sexuality are illustrated by the response to Michelangelo's marble statue of a nude, resurrected Christ that was commissioned in 1514. For almost 500 years, the public has been protected from viewing the marble genitalia on this statue by the addition of a bronze loincloth (Steinberg, 1984). Among the travails of those attempting to study human sexual behavior were the rejection of Freud by most of his fellow physicians, the vilification of Kinsey, the threats made against Masters' offspring, and the F.B.I.'s categorization of Bullough as a "subversive."

It follows that anyone with the desire to investigate sexuality must work within the context of myths, taboos, legal restrictions, emotional inhibitions, fears, and ethical constraints. Imagine for a moment three sexologists raised in somewhat different settings. One comes from Khomeini's Iran and learns from childhood that the penetration of a vagina by a penis causes both partners to become impure and that the milk of a sodomized cow, ewe, or camel may not be consumed (Hendra, 1984). A second was raised on the repressive Irish island of Inis Beag, where *Time* magazine is considered pornographic and marital intercourse takes place only infrequently under cover of darkness with underclothing left on (Messenger, 1971). A third investigator grew up in the sexually permissive atmosphere of Elcho Island, near the Australian coast, where nudity is common and adults think it is amusing for children to sing about and give playful demonstrations of nigi nigi—sexual intercourse—(Money, Cawte, Bianchi, & Nurcombe, 1970). One might guess that the scientific inquiries of these three scientists would differ in a dramatic fashion.

In some respects, the most surprising aspect of the scientific study of sex is the fact that it has taken place at all, that theories have been formulated and tested, and that empirical data have accumulated in a rapidly accelerating fashion over the last century. What is known about sexuality in the 1980s is light years in advance of what was known in the 1950s, not to mention what was known prior to 1900.

Keeping in mind the numerous societal and personal biases and barriers involved in studying sexual behavior, we now turn to the partially analogous difficulties raised by the fact that several independent scientific disciplines have undertaken the task (Allgeier, 1984). Different fields of science often use totally different methodologies, are guided by completely different conceptual systems, and are likely to seek quite different types of data. Note that no hierarchical distinctions are implied—no better–worse, central–peripheral, or even basic–applied—simply *different*.

ONE ELEPHANT, BLIND INVESTIGATORS, NO MAHARAJA

There is an often quoted children's fable about five blind men (it was a fable spun prior to our awareness of sexism) who examined an elephant in an attempt to make sense of this previously unknown creature. The one who felt the trunk obtained a particular set of data that was unlike that obtained by the one who felt the tusks, and so on. Those men and women who have studied various aspects of sexuality over the past decades closely resemble those apocryphal blind investigators. One who records case histories of deviants provides different data from one who determines the anatomical and physiological components of arousal and orgasm. One who examines differences in foreplay and copulatory positions across cultures is dealing with quite different evidence than one who manipulates exposure to various types of pornographic stimuli in order to discover their effect on subsequent emotions, attitudes, intentions, and behavior. Questionnaires that reveal sex and social class differences tell us something only distantly related to studies of the therapeutic effects of guided fantasy on orgasmic dysfunctions. Studies of sexual excitement and its expression in other species seem not to overlap with the study of the guilt and phobic reactions learned by human beings with respect to masturbation, nudity, and the verbalization of erotic concepts.

These and endless other possible examples suggest that the study of sex engages platoons of "blind men and women" who bring back seemingly unrelated bits and pieces of the total phenomenon—either as factual material or in the form of specialized explanatory theories. Is sexuality as elusive as the elephant? The economist Martin Feldstein (1983) has taken the fable one step further. He points out that an intelligent potentate who carefully studied the findings of his five subordinates could probably assemble an acceptable model of this strange pachyderm.

Sexology may still be waiting for someone to play the role of grand amalgamator, but that individual can be expected to benefit from the efforts of behavioral scientists such as those who contributed to this volume. The chapters that follow provide far more than narrowly isolated views of sexual functioning. It should be noted that we asked the contributors to focus on specific aspects of sex research, but it should clearly not be assumed that they are unaware of or unappreciative of other aspects of such research. It may detract from the analogy with the elephant fable, but each contributor is, in fact, much closer in functioning to the maharajah than to those narrowly trying to make sense of limited parts of the unseen animal.

APPROACHES TO THE SCIENTIFIC STUDY OF SEX

Probably the case history was the earliest approach to the study of sex (Byrne & Kelley, 1984), and medical practitioners were usually at the forefront of this work. Beginning in the 19th century, observers such as Krafft-Ebing (1886/1894), Ellis (1899/1936), and Freud (1905/1962) obtained detailed accounts of what others did sexually, what they thought and felt, and even what they dreamed and daydreamed. The reasons for accumulating these voluminous details of individual lives ranged from the desire to construct a taxonomy of deviancy to the belief that such data would provide the basis for understanding all of human behavior. Whatever one's views as to the utility of case histories, it can be agreed that those who first used this approach acted as pioneers who helped bring sexual functioning into the bright light of acceptable scientific inquiry.

The investigation of sex soon expanded beyond the novelistic tone of case histories. The six chapters that follow provide examples of how sexuality is studied and also a summary of some of what is known at this point in the development of the field. The contributions may be conceptualized as falling into three general scientific modes: biosexology, sociosexology, and psychosexology.

Biosexology

The biological basis of sexual functioning is conceptualized in two complementary ways. As shown by Gallup in chapter 2, it is possible to attain greater understanding of human behavior by examining the behavior of other species. The overriding conceptual set is that any genetically determined physical or behavioral characteristic that facilitates reproductive success will be more likely to be retained in subsequent generations than those entities that do not. Thus, much of what is observed in contemporary human sexual expression—from sex differences in promiscuity to the worldwide prevalence of nocturnal intercourse—can be explained in terms of the way in which such behavior has played an historic role in enhancing reproductive success. Those working within this sociobiological framework recognize that some characteristics may be successful in evolutionary cul-de-sacs and yet be unrepresented in the anatomy or behavior of most other species. An example is the insect, *Plecia nearctica,* 47% of whose 120-hour lifespan is spent mating (Male lovebug, 1984). It is also acknowledged that learning occurs; human beings are obviously not genetically programmed to behave in unvarying patterns of behavior. Nevertheless, many biosexologists stress the biological substrate that has a directive influence on which responses we make to which stimulus conditions; in effect, broad limits are set by our evolutionary heritage, and our learned behavior varies within those limits.

Shifting from an historical–biological perspective to a contemporary one, other investigators focus on the physiological aspects of sexual response, as described by Rosen and Beck in chapter 3. Human sexuality may be interwoven with love and many other splendored things or with hate and other totally non-splendored things, but in either event it also remains a matter of some quite specific physical structures and functions. With respect to arousability, arousal, and orgasm, the sexual response cycle can be envisioned as a complex anatomical arrangement involving vasocongestion, lubricatory fluids, myotonia, and electrophysiological discharge.

Laboratory research on these physical aspects of sexuality seems to have begun at Johns Hopkins University when John B. Watson and a female research assistant served as participant observers in a short-lived project (Magoun, 1981). Unfortunately for the rapid progress of sex research, this venture was not appreciated by either Mrs. Watson or the university administration. By the time that Masters and Johnson (1966) engaged in infinitely more defensible research in St. Louis several decades later, it was at last possible to begin documenting and disseminating the details of male and female sexual physiology. As is pointed out in chapter 3, one important aspect of this research involves the technological advances that permit the assessment of each of the multifaceted components of the physiology of sex (cf. Geer, 1980; Jovanovic, 1971; Kelley & Byrne, 1983; Zuckerman, 1971). It should be noted in passing that the endocrinological aspects of sex were purposely omitted from this chapter because they will be described in detail in a related volume (Kelley, in press).

Sociosexology

If biosexology can be characterized as emphasizing the similarities across species and among individuals, sociosexology takes a different conceptual set and emphasizes the differences. In a well-established anthropological tradition, Gregersen in chapter 4 points out the value of examining the variations in sexual behavior across cultures. For one thing, each of us tends to assume that one's own attitudes, beliefs, values, and customs are normal and natural, whereas those of other cultures are odd, disgusting, or at best "interesting" and "quaint." The importance of experience versus biological determinism is suggested when it is discovered that kissing is an expected practice in many cultures and unknown in others or that the modal position used in intercourse varies across groups living in different parts of the world. Polynesians of both sexes expect the female to have an orgasm, whereas a male in an isolated Irish community could only interpret this strange phenomenon in a female tourist as an epileptic seizure (Messenger, 1971). From the prospect of anthropological data, it is difficult to conceptualize "natural" sexuality as involving much beyond tactual stimulation of the genitals accompanied by the physiological processes described by Rosen and Beck. Most of the additional sexual cues to which we respond, our assumptions about what is acceptable to do with whom, and the precise activities in which we engage are primarily a matter of what we have learned in the specific culture in which we live.

Sociologists, as exemplified by McKinney in chapter 5, take the observations of behavioral differences a step further. Especially in large, complex, highly developed societies, there are variations across subgroups in that sexual behavior depends in part on one's social class, age, race, sex, and other demographic factors. There is also an attempt by sociologists to document the way in which group members acquire their particular sets of beliefs, attitudes, and ways of behaving. Research is most likely to involve either observing what people do in everyday settings or asking them about their sexual lives by means of interviews and surveys. The general public first acquired detailed knowledge of the sexual mores of their fellow citizens from the survey studies beginning with Davis (1929), Hamilton (1929), Terman, Buttenwieser, Ferguson, Johnson, and Wilson (1938), and Kinsey (Kinsey, Pomeroy, & Martin, 1948; Kinsey, Pomeroy, Martin, & Gebhard, 1953) and continuing with Reiss (1960), Hunt (1974), and major circulation magazines ranging from *Redbook* to *Playboy*. The individuals engaged in such research have not always been sociologists, but the methodology is a product of that field. Sociological theorists have also developed extensive ways of conceptualizing how our behavior, beliefs, and interactions are patterned by norms expressed in scripts and roles. Our seemingly spontaneous activities thus represent the enactment of culturally assigned parts in an ongoing, real-life miniseries.

Psychosexology

Extending the sociological tradition of focusing on what individuals do and the detailed way in which behavior is acquired and modified, psychologists such as Fisher in chapter 6 often focus on the learning process. If much of human sexual functioning is learned, it is important to understand those variables that determine what is learned and how the behavior of individuals depends on their specific experiences. In addition, there is increasing emphasis among psychologists on the fact that we learn more than behavior, beliefs, and attitudes. There is also concentration on the importance of affective responses, expectancies, and fantasies. Not only do such processes affect overt behavior, but they also serve as sources of motivation. In addition, these "psychological" processes can have profound effects on such "physiological" events as arousal and orgasm. The conceptual emphasis on sexual behavior as the product of learning leads to another emphasis—the possibility of changing behavior by means of interventions ranging from education to therapy.

Chapter 7 presents an intriguing theoretical formulation by Zillmann, who consolidates a number of themes in this volume. The scope ranges from neurophysiological and endocrinological considerations of the interrelations among intense emotions to the way in which physiological arousal is cognitively processed. At the center of this conceptualization is the empirically documented proposition that arousal based on nonsexual events can be "transferred" under specific conditions such that sexual excitement is facilitated and hence intensified. Among other considerations, it is pointed out how anger, fear, pain, disgust, and other emotional states can play a central role in sexual motivation and performance.

In the final chapter, Kelley returns to the theme of integrative sex research that is briefly discussed in the following section.

INTEGRATING DIVERSE APPROACHES TO SEXUALITY

Though the study of sexuality has not yet become a mature field of science with its own methodological and theoretical paradigm, it might at least be helpful to suggest the way in which seemingly diverse approaches can be fit into the same schema. No special claims are made for the schema in question, but the general point to be made is that biosexual, sociosexual, and psychosexual research can be combined within a single framework. They are complementary rather than in conflict, and together they provide an integrative picture of human sexual functioning.

It has been suggested (Byrne, 1977, 1982) that sexuality can be studied in terms of a series of cross-sections, each constituting a sexual behavior sequence. As shown in Fig. 1.1, any given sequence involves a series of constructs consisting of stimulus events (external, environmental influences—both learned and unlearned), internal processes (emotional, informational, imaginal, and physiological processes), overt behavior (both instrumental acts and goal responses), and an outcome that may be rewarding, punishing, or neutral. These behavioral consequences influence subsequent sequences in that they feed back into the system and change the valence of stimulus events, arouse specific positive and negative emotions, provide new information, alter expectancies, and so forth.

As an illustration of the descriptive uses of the model, consider an example. A married man is out of town on a business trip and at the end of a busy day stops at his hotel bar for a drink before going up to his room. Sipping a scotch at the bar, he is startled when the hand of a female sitting on an adjoining stool gently grazes his inner thigh. This *unlearned sexual stimulus* (touch) combined with several *learned cues* (her perfume, clothing, smile, etc.) elicit the first stages of a physiological response in that vasocongestion begins to occur. In a simpler species, a sequence begun in this way would almost always lead directly to sexual intercourse. With humans, however, five other processes are simultaneously activated. Each one can contain positive or negative forces that make

EXTERNAL STIMULI   INTERNAL PROCESSES   OVERT BEHAVIOR

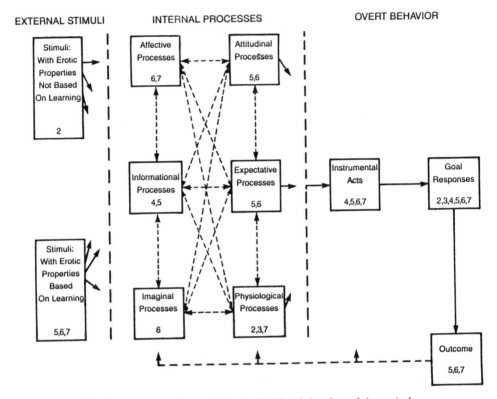

FIG. 1.1.   One theoretical model that has both heuristic value and, increasingly,
predictive utility is the Sexual Behavior Sequence. In its most general form, it
describes a unit of sexual behavior (both instrumental acts and goal responses) as a
function of external stimuli (both learned and unlearned) and internal processes
(affective, attitudinal, informational, expectative, imaginal, and physiological).
The positive or negative outcome of any behavior sequence feeds back into the
system, often causing alteration, and hence influences subsequent sequences. The
extent to which different research traditions focus on different aspects of sexual
functioning is suggested by the numbers in each box that correspond to the chapters in this book.

sexual activity more or less likely to occur. The man's *emotional state* is generally positive in that he enjoys being the target of this stranger's desires and enjoys
the prospect of a sexual interaction. When he thinks of his promises to his wife,
negative affect is also aroused in the form of guilt. His *attitudes* about sex are
very positive whereas those dealing with infidelity are quite negative. At the
same time, his *cognitions* are also activated. He knows how pleasurable sex can
be, but he is also aware of the possibility of contracting a sexually transmitted
disease from this unknown individual—the traditional ones or the as yet incur-
able Herpes II. There are also other considerations such as the possibility that this

woman is a criminal with plans to rob him or that she is a vice cop with plans of entrapment. In addition, there is the possibility that his wife will somehow discover what he did and will be sufficiently hurt or angry as to discontinue their marriage. Each of these *expectancies* involving positive and negative outcomes can be assigned a probability estimate (How likely is it to occur?), and a value can be placed on each outcome (How positive is sexual pleasure and how negative is a disease, robbery, etc.?). These various beliefs, expectancies, and values each exert an influence on the possible behavioral outcomes in a way outlined by various theorists (e.g., Fishbein & Azjen, 1975; Rotter & Hochreich, 1975). Finally, there are *fantasies* evoked by the situation—imagined scenes of pleasure and erotic stimulation that add to his arousal and increase his motivation to respond positively to her overtures. There also can be imagined scenes of negative eventualities that are behaviorally inhibiting.

What does he actually do? The answer depends on the relative magnitudes of the various internal and external forces that are operating with respect to this specific individual at this specific time. If the negative forces predominate, he will resist temptation and end this sexual behavior sequence. If the positive forces predominate, he will proceed with various *instrumental acts* (e.g., asking her to his room) that increase the probability of a *goal response* (e.g., sexual interaction). The *outcome* of this completed sequence (positive or negative, short-term or long-term) will affect his future responses to similar situations.

It should not be assumed, by the way, that this is simply a descriptive model that allows us to identify some of the variables that are operating in a given situation and to "understand" what happened by offering post hoc explanations once the behavior has occurred. In a growing body of recent research, it has been possible to assess the content and magnitude of stimulus events (e.g., Greendlinger & Byrne, 1985), affective state (e.g., Byrne, Fisher, Lamberth, & Mitchell, 1974), attitudes (e.g., Fisher, Byrne, & White, 1983; Smeaton & Byrne, 1985), beliefs (e.g., Aguero, Bloch, & Byrne, 1984), expectancies (e.g., Fisher, 1978), fantasies (e.g., Greendlinger & Byrne, in press), and physiological arousal as indicated by self-reported self-descriptions of physiological responses as well as direct assessment of physiological responses (e.g., Geer, 1975; Kelley, Miller, Byrne, & Bell, 1983; Przybyla & Byrne, 1984; Przybyla, Murnen, & Byrne, 1985: Steinman, Wincze, Sakheim, Barlow, & Mavissakalian, 1981). These variables, in turn, have been utilized to predict subsequent overt behavior, including use of contraceptives (Fisher, Byrne, Edmunds, Miller, Kelley, & White, 1979; Kelley, Smeaton, Byrne, Przybyla, & Fisher, 1984), response to a homosexual stranger (Aguero, Byrne, & Heslin, 1984), proclivity to commit rape (Greendlinger & Byrne, in press), self-regulated exposure to erotic stimulation (Becker & Byrne, 1985), and sexual satisfaction of spouses (Byrne & Becker, 1985). It is proposed that with sufficient knowledge of genetic influences, past experiences, the resulting internal processes, and current stimulus events, all of the sexual acts of an individual could be predicted with greater than chance accuracy.

This particular model may be utilized to encompass the various approaches to understanding sexuality that are described in the following chapters. As indicated by the chapter numbers in the boxes in Fig. 1.1, all approaches represented here are interested in sexual behavior; it is in the other constructs of the model where differences in focus become apparent. It is hoped that the juxtaposition of these approaches in books such as this will encourage each of us to look beyond a single scientific focus in viewing human sexuality. As a relatively typical social psychologist in this respect, I must confess to all too frequently succumbing to the tendency (as Gallup phrases it) to pay lip service to genetic influences—and to cultural and physiological ones as well. A broadened perspective could be expected for all of us if there were an increase in interdisciplinary research (Allgeier, 1984).

Given the growing interest in research on sexuality, the rapid development of appropriate methodologies, the avalanche of empirical data, and the generation of new theoretical formulations (e.g., Abramson, 1982; Mosher, 1980; Storms, 1981; Zillmann, 1983), the future of this field is both exciting and an occasion for scientific optimism.

REFERENCES

Abramson, P. R. (1982). *The sexual system: A theory of human sexual behavior.* New York: Academic Press.

Aguero, J. E., Bloch, L., & Byrne, D. (1984). The relationships among sexual beliefs, attitudes, experience, and homophobia. *Journal of Homosexuality, 10,* 95–107.

Aguero, J. E., Byrne, D., & Heslin, R. (1984). *The effects of attitude similarity on heterosexual dislike of homosexuals.* Manuscript submitted for publication.

Allgeier, E. R. (1984, April). *State of the science: Sex research—contrasts and compliments.* Paper presented at the meeting of the Eastern Region of the Society for the Scientific Study of Sex, Philadelphia.

Becker, M. A., & Byrne, D. (1985). Self-regulated exposure to erotica, recall errors, and subjective reactions as a function of erotophobia and Type A coronary-prone behavior. *Journal of Personality and Social Psychology, 48,* 228–235.

Byrne, D. (1971). *The attraction paradigm.* New York: Academic Press.

Byrne, D. (1977). Social psychology and the study of sexual behavior. *Personality and Social Psychology Bulletin, 3,* 3–30.

Byrne, D. (1982). Predicting human sexual behavior. In A. G. Kraut (Ed.), *The G. Stanley Hall lecture series* (Vol. 2, pp. 207–254). Washington, DC: American Psychological Association.

Byrne, D., & Becker, M. A. (1985, March). *Sexual interaction as a function of husbands' and wives' sexual attitudes.* Paper presented at the meeting of the Eastern Psychological Association, Boston.

Byrne, D., Fisher, J. D., Lamberth, J., & Mitchell, H. E. (1974). Evaluations of erotica: Facts or feelings? *Journal of Personality and Social Psychology, 29,* 111–116.

Byrne, D., & Kelley, K. (1984). The role of case histories in psychosexology. In P. R. Abramson (Ed.), *Sarah: A sexual biography* (pp. 1–12), Albany, NY: SUNY Press.

Davis, K. B. (1929). *Factors in the sex life of 2,200 women.* New York: Harper & Row.

Ellis, H. (1936). *Studies in the psychology of sex.* New York: Random House. (Originally published in 1899.)

Feldstein, M. (1983). *Inflation, tax rules, and capital formation.* Chicago: University of Chicago Press. Reading, MA: Addison-Wesley.

Fishbein, M., & Azjen, I. (1975). *Belief, attitude, intention, and behavior. An introduction to theory and research.* Reading, MA: Addison-Wesley.

Fisher, W. A. (1978). *Affective, attitudinal, and normative determinants of contraceptive behavior among university men.* Unpublished doctoral dissertation, Purdue University, West Lafayette.

Fisher, W. A., Byrne, D., Edmunds, M., Miller, C. T., Kelley, K., & White, L. A. (1979). Psychological and situation-specific correlates of contraceptive behavior among university women. *Journal of Sex Research, 15,* 38–55.

Fisher, W. A., Byrne, D., & White, L. A. (1983). Emotional barriers to contraception. In D. Byrne & W. A. Fisher (Eds.), *Adolescents, sex, and contraception* (pp. 207–239). Hillsdale, NJ: Lawrence Erlbaum Associates.

Freud, S. (1962). *Three contributions to the theory of sex.* New York: Dutton. (Originally published 1905.)

Geer, J. H. (1975). Direct measurement of genital responding. *American Psychologist, 30,* 415–418.

Geer, J. H. (1980). Measurement of genital arousal in human males and females. In I. Martin & P. H. Venables (Eds.), *Techniques in psychophysiology* (pp. 431–458). New York: Wiley.

Greendlinger, V., & Byrne, D. (in press). Coercive sexual fantasies of college males as predictors of self-reported likelihood to rape and overt sexual aggression. *Journal of Sex Research.*

Greendlinger, V., & Byrne, D. (1985). *Dispositional variables as predictors of emotional and evaluative responses to heterosexual and homosexual films.* Manuscript submitted for publication.

Hamilton, G. V. (1929). *A study in marriage.* New York: Boni.

Hendra, T. (Ed.). (1984). *Sayings of the Ayatollah Khomeini: Political, philosophical, social, and religious (The little green book).* New York: Bantam.

Hunt, M. (1974). *Sexual behavior in the 1970s.* Chicago: Playboy Press.

Jovanovic, U. J. (1971). The recording of physiological evidence of genital arousal in human males and females. *Archives of Sexual Behavior, 1,* 309–320.

Kelley, K. (Ed.). (in press). *Females, males, and sexuality.* Albany, NY: SUNY Press.

Kelley, K., & Byrne, D. (1983). Assessment of sexual responding: Arousal, affect, and behavior. In J. Cacioppo & R. Petty (Eds.), *Social psychophysiology* (pp. 467–490). New York: Guilford.

Kelley, K., Miller, C. T., Byrne, D., & Bell, P. A. (1983). Facilitating sexual arousal via anger, aggression, or dominance. *Motivation and Emotion, 7,* 191–202.

Kelley, K., Smeaton, G., Byrne, D., Przybyla, D. P. J., & Fisher, W. A. (1984). *Predicting contraceptive behavior across divergent college populations.* Manuscript submitted for publication.

Kinsey, A. C., Pomeroy, W., & Martin, C. (1948). *Sexual behavior in the human male.* Philadelphia: W. B. Saunders.

Kinsey, A. C., Pomeroy, W., Martin, C., & Gebhard, P. (1953). *Sexual behavior in the human female.* Philadelphia: W. B. Saunders.

Krafft-Ebing, R. von. (1894). *Psychopathia sexualis.* Philadelphia: F. A. Davis. (Originally published 1886.)

Magoun, H. W. (1981). John B. Watson and the study of human sexual behavior. *Journal of Sex Research, 17,* 368–378.

Male lovebug. (1984 May 5). Believe it or not. *Albany Times–Union.*

Masters, W., & Johnson, V. E. (1966). *Human sexual response.* Boston: Little, Brown.

Messenger, J. C. (1971). Sexual repression: Its manifestations. In D. S. Marshall & R. C. Suggs (Eds.), *Human sexual behavior* (pp. 14–20). Englewood Cliffs, NJ: Prentice-Hall.

Money, J., Cawte, J. E., Bianchi, G. N., & Nurcombe, B. (1970). Sex training and traditions in Arnhem Land. *British Journal of Medical Psychology, 43,* 383–399.

Mosher, D. L. (1980). Three dimensions of depth of involvement in human sexual response. *Journal of Sex Research, 16*, 1–42.

Przybyla, D. P. J., & Byrne, D. (1984). The mediating role of cognitive processes in self-reported sexual arousal. *Journal of Research in Personality, 18*, 54–63.

Przybyla, D. P. J., Murnen, S., & Byrne, D. (1985). *Emotional arousal and sexual attraction: Misattribution versus anxiety reduction*. Manuscript submitted for publication.

Reiss, I. (1960). *Premarital sexual standards in America*. New York: Free Press.

Rotter, J. B., & Hochreich, D. J. (1975). *Personality*. Glenview, IL: Scott, Foresman.

Smeaton, G., & Byrne, D. (1985). *The relative importance of erotophobia-erotophilia, loneliness, and situational variables in predicting male contraceptive use*. Manuscript submitted for publication.

Steinberg, L. (1984). *The sexuality of Christ in renaissance art*. New York: Pantheon/October Book.

Steinman, D. L., Wincze, J. P., Sakheim, D. K., Barlow, D. H., & Mavissakalian, M. (1981). A comparison of male and female patterns of sexual arousal. *Archives of Sexual Behavior, 10*, 529–547.

Storms, M. D. (1981). A theory of erotic orientation development. *Psychological Review, 88*, 340–353.

Terman, L. M., Buttenwieser, P., Ferguson, L. W., Johnson, W. B., & Wilson, D. P. (1938). *Psychological factors in marital happiness*. New York: McGraw-Hill.

Watson, J. D. (1968). *The double helix*. New York: Atheneum.

Zillmann, D. (1983). *Connections between sex and aggression*. Hillsdale, NJ: Lawrence Erlbaum Associates.

Zuckerman, M. (1971). Physiological measures of sexual arousal in the human. *Psychological Bulletin, 75*, 297–329.

2 Unique Features of Human Sexuality in the Context of Evolution

Gordon G. Gallup, Jr.
State University of New York at Albany

There have been a number of recent attempts to characterize the role of evolution in human sexuality (e.g., Daly & Wilson, 1983; Symons, 1979). The purpose of this chapter, however, is to examine some distinctive features of human sexual behavior and anatomy from the standpoint of adaptive considerations related to the evolutionary history of our species.

EVOLUTION

Evolution is of interest for more than just historical reasons. It is an ongoing process in which we are each involved, wittingly or not. The part we play in evolution is largely predicated on our sexual behavior. None of us would be here if it were not for sex. If at any point in the past our ancestors had stopped having sex the human race would have disappeared.

Rather than being represented by "the survival of the fittest," evolution is based on the perpetuation of the most viable reproductive configurations of genes. As most people conceive of it, survival of the fittest is a tautology or what amounts to an instance of circular reasoning. Consider why one species survived while members of another went extinct. As traditionally conceived, the answer would be that the survivors were more fit. But how do you know they were more fit? Because they survived! All of which is tantamount to saying that they survived because they survived, and the concept of fitness is superfluous.

Psychology is replete with tautologies. Why does the rat press the bar in a Skinner box? Because it has been reinforced to do so. But how do you know it has been reinforced? Because it is pressing the bar! Thus, in an analogous way, it is pressing the bar because it is pressing the bar. The problem is that reinforcement has not been defined independent of the behavior it is supposed to explain. Survival is not the central issue of evolution. No one survives forever. Death is an inevitable consequence of life. Life, in one sense, is a terminal disease. Likewise, common sense notions of fitness have little or nothing to do with evolution. You could be the fittest person imaginable—in terms of strength, vitality, intelligence, and so on—but if you do not reproduce, or at least behave in ways that contribute to the reproductive success of relatives, your contribution to evolution is zero.

For our purposes, the best way to conceptualize evolution is to think of what happens in terms of gradual changes in the composition of a gene pool over time. A gene pool is a hypothetical conglomerate of all the genes carried by members of a particular species. Indeed, different species can be thought of as being represented by nonoverlapping gene pools, whereas members of the same species share enough genes in common that they can breed and reproduce. Evolution implies change, and the basis for all such change is genetic. Changes that may occur in individuals as a result of environmental influences (e.g., body building, face lifts, obtaining a Ph.D., or being circumcised) are not genetically transmittable. Much of what we strive to achieve in a lifetime is of indirect consequence at best. The key to evolution is differential or nonrandom reproduction. If every individual in a population has an equal chance of reproducing with every other individual, and who bred with whom was random, then the composition of a gene pool would remain static over time. Only if certain individuals leave more or fewer descendants than others will there be any change. Sex is the final common path for all evolutionary change. The composition of a gene pool at any particular point in time can be thought of as a consequence of the reproductive success of the immediately preceding generation. In order for anything to evolve, it has to contribute directly or indirectly to reproductive success. Such success, however, is not defined merely by the number of offspring you produce, but rather by the number of offspring that your offspring produce, and so on.

Instead of being an issue of your survival or mine, evolution is based on the survival of the gene. Which came first, the proverbial chicken or the egg? The egg did. In an evolutionary sense a hen can be thought of as an egg's way of producing another egg. The hen is nothing but a transient, protoplasmic superstructure that provides for the perpetuation of genes. From the standpoint of biology, the principle purpose in life is to reproduce. Failure in an evolutionary sense is defined by not passing on your genes.

Contrary to the impression many people have, evolution does not occur by design. It is not a purposive, deductive process. The reason it may appear to be driven by some grand plan is that all we typically see are the instances of success. Yet of all the species that have ever existed, fewer than 1% are alive today. Evolution occurs by selection, rather than by design, and the raw material for such selection is genetic accidents. Selection is neither a conscious, an intentional, or a deliberate process. Certain genetic accidents merely enhance the chances of reproductive success and therefore get perpetuated. Others detract from the chances of gaining genetic representation in subsequent generations and disappear. Unlike trial-and-error learning, evolution cannot profit from its mistakes. Mistakes are genetic dead ends.

Thus, rather than being defined by the survival of the fittest, selection can be thought of more precisely as a correlation between genotype and reproductive success. Whether the correlation is positive or negative determines the extent to which the trait becomes more or less prevalent. It is important to realize that in either case, it is not the size of the correlation that counts. As long as it remains in effect long enough, the end result will be the same. The size of the correlation simply determines the rate of selection. If the correlation between the genotypic basis for some trait and reproductive success was 1.0, there would be complete selection for the trait in one generation. That is, all surviving members of the population in the next generation would be carrying that trait. On the other hand, even if the correlation was a mere .001, if it remained in effect long enough, practically all members of the population, somewhere far down the line, would eventually carry the genes for that trait.

Evolution presupposes two things: individual differences, based on genetic variation, and nonrandom reproduction. Differences among people, whether physical or psychological, are the raw material for evolutionary change. Not only is there variation among species, but more important, there is variation within species. With the possible exception of monozygotic twins, no two people look alike, think alike, or have exactly the same set of interests. God did not create all men equal, Thomas Jefferson did. Genetic variation defines the limits of evolutionary change, but not the direction. The direction of such changes is a consequence of environmental factors that favor one genetic configuration over another.

Exemplars

Perhaps the best way to illustrate evolutionary principles is to examine their applicability to some tangible cases.

Increasingly more and more people succumb to cancer. As cancer becomes an ever more frequent cause of death, what are its long-term evolutionary consequences likely to be? Substantial individual differences in susceptibility to cancer have a genetic basis. Does that mean that there will be selection against those people showing greater degrees of susceptibility or vulnerability to carcinogens? Probably not. Most forms of cancer do not appear until after one's reproductive years are about over; that is, most people die of cancer in their 50s and 60s, not in their 20s or 30s. Therefore, whether you die of cancer, heart attack, or old age is of little consequence. We all die. Only if different forms of cancer begin to affect people at earlier ages and thereby impinge on their reproductive success will there be any direct basis for selection. One could always argue that a parent's dying prior to his or her offspring's achieving adulthood could affect their fitness and as a consequence could be a basis for selection. Although that may have been true during human evolution, presently, particularly in this country, it is much less likely to have a significant impact with all of the social support and entitlement programs.

Consider homosexuality as another case in point. Why do people become homosexual? The theories range from problems in early socialization and gender identification, to hormonal and neurochemical imbalances, to the notion that homosexuality might be a genetic trait. If homosexual inclinations were genetic, what would be the fate of such genes? In the case of exclusive homosexuality, those genes would never get passed on and therefore would disappear from the gene pool. Other things being equal, reproductive success (at least for males) ought to be directly proportional to the frequency of heterosexual intercourse. This even applies to instances in which people use various birth control devices. Short of sterilization, no device is completely effective. Thus, even if people partitioned their lives into both homosexual and heterosexual pursuits (as in the case of bisexuals), their relative genetic contributions to subsequent generations would be less than that of heterosexuals, and as a consequence the proportion of such genes in the population would diminish over time. To the extent that an individual might distribute or time-share his or her sexual activity among both heterosexual and other pursuits, one's reproductive success would be reduced in proportion to the amount of reproductive effort expended in other than heterosexual encounters. Unless homosexual tendencies were to somehow contribute to reproductive success, they would have disappeared long ago if they had a genetic basis. Homosexuality in the context of evolution is discussed at a later point. Suffice it to say, for the time being, that as far as homosexuality is concerned it is sexuality (not the prefix) that has a genetic basis.

Finally, consider the consequences of making birth control devices freely available in underdeveloped countries around the world in a would-be humanitarian effort to help them cope with runaway population explosions. To be effective, most birth control devices require careful, conscientious use coupled with a knowledge of their appropriate application. It is not unreasonable to assume that it takes some minimal level of intellectual ability to use birth control devices effectively. Therefore, people who lacked the intellectual wherewithal to deploy such techniques correctly would, other things being equal, have a reproductive advantage over those who did, and as a result would make a disproportionately greater genetic contribution to subsequent generations. In other words, there would be selection against those who had the capacity to use birth control devices effectively.

GENETIC INFLUENCES VERSUS GENETIC DETERMINATION

Some readers may not react well to the foregoing examples. After all, everyone knows that intellectual functioning has nothing to do with genes. Right? Wrong. It is inconceivable that reliable differences among individuals along any dimension, psychological or otherwise, could be free from genetic influences. Although an attempt to explain behavior exclusively in terms of genes would and should be dismissed as naive, it is important to realize that the same holds true for an environmental approach. When it comes to identifying the sources of any particular behavior, social scientists have often been guilty of dichotomizing the world. Things are rarely that simple. Genetic and environmental influences always combine to determine behavior. Behavior is not determined by environmental effects or by genes. Each influence presupposes the other. Environmental factors merely exert an influence, which in one sense is only made possible by genes. Environmental effects on behavior presuppose an organism, and the existence of organisms presupposes genes.

In order to affect behavior an environmental event must impinge on a receptor surface and be encoded in the form of a neuronal message that travels over afferent pathways to some part of the central nervous system, where it then gets translated into an efferent impulse that terminates at an effector organ and activates a change in behavior. Much of the activity that intervenes between stimulus and response is a consequence of the genetic makeup of the organism in question. Although genetic and environmental influences may vary from organism to organism and situation to situation, it is inconceivable that either could ever equal zero. There has never been an instance in which selective breeding based on a behavioral trait has failed to produce an effect (Hirsch, 1967). The existence of any organism presupposes both genes as well as an environment, and either set of influences never operate independent of the other. Although most psychologists pay lip service to genetic effects, many continue to act as if they did not exist (e.g., Epstein, Lanza, & Skinner, 1981). To focus on one set of influences while ignoring the other is like trying to calculate the area of a field based on its width but not on its length.

Inclusive Fitness

The real breakthrough in evolutionary theory came with the realization that the unit of selection is the gene, not the individual. Your *inclusive fitness* is represented by your net genetic representation in subsequent generations. Whether any of your genes find their way into the next generation is not only a reflection of your individual reproduction success, but it will also be influenced by the reproductive efforts of your kin. For example, you share approximately 50% of your genes in common with your brother. Therefore, if your brother has a child it will be carrying 25% of your genes and those will count toward your net genetic representation.

According to evolutionary theory, if you found yourself in a situation in which your father and your brother were drowning and you could only save one or the other, even though you may share the same proportion of genes in common with both, you should opt to save your brother. The reason for this prediction is simple. If your brother were saved, he may survive to have children of his own, which would contribute to your inclusive fitness. Saving your father, however, would be less likely to enhance your long-term genetic best interests. Indeed, because of paternal uncertainty you and your brother have a better chance of sharing genes in common than you and your ostensible father (see section on Optimal Heterosexual Strategies). You have no guarantee that your father is in fact your father. Thus, if the choice were between your father and your mother, you should save your mother.

Coupled with the notion of cost/benefit ratios, the concept of inclusive fitness provides a compelling account of why organisms do certain things. Take bystander apathy as a case in point. Psychologists have agonized over this phenomenon for some time. Bystander apathy is represented by a situation in which someone is being robbed, mugged, or raped, and bystanders witnessing the episode do nothing to help the victim or even summon aid from authorities. Aid giving or helping behavior always involves a reproductive risk. Consider the following hypothetical examples in order of the degree of such risk. Helping a little old lady across a busy intersection. There is a chance, albeit remote, that you could be run over in the process. What about breaking up a fight? You could easily become involved in the fight as a consequence and sustain serious injury. Or, what about jumping into the icy waters of the Potomic River to save drowning victims of an airline crash? Clearly, you could die in the process. Putting yourself at risk at someone else's behalf only makes sense evolutionarily when viewed in terms of cost/benefit ratios. If someone were being mugged or raped, intervention on your part would entail considerable risk and therefore a high cost. Whether you are willing to incur such a risk ought to be intimately related to the status of your inclusive fitness and the characteristics of the victim.

Evolutionary theory would predict that bystander apathy ought to be most prevalent under conditions in which the victim is unknown to the witnesses and, therefore, the chances of ever having the favor repaid (*reciprocal altruism*) is remote. For instance, the probability of witnesses remaining apathetic should be much higher in a big city than in a small rural community. Similarly, it is unlikely that you would remain passive if the victim were a close friend or relative. In the former case reciprocal altruism would be the deciding factor, whereas in the latter your inclusive fitness would be at stake.

From the standpoint of evolution the only kinds of genes that can ever evolve are selfish ones (Dawkins, 1976). Individuals who forego their own reproductive best interests in favor of enhancing the reproductive potential of other unrelated individuals will be selected against. In order to survive, apparent instances of altruistic behavior have to ultimately be selfish. Genes being carried by persons who consistently behave in ways where the cost exceeds the benefit are doomed to oblivion. Scratch an altruist and watch a hedonist bleed.

Random Reassortment

In the case of sexually reproducing species, each parent contributes half of their genes to an offspring. Gamete formation is based on a process called *meosis,* in which half of the number of available chromosomes are carried by each sperm and each egg. Underlying this process is a phenomenon called *random reassortment,* which means that each time a new gamete is formed the genes it carries will be drawn randomly from all those available (this is an ideal case of what statisticians call *random sampling* with complete replacement). It is for this reason brothers and sisters only share half of their genes in common. Even though they have the same father and mother, on the average only half of the genes being carried by any given spermatophore will be carried by any other, and the same holds true for eggs. Thus, sibling resemblance will be the sum of .25 and .25 or 50%. Although it is theoretically possible for two siblings conceived at different times to be genetically identical, it is equally possible, but just as unlikely, for two full siblings to share none of their genes in common. Either of these cases is extremely remote, and statistically the best estimate is always 50%.

The role of random reassortment in gamete formation has some interesting implications. Through reproduction you do not pass on all of your genes, only some of them. Table 2.1 details the statistical estimate of an individual's proportinate genetic representation in the next generation as a function of the number of offspring generated. With each succeeding child, the number of genes not already represented declines precipitously, and by the time a person has seven children over 99% of all their genes will have been transmitted. In effect, by producing seven or more children you achieve what amounts to the statistical equivalent of an extended clone.

Although some sociobiologists have argued that behaving in ways that allow each of two siblings to have a child would be equivalent to having one of your own, the role of random reassortment precludes this from happening. Although it is true that each of their offspring will be carrying 25% of your genes this does not equal 50% because the genes you share in common with your siblings are independent. Indeed, two siblings, just like two of your own children, will be carrying only 75% of your genes, therefore, the total of your genes being carried by nieces or nephews conceived by each of your two siblings will only amount to 37.5%. Even if your brother, with whom you share 50% of your genes, had 10 children the total of your genes being represented would be slightly less than 50% (this would remain true even if he had 100 children).

Table 2.1
What Proportion of Your Genes Will Be Represented?

Number of Offspring	Proportion of Genes Not Previously Represented	Total Representation
1	.50	.50
2	.25	.75
3	.125	.875
4	.0625	.9375
5	.03125	.96875
6	.015625	.984375
7	.0078125	.9921875

OPTIMAL HETEROSEXUAL STRATEGIES

In spite of what various factions might have us believe about how sex differences in behavior are simply due to social and cultural influences, there is no such thing as equality when it comes to reproduction. The genetic best interests of males and females are so different that one writer (Symons, 1979) was prompted to conclude that for a member of one sex to adopt the reproductive strategy of the opposite sex would be tantamount to a ticket to reproductive oblivion.

There is a basic and irreconcilable conflict between males and females in terms of their respective roles in evolution. When it comes to inclusive fitness, the best interests of females serve to constraint those of males, and vice versa. When viewed in the context of competition for inclusive fitness there may very well be a biological rather than merely a cultural basis for the sexual double standard. Table 2.2 depicts the three dimensions that are central to an understanding of why males and females have evolved to practice conflicting reproductive strategies. First, consider the question of genetic assurance, or conversely paternal uncertainty. Females have what amounts to an iron-clad guarantee of sharing 50% of their genes in common with each of their offspring. Even if the female does not know who the father is (as a consequence of being unconscious when conception occurred or being promiscuous), she still can be assured that her baby is carrying half of her genes. Males, on the other hand, confront a much different set of circumstances—males can be cuckolded.

Cuckoldry gets it name from the cuckoo bird, which is a parasitic egg layer. The female cuckoo bird lays an egg in the nest of another species, and because the egg resembles those of the other bird it is cared for and nutured by the host species. In other words, the bird of another species is duped into caring for and raising an offspring other than its own. Because of the ever present possibility of adultery or rape, males of any species that provision females and offspring run a similar risk. This has led to some bizzare anti-cuckoldry tactics among humans, ranging all the way from the use of chastity belts to infibulation. The latter

Table 2.2
Gender-specific Differences
in Optimal Heterosexual Strategies

	Females	Males
Genetic Assurance	Complete	Uncertain
Biological Commitment	Awesome	Negligible
Reproductive Potential	Low	High

consists of sewing the labia together in such a way that they grow together and have to be cut open to allow intercourse (see Daly, Wilson, & Weghorst, 1982).

The second and most obvious difference between males and females involves the degree of parental investment required for procreation. Males do not get pregnant. When it comes to reproduction females pay the freight. In terms of sex there is no such thing as "dutch treat." Because of her basic biology, the female must bear the burden of pregnancy, childbirth, and lactation. Females also typically assume primary responsibility for child care and child rearing. As such, reproduction requires an awesome commitment from females. In stark contrast, the male's role in many species is limited to serving solely as a source of sperm. Sperm are a dime a dozen, but eggs are scarce. Males produce hundreds of thousands of sperm on a daily basis. Human females, on the other hand, only release one egg per month. Moreover, unlike males, infant survival presupposes that mammalian females will live with and care for the consequences. Therefore, when it comes to mate selection the effects of having made a poor choice fall squarely on the shoulders of females. Because of these kinds of considerations it is reasonable to assume that females have been selected to be careful comparison shoppers when it comes to picking a mate. Given the biological commitment that will be required of her, she can ill afford to risk that investment on a mate that might be carrying genetic deficiencies.

Finally, as we have already implied, there is an enormous difference between the sexes in their reproductive potential. Males produce billions of sperm in a lifetime and, if given sexual access to enough ovulating females, could father hundreds of offspring. The situation for females is again quite different. Among human females ovulation occurs only once a month and there are no obvious external cues that can be used to index her ovulatory status (see section on Concealed Ovulation). Moreover, because gestation lasts for nine months and lactation creates hormonal changes that tend to inhibit ovulation (e.g., Anderson, 1983), the practical upper limit for reproduction among women would amount to 12 to 15 offspring in a lifetime. The period of time during their lives that females remain reproductively viable is also truncated, relative to that of males, even though they live longer. Many men continue to produce viable sperm until they die. Whereas the reproductive capacity of males only tapers off with age, in women it comes to a rather abrupt halt usually in the early to mid-40s. Thus, human females are fertile for only about 50% or less of their lives.

The cessation of reproductive activity among females, or what is called *menopause,* is a good illustration of how selection has operated differentially on males and females. Maternal age, but not paternal age, is correlated with a number of deleterious reproductive side effects, such as fetal deaths, fetal abnormalities (e.g., Down's Syndrome), and even maternal deaths attributed to childbirth or pregnancy. Because the risks associated with reproduction increase with age among females, a point where the costs incurred begin to outweigh the benefits is eventually reached, and females who underwent menopause would have had the advantage of being able to continue to provide for surviving offspring as well as invest in grandchildren and thereby protect and fortify their existing investment.

In this context, it is curious to note that females are born with all the eggs they will ever have. Unlike spermatogenesis, ovulation involves the release of a preformed egg. Ovulation does not involve egg production. Each human ovary contains approximately 1 million eggs, the vast majority of which never get used. Given that the average female ovulates about once a month over a period of 30 years (assuming she never gets pregnant), that involves the release of fewer than 400 eggs or far less than even 1% of the total. How are we to explain such an anomaly? It is fine to have a reserve, but this borders on the ridiculous. Evolution is a conservative process. Things do not typically evolve unless they are needed. Perhaps such an enormous surplus of eggs is a vestige from a point in our very distant evolutionary past when our forebearers used to litter, or maybe even spawn. The fact that the female is born with all the eggs she will ever have may be the underlying reason for the correlation between fetal abnormalities and maternal age. Unlike males who are producing sperm all the time, the female's eggs are subjected to low levels of ambient radiation from the time she is born until she conceives, the effects of which may cumulate with age to the point of producing genetic damage.

Now we can refer back to Table 2.2 to consider how all this translates into differences between males and females in terms of strategies for optimizing their genetic representation in subsequent generations. Because females have complete assurance about their genetic relationship to offspring, but must make an awesome biological investment, and have only a very limited reproductive potential, they have been selected to emphasize careful discrimination when it comes to mate selection. Females can maximize their chances of gaining genetic representation by selecting a mate with high genetic quality who is willing to make a long-term commitment to provisioning the female and her offspring.

Although the existence of female promiscuity might seem to undermine this analysis, it is important to emphasize that individual differences are the raw material of evolution. Modal characteristics or normative behaviors are those that most clearly reflect the influence of evolution. Promiscuous women are the exception, not the rule. Prior to the advent of civilization the sexually indiscriminate female would have been at a distinct disadvantage. Being unable to identify the father of her offspring and/or being seen as a cuckoldry risk by males in general, she would probably not have received the paternal aid and caregiving behavior, as well as other resources, which would have been essential for infant survival and child rearing. Although females cannot be cuckolded, they can be abandoned. Although not true now, 100,000 years ago abandonment could have had devastating consequences for a female and her offspring.

For males the situation is quite different. Never knowing for certain that their ostensible offspring are indeed their own, but being required to make much less of an investment in procreation and having an almost unlimited reproductive potential, males have been selected to attempt to copulate with many females on a high frequency basis. The faithful, but cuckolded male would lose the entire genetic ball of wax when it comes to evolution.

In the case of humans, evolutionary theory would predict that when it comes to mate selection, females should attempt to postpone copulation for purposes of assessing mate quality and making a judgment about the male's willingness to enter into a long-term relationship for purposes of provisioning. Males, on the other hand, should be motivated by relatively immediate sexual gratification. Thus males may have been selected to be effective at perpetrating instances of deception, by way of feigning good intentions and a commitment, for purposes of gaining sexual favors (i.e., "I love you, so let's go to bed"). Females, however, under such conditions would have been selected to detect deception and make judgments about the fidelity of an intent to form a lasting relationship. All of which might account for the so-called women's intuition or sixth sense. Indeed, one testable implication of such differential selection would be that males should be better than females when it comes to deception, but females should be superior to males when it comes to detecting deception. It would be interesting to test this hypothesis using a paradigm modeled after the once-popular television program entitled "To Tell the Truth." By varying the gender of the actors and the audience one should be able to demonstrate sex differences in the ability to perpetrate and detect deception if this hypothesis is correct.

The Role of Female Choice

Among many vertebrate species, copulation occurs as a consequence of female invitation or choice. That this is consistent with evolutionary principles should come as no surprise because females have to "pick up the tab" when it comes to reproduction. Because of their limited potential females cannot afford to make many reproductive mistakes.

Along what dimensions do females make reproductive choices? Among many species it is correlated with the position of males in the dominance hierarchy. The Wyoming sage grouse is an excellent case in point (Allee, 1938). A few weeks prior to the breeding season, the males congregate in areas called strutting grounds where they fight with one another for status. As a result of this competition about 1% of the males can be clearly identified as occupying the position of alpha or most dominant, and another 2% are next in line or what are known as beta males. After these contests are over the females arrive on the scene to take stock of the available males, who all frantically display in an attempt to attract a mate. In sage grouse (as is true of many species) copulation only occurs on the basis of female invitation. Careful recordings of who breeds with whom reveal that during a single breeding season 74% of all matings involve alpha males, and 13% involve beta males. Therefore, 87% of the entire crop of baby sage grouse are being fathered by a mere 3% of the male population! Although not quite as extreme, similar instances of a few males inseminating a disproportionately large number of females has been reported for a variety of other species (e.g., LeBoeuf & Peterson, 1969).

The advantage to females in being so selective should be apparent. Because the position of males in the dominance hierarchy is pretty much a direct reflection of strength, stamina, and vitality, favoring such males enhances the female's chances of producing offspring that will exhibit similar traits and stand a good chance of passing on their genes. Contrary to popular opinion, males may not in actuality compete among one another for females. Rather, they compete among one another for dominance which, in turn, provides greater access to females.

Goodall (1971) has described an intriguing instance among chimpanzees of a male's rise to dominance that has some interesting implications for humans. One day she saw a subordinate male pick up a pair of empty kerosene cans from around her camp, and proceeded to climb a hill that overlooked an area where a group of dominant males were eating bananas that had been set out as bait. Having reached the top of the hill, the chimpanzee proceeded to charge down the hill running directly at the other animals while banging the cans together. Startled by the clamor, the males dropped their bananas and ran for cover. Not only did this prove to be a highly effective technique for intimidating physically superior animals and gaining access to food, but as a consequence the innovator became the alpha male. Under certain circumstances, therefore, intellectual prowess can supplant physical powess as a means of achieving upward mobility and status in a dominance hierarchy. This is clearly the case among humans, and may provide a clue as to the reason for the rapid expansion of man's cranial capacity during the past several million years.

In an unpublished survey of college students, (Gallup & Suarez, 1983c), we found data that bear directly on the issue of mate selection among humans. College students were asked to respond to two questions. "What physical characteristics of members of the opposite sex do you find most attractive?" "What psychological characteristics of members of the opposite sex do you find most attractive?" In response to the second question, the traits most frequently mentioned by females were intelligence and a sense of humor. Among males, in response to the first question, the leading indicator of sexual attraction were breasts, and the reason for this becomes apparent in a subsequent section (see Permanent Breast Enlargement). But suffice it to say that females respond in ways that may place them at the cutting edge of the selective pressure that gave rise to our formidable brains.

Indeed, the role of female choice may very well be a deciding factor in dictating a variety evolutionary change. In many respects males are nothing but an evolutionary experiment being run by females. Except for providing a complimentary set of gametes the male's role in reproduction is frequently negligible. Therefore, although females are in effect calling the shots when it comes to evolution, it is important to recognize that this cuts both ways. If there are male traits that some females find objectionable (e.g., domineering) they have no one to blame but themselves and their female predecessors.

Sexual Pleasure

If at least one of your parents had not found sex pleasurable, you probably would not be here. Sexual appetite and sexual pleasure can be thought of as evolutionary adaptations, or what are called proximate causes that provide for appropriate timing and reoccurrence of sexual activity.

The frequency with which different organisms engage in sex varies from once in a lifetime to many times per day. The Pacific salmon is a good illustration of the former case. The eggs of the Pacific salmon (of which there are five species) hatch in fresh water streams (or lakes that empty into streams), and the fingerlings eventually migrate downstream and wind up in the ocean. There they remain and grow for 2 to 5 years. Once they achieve sexual maturity they return to the stream where they were hatched and travel back to approximately the same place they started. Males and females pair off and spawn, the female beating a depression in the bed of the stream with her tail and the male positioning himself slightly upstream so that the semen will drift over and fertilize at least some of the thousands of eggs she deposits in the nest. Within only a few days after spawning both participants die.

For an organism where reproduction is a once in a lifetime opportunity, there need to be powerful motivational mechanisms that ensure for a high probability of mating. If you have only one chance at genetic perpetuation you cannot afford to miss it. Indeed, for Pacific salmon that encounter obstacles (such as dams that have been erected for purposes of generating hydroelectric power) on their migratory trip back upstream it is not uncommon for them to continue to jump, plunge, and smash into the obstruction until they literally kill themselves in a futile effort to complete the spawning run. So even though the motivation to spawn must be intense, it can be argued that salmon probably experience no intrinsic sensory pleasure from the act of spawning. Although it is very important that they spawn, there is no need to have any provisions for the reoccurence of the reproductive act because they die shortly afterward. In other words, pleasure derived from sex is only important for species that need to engage in sex more than once. If you could sire as many as several hundred or even thousands of offspring on a single occasion, it would not be essential to do it very often.

Orgasm, therefore, can be thought of as an evolved neurological capacity that serves to make the reoccurence of sexual activity a fairly high probability event for species with low reproductive rates. Thus, we can derive two generalizations about the degree to which sexual behavior should be accompanied by sexual pleasure across different species. In principle, sexual pleasure should be inversely proportional to reproductive rate. Humans, for example, have very low reproductive rates. People typically have only one offspring at a time. Gestation takes nine months, breast feeding lasted for 3 or 4 years (prior to the availability of alternative forms of nursing) and children remain parent dependent for 12 years or more.

The other factor that needs to be considered in terms of trying to build a predictive model of the extent to which different species should find sex pleasurable is the question of synchrony. With a few notable exceptions, involving females of species (such as bats, seagoing turtles, and some insects) that can store sperm in a viable state for prolonged periods, copulation needs to occur in close temporal proximity to ovulation in order to achieve conception. Different species synchronize these two events in different ways. Among seasonal breeders, reproductive activities are triggered by hormonal changes that occur in response to changes in the photoperiod. In other species, ovulation is accompanied by cues that serve to advertise that condition to males. As any dog owner can testify, female dogs, for example, produce olfactory cues that attract males and incite sexual arousal. Among chimpanzees, ovulation is accompanied by swelling and color changes in the female's anal-genital region that have a powerful effect on males by way of producing sexual attraction. Humans, however, represent a fundamentally different case. Human females produce no observable cues that can be used by males for purposes of synchronizing copulation with ovulation. In the absence of any means of detecting ovulation the only effective means of achieving synchrony is through frequency. Therefore, in species that do not signal ovulation, one would expect to find high rates of copulation driven by powerful proximate causes related to sexual pleasure.

The Rare Male Mating Advantage

Contrary to the way most people have been taught to think about it, evolution does not appear to have occurred in a continuous or gradual fashion. A careful reading of the fossil record reveals the presence of sudden, sporadic changes interspersed by periods of relative equilibrium (Eldridge & Gould, 1972). In one sense, discontinuity is the order of the day among biological phenomena. Not only has evolution proceeded in an erratic stepwise fashion, but few if any existent species are ancestral to one another. For instance, we did not evolve from chimpanzees or vice versa. Humans and chimpanzees are related only by virtue of sharing a common ancestor that is now extinct. Even different species, as defined by nonoverlapping gene pools, represent fundamentally discontinuous distinctions.

One way to account for this stepwise feature to evolution is in terms of the rare male mating advantage. If, within a particular population, a mutant male should appear that is distinctively different from other males, and this difference is one that females find attractive, then because of the greater reproductive potential of males in general, that male and his progeny could rapidly infuse the mutant configuration of genes into the gene pool so as to provide for the "sudden" appearance of a new trait. Consider blue eyes among humans. Eye color is invariant across all racial groups except caucasians. Only among caucasians is eye color anything other than brown. If among the caucasians indiginous to Europe many thousands of years ago, there appeared a male with blue eyes, that trait could have conferred such an advantage. The fact that it no longer operates in this way is probably a consequence of the fact that the trait has been so widely diffused that it is now commonplace. Yet, even now if you ask females to indicate their favorite color among the four primary colors, blue is named more frequently than any other (Gallup, 1984).

Concealed Ovulation

As already noted, human females are concealed rather than signalled ovulators. One cannot walk into a class and tell which coeds are ovulating or about to ovulate, yet within a group of chimpanzees it would be obvious at a glance.

A variety of interpretations have been advanced to account for the fact that ovulation in humans is not accompanied by any external cues. One of the most popular was put forth by Burley (1979). She argues that ovulation is not only indetectable by others but it is concealed even to the female who is ovulating. According to her hypothesis, the reason ovulation became indetectable in humans was a consequence of the realization among women that childbirth was painful, and therefore those who could detect ovulation and avoided intercourse during periods when the likelihood of conception was high were selected against, leaving only those in which ovulation was not accompanied by any cues.

Although this might sound plausible, on closer inspection it may be shown untenable. In the first place, we have no evidence that ovulation is accompanied by internal cues in any species. Moreover, implicit in Burley's (1979) hypothesis is the assumption that the relationship between intercourse and conception was widely known and appreciated during the course of human evolution. Yet, if you think about it, the discovery that sex is the basis for procreation is no mean task. Although there is a correlation between intercourse and conception, it is very small. Copulation among adolescents is less likely to result in pregnancy because adolescent females are often anovulatory (see section on Permanent Breast Enlargement). Likewise, intercourse with menopausal females, menstruating females, pregnant women, and lactating females is unlikely to result in conception. In addition, sperm viability is short lived. Intercourse at any point in the menstrual cycle other than plus or minus 12 hours of ovulation is unlikely to produce conception. Many people have sex on a regular basis for months or even years but do not conceive. Indeed, some people have had sex all their lives but remain childless. Furthermore, the same kind of ambiguity applies to conception itself. Whether conception has occurred does not become obvious for weeks or even months afterward, which further complicates and obscures the relationship between conception and copulation. As support for the notion that this realization was achieved only very recently in evolutionary time, there are groups of primitive people even now who see no connection between copulation and reproduction and believe that conception occurs as a result of spiritual intervention (Malinowski, 1929).

To my mind one of the most plausible accounts of why ovulation became concealed in humans was the need to ensure for continuous male provisioning. If humans were signalled ovulators, the only time females would have been the object of male attention was when they were ovulating. Becoming concealed ovulators allowed females to extract provisioning from a male on a more or less continuous basis and provided a means of accommodating high levels of male sexuality. Concealed ovulation also raises the spector of paternal uncertainty by providing females with a means of cuckolding their mates. Although a male might be able to sequester his mate in such a way as to preclude access by other males for a few days each month, clearly this cannot be done on a continuous basis. It is also important to acknowledge that because ovulation is cued by anal-genital swelling in many primates, the adoption of an upright posture would have favored the survival of females who were not hampered by such a motorically cumbersome means of advertising ovulation (see Gallup, 1982).

Permanent Breast Enlargement

Humans are the only species where females show breast enlargement beginning in puberty that is independent of lactation. Among most mammals, breast enlargement is occasioned only by lactation. Why should humans be unique in this respect? Is this merely an anatomical anomaly or does it have some kind of functional significance?

It is important to acknowledge at the outset that the size of the nonlactating breast bears no relationship to the quantity or quality of milk a woman is capable of producing should she become pregnant and have a child (Anderson, 1983). In order to put this issue in perspective there are essentially two questions that need to be answered: (a) Why do human females have enlarged breasts? and (b) why do males find breast enlargement sexually attractive? Although there have been several attempts to account for breast enlargement, they focus exclusively on the first question. Morris (1967), for instance, argues that breasts mimic buttocks and that they have evolved to compensate for the development of an upright posture and frontal or face-to-face sexual encounters. Morgan (1972) claims that breasts evolved as an appendage for infants to hold on to, whereas Frisch (1983) sees the breast as a cooling fin for dissipating body heat. It has been argued (Gallup, 1982) that even as far as the first question is concerned, the interpretations advanced by Morris and Morgan are flawed for a number of reasons, and as far as Frisch's hypothesis is concerned one would expect to find a comparable adaptation in males if heat dissipation was a critical factor. In what follows I attempt to summarize my own theorizing about breast enlargement in human females (see Gallup, 1982).

It would be well to start with the basis for the enlargement because therein lies a subtle clue as to the significance of the phenomenon. Figure 2.1 depicts the life-span developmental changes in the human breast. Note that the enlargement that begins during puberty is almost entirely a consequence of the localized accumulation of fat deposits. A programatic series of studies by Frisch (1975, 1978, 1980) has shown that there is an intimate relationship between stores of body fat and reproductive function in human females. It has been known for some time that the age of first menstruation among females entering puberty has been decreasing in the western world for the last 100 years (see Tanner, 1970). This has been attributed primarily to improved nutritional status. Frisch argues, however, that it is not a consequence of better nutrition per se, but rather that the daily caloric intake has increased and therefore females are accumulating critical stores of body fat at earlier ages. For example, Frisch has shown that the onset of menstruation requires that at least 17% of body weight be represented by body fat; that is, menarche is not a function of age per se but achieving a critical body fat to body weight ratio. This is why obese girls begin menstruating sooner than their nonobese counterparts (Frisch, 1980). Frisch has also found that ovulation in females does not begin until they have accumulated about 26% of their body weight in body fat. Therefore, the typical adolescent female who has begun to menstruate remains relatively infertile until additional stores of body fat are acquired. If the proportion of body fat on the part of an adult female ever drops below 22% of body weight, menstruation stops. In keeping with these data, it has been discovered that excessive loss of body fat due to vigorous exercise, such as jogging, can lead to anovulation (Frisch et al., 1981), and the same holds true for starvation (as in the case of women who suffer from anorexia nervosa).

Given the biological investment that is required for pregnancy and lactation, the relation between body fat and reproductive function appears highly adaptive. In the absence of adequate energy stores, and by implication reliable food supplies, pregnancy would not only be a risky proposition from the standpoint of the fetus, but the mother as well. Frisch (1983) estimates that the average young adult female with access to adequate nutrition has accumulated about 16 Kg of body fat, and contained therein are approximately 144,000 calories of stored

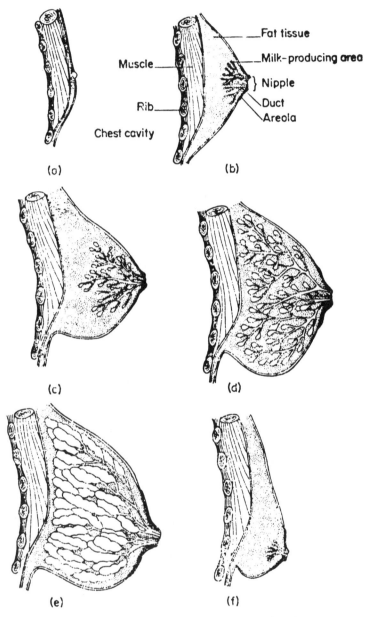

FIG. 2.1.   Changes in the female breast from preadolescence through menopause (from Gallup, 1982). (a) child; (b) adolescent; (c) adult; (d) pregnant adult; (e) lactating adult; (f) adult after menopause.

energy. To go full term, pregnancy requires 50,000 calories in excess of normal energy requirements, whereas lactation takes an additional 1,000 calories per day. Therefore, the typical woman has enough excess energy represented in fat reserves to sustain a successful pregnancy and about 3 months of lactation.

Although very interesting, the relation between body fat and reproduction does not, by itself, explain breast enlargement in human females. Fat can be stored in a variety of ways. Most mammalian species probably also have to acquire adequate energy stores before becoming fertile, yet we are the only ones to show permanent breast enlargement.

According to the theory I have developed, breast enlargement is a byproduct of concealed ovulation. In principle, the males of most sexually reproducing species should have been selected to copulate with females who have a high probability of ovulating. The emphasis, as we have already seen, is on synchronizing insemination with ovulation. Human females no longer produce obvious external cues that would allow males to index their ovulatory status. How has human evolution been affected by the absence of any apparent means of achieving synchrony in terms of gamete exchange?

There is another strategy, however, that is much like the one that can be employed by the sophisticated student on a multiple choice test. If confronted with an item for which you do not know the correct answer, one approach is to change your set and try to identify those alternatives that are incorrect. If you can rule out one or more as being wrong, you can substantially increase the probability of getting the right response even when you do not know the correct answer by guessing among the remaining alternatives. By analogy, being unable to detect ovulation, an alternative approach would be to identify and avoid making sexual investments in females who have a low probability of ovulating.

In fact, there are a number of discernable periods during which the probability of conception is greatly reduced in human females. Most females are relatively anovulatory prior to attaining sexual maturity and during periods of starvation. The same holds true for menstruation, pregnancy, lactation, and menopause. If there was a male who showed an exclusive preference for copulating with prepubertal, menopausal, or pregnant females it is doubtful that many of his genes would find their way into subsequent generations. Conversely, if males refrained from pursuing anovulatory females and focused their sexual interests on those who had a higher probability of ovulating that should translate into a reproductive advantage. However, if males have been selected against copulating with females during periods of anovulation that would presuppose the existence of reliable cues that could be used to index such periods. Table 2.3 details the different conditions of relative anovulation in human females and the primary cues associated with each state.

Ovulation stops during pregnancy. The most obvious way to tell if a female is pregnant is by the gradual enlargement of the abdomen and the loss of an ''hour glass'' figure. Not only is the frequency of intercourse lower during pregnancy

Table 2.3
Conditions of Relative Anovulation in Human Females

Condition	Cues
1. Pregnancy	Abdominal enlargement
2. Menstruation	Menstrual flow
3. Lactation	Augmentation of breast size
4. Menopause	Changes in breast configuration
5. Sexual immaturity	Absence of breast enlargement
6. Starvation	Loss of breast enlargement

(Tolor & DiGrazia, 1976), but most males are less attracted to females with abdominal enlargement (Hagen, 1979). When it comes to physical attraction, males are highly sensitive to weight distribution and female waist configuration (Lerner, Karabenick, & Stuart, 1973), which is consistent with the notion that men have been selected to prefer nonpregnant females as sex partners. Much the same appears true of the way males react to females who are menstruating. The primary cue of menstruation is the presence of menstrual flow, and males are much less likely to copulate with females during menstruation than at any point in the menstrual cycle (McCary, 1978; Udry & Morris, 1968). Indeed, among some cultural and religious groups intercourse is forbidden during menstruation.

In the context of this hypothesis, it is of more than passing curiosity to note that the principle cue to all of the four remaining conditions of anovulation in women depicted in Table 2.3 are changes in either breast configuration and/or breast size. Breast development during puberty is highly correlated with emerging reproductive function in females. In the absence of breast enlargement, either because of sexual immaturity or inadequate food supplies, the probability of ovulation remains low. Likewise, the change in breast shape and reduction in size that accompanies menopause (see Fig. 2.1) could be used to index the status of egg production. Thus enlarged breasts, by virtue of signalling ample energy stores and ovulatory potential, could function as a means of which males access (consciously or not) the probable reproductive status of females, and as such breast enlargement may compensate for concealed ovulation.

Are breasts a sexual appendage, as the present analysis would suggest, or do they merely exist to provide a source of nutrition for neonates? Although there are cultural differences in the value that men attach to different parts of the female anatomy, there is general agreement that the female breast is a universal sex symbol among human males (Wickler, 1972). Fondling and stimulation of the female breast is practically invariant across cultures as a prelude to intercourse (Ford & Beach, 1952). The sexual attraction that many males have to enlarged female breasts (e.g., Kleinke & Staneski, 1980; Wiggins, Wiggins, & Conger, 1968) is highly compatible with this model. If, in fact, breast development does function as a reliable cue to ovulatory potential, then during human evolution the males who showed a preference for copulating with such females would have had a clear reproductive advantage over those who were indifferent to enlarged breasts, or those who were repelled by enlarged breasts.

One obvious objection to this theory might be that the relationship between stores of body fat and reproductive function in females could just as easily produce selection for males who were attracted to obese females, as opposed to those merely exhibiting breast enlargement. There are at least two problems with this interpretation. First, obesity is almost invariably accompanied by abdominal enlargement, and therefore would serve to simulate pregnancy. Thus obesity can be viewed as a pregnancy mimic. Second, just as insufficient body fat can impair, retard, or even preclude reproductive function, the same appears to hold for obesity. Excessive body fat causes amenorrhea (Iizuka & Kawakami, 1968).

The one exception to the theory that breast enlargement evolved to compensate for concealed ovulation by signalling ample energy stores and ovulatory potential, is the additional augmentation in breast size that occurs prior to and during lactation (see Fig. 2.1). During lactation, endocrine function changes so that ovulation is initially inhibited, and the prevailing view of this effect is that it is an evolved means of achieving some semblance of birth spacing (Anderson, 1983; Daly & Wilson, 1983). The significance of a lactational augmentation of breast size might be that it served as a means of enhancing the pre- and postpartum pair bond and functioned to increase the likelihood of aid-giving by the male during a period in which provisioning would have been particularly crucial for infant survival.

Finally, there is the question of trying to anticipate future evolutionary change. If males have been selected to prefer sex partners with enlarged breasts, will breast enlargement in human females become even more exaggerated in succeeding generations? This is doubtful partly because of the fact that too much fat can interfere with reproductive function. It is also important to remember that changes in the shape and contour of the female breast tend to be associated with menopause (see Fig. 2.1). Thus, males have probably been selected to respond to breast shape as well as breast size. Selection for shape, therefore, may serve as a limiting factor on size. In fact, beyond a certain size there is evidence that breast enlargement ceases to have attractive properties (Kleinke & Staneski, 1980).

IMPACT OF BIPEDALISM ON HUMAN REPRODUCTION

In addition to concealed ovulation and permanent breast enlargement, humans are also unique among primates in terms of their sexual posturing during intercourse. Among most terrestrial forms, copulation occurs in the dorsal-ventral position with the male typically mounting the female from behind. Although humans can and occasionally do employ what amounts to an almost limitless variety of copulatory positions, the most prevalent is in the ventral-ventral mode with the female in a supine position and the male on top. The evidence suggests that among humans ventral-ventral copulation may be a unique adaptation to an upright posture.

The assumption of an upright posture and the use of only two limbs to affect locomotion (bipedalism) carries the advantage of freeing up the hands for a variety of other uses. But bipedalism also entails some very real reproductive hazards, not the least of which is sperm retention. Among quadrupeds that employ dorsal-ventral patterns of copulation the female reproductive tract is positioned parallel with gravity. However, for humans standing upright the situation is quite different. In an upright posture the vaginal tract is placed perpendicular to gravity and therefore poorly suited for sperm retention. In some species the male leaves a mucous plug as part of the ejaculate that serves to prevent sperm loss. Plugs are particularly advantageous for arboreal species, because climbing and brachiating frequently results in moments when the female reproductive tract is brought into a perpendicular orientation to gravity. Human males do not produce plugs. But contained in human ejaculate are mucous particles that apparently represent the vestigal remains of what used to be a plug (Quiatt & Everett, 1982).

In our view (Gallup & Suarez, 1983b) the significance of ventral-ventral copulation is that it brings the female reproductive tract back into a parallel position with gravity and thereby functions to increase the chances of sperm retention. Several aspects of human reproductive anatomy serve to bolster this hypothesis. For instance, the vaginal angle in human females has shifted in such a way as to make intromission easier in the ventral-ventral mode (Morgan, 1972) and it also maximizes the chances of sperm pooling in the vicinity of the cervix when the female is lying on her back (Masters & Johnson, 1966). Morris (1967) has called attention to the fact that humans are distinctive among primates in having the largest penis. As shown in Table 2.4, this is indeed the case relative to other great apes. We contend that this may also be an adaptation to an upright posture. The obvious advantage of a long penis is that it would provide for the release of sperm deep within the vaginal barrel so as to maximize sperm retention.

Because the resumption of an upright posture following copulation would endanger sperm retention, if our analysis is correct, you would expect to find some unique behavioral adaptations among humans that compensate for or at least postpone this eventuality. Although many writers continue to cling to the antiquated and specious notion that human females are unique in their capacity to experience orgasm (e.g., Anderson, 1983; Symons, 1979), data from nonhuman primates (reviewed by Allen & Lemmon, 1981) make it clear that many female monkeys and apes show responses that are virtually indentical to those exhibited by women during orgasm. Orgasm in human females, however, may also function to aid and abet sperm retention. Vaginal contractions during orgasm facili-

Table 2.4
Penis Length and Body Weight
among Great Apes and Humans

Species	Body Weight (kg)	Length of Erect Penis (cm)
Gorilla	169·0	3
Orang-utan	74·6	4
Chimpanzee	44·3	8
Human	65·7	13

Data from Short (1979) and Harcourt, Harvey, Larson, and Short (1981). Adapted from Gallup & Suarez (1983b).

tate sperm transport (Masters & Johnson, 1966), and it is widely acknowledged that orgasm frequently acts as a mild sedative that may serve to postpone the resumption of an upright posture.

Nocturnal copulation can also be understood in this context. If the incidence of copulation was randomly distributed across all hours of the day, we would predict that the probability of conception should be higher during the dark portion of the light cycle than at any other time. The reason for this is that, coupled with the sedative effects of orgasm, the latency to stand up following intercourse should be longer at night. Moreover, the capacity of human females to have multiple orgasms with no refractory period may likewise function to aid and abet the probability of remaining supine, and thus facilitate sperm retention and transport. Nocturnal copulation may have also functioned in other ways. Copulation in the ventral-ventral position entails certain risks. Among other things the participants would have been more vulnerable to predation in that the ability to continue to monitor the environment would be impaired as would the latency to engage in effective escape and predator evasion tactics. Thus copulation at night may represent a convergent solution that minimized vunlerability to predation and maximizes sperm retention.

Then there is the issue of concealed copulation. Imagine yourself as an intergalactic traveler, an intelligent life form but of another species, who visits planet earth for purposes of cataloging different life forms. In the process of developing such a taxonomy, one of the peculiar features of *Homo sapiens* that you might notice is the question of how they reproduce. Even after several weeks of careful observation it is unlikely you would witness even a single instance of copulation (when was the last time you were walking down the street and stopped to watch someone copulate?). In marked contrast with other species, human sexual activity almost invariably occurs in private (Ford & Beach, 1951). Millions upon millions of people are copulating every day, but few of us ever bear witness to it as anything other than participants. Copulation during the dark portion of the light cycle also serves to make such activity inconspicuous, and may have functioned to prevent other males from becoming aroused and attempting to mate with a female who had already developed a pair bond. This may also have some bearing on the widespread tendency of couples to sleep together. The significance of sleeping together, in addition to synchronizing insemination with a period in which the likelihood of remaining in a prone position is enhanced, is that it could have served as an anticuckoldry strategy. One testable implication of this hypothesis is that the incidence of sleeping together should drop dramatically at about the time a female reaches menopause.

HOMOSEXUALITY

The final topic we consider is homosexuality. As a result of paternal uncertainty and an almost limitless reproductive potential, males, as we have seen, have been selected to seek high-frequency sex with a variety of different females. Females, on the other hand, can maximize their inclusive fitness by holding out for loving, lasting, caring relationships that insure for provisioning. It should be apparent that because of these differences the best interests of females serve to constrain those of males and vice versa.

Homosexuality allows the gender differences in sexuality to stand out in relief because the participants have congruent sexual interests. In homosexuality we see the basic differences between male and female sexuality in a relatively pure and uncontaminated form (Symons, 1979). Indeed, as I show, the evidence strongly suggests that homosexuals continue to act out what would otherwise be optimal heterosexual strategies. The expression of sexuality in any context is bound by a biological imperative that the participants typically have no insight into nor control over. For instance, male homosexuals tend to be far more promiscuous than their female counterparts. Recent surveys show that as many as 25% of homosexual males have sexual encounters with a thousand or even more homosexual partners (Bell, Weinberg, & Hammersmith, 1981). For females, in stark contrast with males, the median number of homosexual partners is only three (Loney, 1974). Male homosexuality often amounts to a sexual smorgasbord with an almost limitless variety of opportunities, whereas it is clear that lesbians only involve themselves in relatively permanent, monogamous relationships. Also paralleling the heterosexual world, male homosexuals develop attractions to one another primarily on the basis of physical characteristics, whereas females respond to each other along an emotional dimension. Thus, although the choice of sex objects differ, the expression of sexuality remains basically the same in both heterosexual and homosexual contexts.

We have argued (Gallup & Suarez, 1983a) that if the sexual best interests of males and females were not at odds with each other there would be little or no homosexuality. In other words, according to our hypothesis the evolution of optimal heterosexual strategies among humans has created a situation in which the sexual agendas of males and females are so different from one another that homosexuality has become an increasingly frequent outcome. Accordingly, we see the reasons for adopting a homosexual lifestyle as being quite different depending on gender.

Heterosexuals almost invariably have to compromise their sexuality. For males this means far fewer sexual opportunities and fewer sexual partners than they would like, whereas for females it means having to settle for a relationship with a potentially unfaithful mate that will probably lack the deep emotional and psychological ties she would like. The typical adolescent male, for instance, is primarily interested in intercourse and immediate sexual gratification. Females, however, are looking for lasting, caring relationships. Whereas adolescent males have limited access, at best, to heterosexual outlets, females are confronted by just the opposite set of circumstances. Many adolescent females are subject to more potential heterosexual opportunities than they can handle, and early heterosexual experiences often leave the impression that men are "animals" and interested in nothing but sex. Not infrequently females are lied to, taken advantage of, and coerced into sexual encounters that they would just as soon avoid.

Thus, according to our hypothesis, homosexuality in females is a result of becoming progressively disillusioned and disenchanted with heterosexual relations. Witness the fact that although homosexual males no longer see them as sex objects, they usually continue to relate to females in a positive way. For many lesbians, however, the situation could not be more different. Homosexual females often evidence an unbridled hatred and distrust of males. They see males as oppressive, domineering, and abusive. The despise that lesbians hold for males stands as obvious testimony to the validity of our model. Males, on the other hand, become homosexual because of frustration and inadequate opportunities for sexual expression in the heterosexual mode. The relative unavailability of heterosexual outlets for the adolescent male is further complicated by the fact that females show a distinct dating and sexual preference for older males (Daly & Wilson, 1983). The existence of gender differences in age of peak sexual desire may also contribute to putting adolescent males out of phase with females. For males, sexual appetite often reaches its highest level in the late teens, whereas for females it can be delayed into their 30s (Kinsey, Pomeroy, & Martin, 1948; Kinsey, Pomeroy, Martin, & Gebhard, 1953).

As evidence for the fact that lesbians are disenchanted with heterosexual relations, whereas homosexual males are frustrated by a lack of heterosexual opportunities consider the following statistics. Approximately 85% of female homosexuals have had heterosexual intercourse prior to turning to homosexuality, but this holds true for only 20% of the gay male population (Bell & Weinberg, 1978; Schäfer, 1977). In other words, as evidence for having had an ample opportunity to experience dissatisfaction, female homosexuals are over four times more likely to have had prior heterosexual experience than their male counterparts. Loney (1974) reports that prior to adopting a homosexual orientation, females had an average of 5.3 heterosexual partners, whereas among males the mean was only 1.3, with many males never having experienced heterosexual intercourse at all. Ironic as it might seem, but highly consistent with our analysis, homosexual females typically have had more heterosexual than homosexual partners. Similarly, whereas only about 1 of every 17 homosexual males has been involved in a prior heterosexual marriage (Schäfer, 1977), almost 50% of lebsians have been party to a previous marriage with a man (Cotton, 1975). Suffice it to say that the inexperience with heterosexual relations is consistent with the notion of heterosexual frustration among males as a precursor to becoming homosexual, and that the average lesbian has had more than ample opportunity to be rebuffed and become disenchanted with males.

A recent study by Bell, Weinberg, and Hammersmith (1981) also provides support for our model. They found, as a result of a detailed survey, that contrary to popular opinion homosexual sex object choices do not develop in childhood. Rather, adolescent experiences appear to be the important ones in determining adult sexual orientation. This follows from our analysis because heterosexual frustration and/or disenchantment presuppose the kinds of heterosexual conflict that would only emerge during puberty.

Finally, it is important to comment about heterosexual hostility toward homosexuals. Why should some heterosexuals show disdain for persons who have adopted homosexual lifestyles? Aside from the hostility that many lesbians have for males, most homosexuals do not exhibit intense anti-heterosexual attitudes. Lesbians, for instance, do not harbor a disdain for heterosexual females. We think that this phenomenon can also be dealt with in the context of evolution. Under most circumstances, homosexuality would detract from rather than contribute to one's genetic representation in subsequent generations. Thus, homosexuality could pose a threat to heterosexuals to the extent that their offspring might be seduced and/or modeled into developing homosexual tendencies. From the standpoint of evolution and inclusive fitness, exclusive homosexuality is tantamount to sterilization. Therefore, we would predict that reactions to homosexuals by heterosexuals should be context specific. If our analysis is correct, heterosexual hostility toward homosexuals should be directly proportional to the extent to which they pose a perceived threat to a child's emerging sexuality.

The data on anti-homosexual attitudes, or what is known as homophobia, are highly consistent with this interpretation. Many people with anti-homosexual attitudes believe that homosexuals (especially males) will attempt to seduce young children (Morin & Garfinkle, 1978). As would be expected, homosexuals experience more discrimination in teaching than any other profession (Larsen, Reed, & Hoffman, 1980). For instance, although Levitt and Klassen (1974) found that three quarters of persons polled would object to homosexual teachers, far fewer would bar homosexuals from becoming artists, musicians, or florists. If our analysis is correct, similar objections should hold for homosexual babysitters, nursemaids, and athletic coaches, whereas lumberjacks, truck drivers, and construction workers should be relatively immune from such targeted unrest. Although it has frequently been overlooked it is important to acknowledge that to the extent that seduction may be involved in the development of a homosexual orientation its source may often be peer-based rather than enticement by homosexual adults.

This analysis of homosexuality has a number of implications. If homosexuality is a byproduct of selection for optimal heterosexual strategies, then it would follow that homosexuals are not sick, perverted, or deranged. Nor would homosexuality be a consequence of gender-identity problems, genetically based homosexual predispositions, hormonal imbalances, or altered brain chemistry. Indeed, parents would no longer have to bear a burden of guilt, responsibility, or even shame for an offspring's homosexual inclinations if this approach is correct.

Should parents, on the other hand, be concerned about minimizing the chances that their offspring might become homosexual, effective action would require minimizing the likelihood of heterosexual conflict during adolescence. In males, this might take the form of providing greater access to heterosexual opportunities (e.g., legalized prostitution). For females, however, the solution is not as simple, since the problem is one of dissatisfaction rather than frustration as a consequence of inadequate opportunities. Perhaps early education about the source and significance of sexuality and reproduction in the context of evolution, as well as the reasons for the gender differences in optimal heterosexual strategies, might prove to be an effective way of dealing with the development of sexual orientation in females.

EPILOGUE

Some readers no doubt will have taken exception to a variety of points made in this chapter; and that is fine. But bear in mind that the tenability of any interpretation is a function of the degree to which it is consistent with current information, the extent to which it integrates existing data, and whether it has testable implications. Whether you feel comfortable with an interpretation is irrelevant. For most psychologists, thinking in evolutionary terms requires a dramatic change in set, as many of us have been taught to emphasize environmental influences to the exclusion of practically anything else. The ostensible advantage of an environmental approach is that it creates the impression of being able to affect change, particularly when it applies to social and psychological ills. The environment and society is often construed as a convenient scapegoat and a means of avoiding responsibility.

The emphasis in this chapter has been on gender differences in sexuality that are a reflection of our evolutionary heritage, not environmental or cultural influences. Although much of what was said in this chapter about the sexual agendas of males and females may not seem "fair," it is important to realize that evolution does not operate according to preconceived notions of human dignity, equality, or affirmative action. Nor does evolution work to promote human happiness. It serves to propogate the species, and particularly among mammals the female's role, like it or not, is much different than that of the male. These are differences over which we have no control and for which we need not apologize. To rationalize or even to deny such differences is another matter, but that does not change basic human biology. Regardless of whether you are male or female, straight or gay, flat chested, or unattractive, you can spend the rest of your life attempting to buck biology and protesting your unfortunate lot in life, but that will not change the ultimate reasons for these differences, or, for that matter, the rationale for your existence. Differences do not necessarily mean better or worse, equal or unequal, fair or unfair, they are merely facts of our biological heritage. Economically, socially, and politically you might be able to do something about your lot in life, but sexually the gender differences are irrevocably fixed.

REFERENCES

Allee, W. C. (1938). *The social life of animals*. New York: Norton.
Allen, M. L., & Lemmon, W. B. (1981). Orgasm in female primates. *American Journal of Primatology, 1,* 15–34.
Anderson, P. (1983). The reproductive role of the human breast. *Current Anthropology, 24,* 25–45.
Bell, A. P., & Weinberg, M. S. (1978). *Homosexualities: A study of diversity among men and women.* New York: Simon & Schuster.
Bell, A. P., Weinberg, M. S., & Hammersmith, S. K. (1981). *Sexual preference: Its development in men and women.* Bloomington: Indiana University Press.
Burley, N. (1979). The evolution of concealed ovulation. *American Naturalist, 114,* 835–858.
Cotton, W. L. (1975). Social and sexual relationships of lesbians. *Journal of Sex Research, 11,* 139–148.
Daly, M., & Wilson, M. (1983). *Sex, evolution, and behavior* (2nd. Ed.). Boston: Willard Grant.
Daly, M., Wilson, M., & Weghorst, S. J. (1982). Male sexual jealousy. *Ethology and Sociobiology, 3,* 11–27.
Dawkins, R. (1976). *The selfish gene.* Oxford: Oxford University Press.
Epstein, R., Lanza, R. P., & Skinner, B. F. (1981). "Self-awareness" in the pigeon. *Science, 212,* 695–696.
Eldridge, N., & Gould, S. J. (1972). Punctuated equilibria: An alternative to phyletic gradualism. In T. J. M. Schopf (Ed.), *Models in paleobiology* (pp. 82–115).San Francisco: Freeman, Cooper.
Ford, C. S., & Beach, F. A. (1951). *Patterns of sexual behavior.* New York: Harper & Row.
Frisch, R. E. (1975). Critical weight at menarche. *American Journal of Diseases of Children, 129,* 258–259.
Frisch, R. E. (1978). Population, food intake, and fertility. *Science, 199,* 22–30.
Frisch, R. E. (1980). Fatness, puberty, and fertility. *Natural History, 89,* 16–27.
Frisch, R. E. (1983). Comment on Anderson. *Current Anthropology, 24,* 32.
Frisch, R. E., von Gotz-Welbergen, A., McArthur, J. W., Albright, T., Witschi, J., Bullen, B., Birnholz, J., Reed, R. B., & Hermann, H. (1981). Delayed menarche and amenorrhea of college

athletes in relation to age of onset of training. *Journal of the American Medical Association, 246,* 1559–1563.

Gallup, G. G., Jr. (1982). Permanent breast enlargement in human females: A sociobiological analysis. *Journal of Human Evolution, 11,* 597–601.

Gallup, G. G., Jr. (1984). Unpublished survey.

Gallup, G. G., Jr., & Suarez, S. D. (1983a). Homosexuality as a by-product of selection for optimal heterosexual strategies. *Perspectives in Biology and Medicine, 26,* 315–322.

Gallup, G. G., Jr., & Suarez, S. D. (1983b). Optimal reproductive strategies for bipedalism. *Journal of Human Evolution, 12,* 193–196.

Gallup, G. G., Jr., & Suarez, S. D. (1983c). Unpublished survey.

Goodall, J. (1971). *In the shadow of man.* New York: Dell.

Hagen, R. (1979). *The bio-sexual factor.* New York: Doubleday.

Harcourt, A. H., Harvey, P. H., Larson, S. G., & Short, R. V. (1981). Testis weight, body weight and breeding system in primates. *Nature, 293,* 55–57.

Hirsch, J. (Ed.). (1967). *Behavior-genetic analysis.* New York: McGraw–Hill.

Iizuka, R., & Kawakami, S. (1968). Body weight change and sexual function in women. *Sanfujinka No Jissai* (Tokyo), *17,* 388–394.

Kleinke, C. L., & Staneski, R. A. (1980). First impressions of female bust size. *The Journal of Social Psychology, 110,* 123–134.

Kinsey, A. C., Pomeroy, W. B., & Martin, C. E. (1948). *Sexual behavior in the human male.* Philadelphia: Saunders.

Kinsey, A. C., Pomeroy, W. B., Martin, C. E., & Gebhard, P. H. (1953). *Sexual behavior in the human female.* Philadelphia: Saunders.

Larsen, K. S., Reed, M., & Hoffman, S. (1980). Attitudes of heterosexuals toward homosexuality: A Likert-type scale and construct validity. *Journal of Sex Research, 16,* 245–257.

Levitt, E. E., & Klassen, A. D., Jr. (1974). Public attitudes toward homosexuality: Part of the 1970 National Survey in the Institute for Sex Research. *Journal of Homosexuality, 1,* 29–43.

LeBoeuf, B. J., & Peterson, R. S. (1969). Social status and mating activity in elephant seals. *Science, 163,* 91–93.

Lerner, R. M., Karabenick, S. A., & Stuart, J. L. (1973). Relations among physical attractiveness, body attitudes, and self-concept in male and female college students. *Journal of Psychology, 85,* 119–129.

Loney, J. (1974). Background factors, sexual experiences, and attitudes toward treatment in two "normal" homosexual samples. *Journal of Consulting and Clinical Psychology, 38,* 57–65.

Malinowski, B. (1929). *The sexual life of savages in north-western Melanesia.* London: Routledge.

Masters, W. H., & Johnson, V. E. (1966). *Human sexual response.* Boston: Little, Brown.

McCary, J. L. (1978). *McCary's human sexuality.* New York: Van Nostrand Reinhold.

Morgan, E. (1972). *The descent of woman.* New York: Bantam.

Morin, S. F., & Garfinkle, E. M. (1978). Male homophobia. *Journal of Social Issues, 34,* 29–47.

Morris, D. (1967). *The naked ape.* New York: McGraw–Hill.

Schäfer, S. (1977). Sociosexual behavior in male and female homosexuals: A study of sex differences. *Archives of Sexual Behavior, 6,* 355–364.

Short, R. V. (1979). Sexual selection and its component parts, somatic and genital selection, as illustrated by man and the great apes. In J. S. Rosenblatt, R. A. Hinde, C. Beer, & M.-C. Busnel (Eds.), *Advances in the study of behavior* (Vol. 9). New York: Academic Press.

Symons, D. (1979). *The evolution of human sexuality.* New York: Oxford University Press.

Tanner, J. M. (1970). Physical growth. In P. H. Mussen (Ed.), *Carmichael's manual of child psychology* (Vol. 1, 3rd Ed, pp. 77–155). New York: Wiley.

Tolor, A., & DiGrazia, P. V. (1976). Sexual attitudes and behavior patterns during and following pregnancy. *Archives of Sexual Behavior, 5,* 539–551.

Quiatt, D., & Everett, J. (1982). How can sperm competition work? *American Journal of Primatology, 1,* 161–169.

Udry, J. R., & Morris, N. M. (1968). Distribution of coitus in the menstrual cycle. *Nature, 220,* 593–596.

Wickler, W. (1972). *The sexual code.* Garden City, NY: Doubleday.

Wiggins, J. S., Wiggins, N., & Conger, J. C. (1968). Correlates of heterosexual somatic preference. *Journal of Personality and Social Psychology, 10,* 82–90.

Models and Measures of Sexual Response: Psychophysiological Assessment of Male and Female Arousal

3

Raymond C. Rosen
Rutgers Medical School U.M.D.N.J.

J. Gayle Beck
University of Houston

> *It cannot be that the axioms established by argumentation can suffice for the discovery of new works, since the subtlety of nature is greater many times over than the subtlety of argument.*
>
> —Francis Bacon

> *Whatever the poetry and romance of sex, and whatever the moral and social significance of human sexual behavior, sexual responses involve real and material changes in the physiologic functioning of the . . . (individual).*
>
> —Alfred C. Kinsey

INTRODUCTION

Since the publication of Masters and Johnson's (1966) first observational findings on sexual response, laboratory studies of sexual arousal have achieved a degree of respectability and acceptance in the scientific establishment. Considerable impetus has since been given to the empirical study of sexual response by the development of a suitable measurement technology for precise and reliable psychophysiological recording (e.g., Geer, 1980; Hatch, 1979). Along with advances in methodological sophistication, the scope and diversity of laboratory studies has also broadened considerably (Reinisch & Rosen, 1981). This chapter reviews the development of laboratory research methods in this field, focusing particularly on the role of physiological assessment devices in the study of sexual responding. Emphasis is given to the integration of conceptual and methodological advances, with some discussion of the limitations and shortcomings of the psychophysiological approach.

Historically, sex research has been anchored in the study of clinical and applied concerns. Representative examples include studies of sexual dysfunction (Barlow, & Sakheim, 1983; Heiman & Rowland, 1983); contraception and adolescent pregnancy (Chilman, 1979; Zelnik, Kantner, & Ford, 1981); the effects of drugs and illness on sexuality (Kolodny, Masters, & Johnson, 1979); sexual misconduct and aggression (Abel, Barlow, Blanchard, & Guild, 1977; Greer & Stuart, 1983); and a variety of gender identity issues (Weinberg, & Hammersmith, 1981; Lothstein, 1980). One positive outcome of this association with clinical concerns has been a growing empirical focus on the mechanisms and efficacy of sex therapy, as well as more thorough understanding of the nature of the various sexual disorders. Increasingly refined assessment and diagnostic procedures have resulted from this association as well.

An unintended and unfortunate consequence, however, of the continuing link between clinical applications and basic methodology in sex research has been a degree of neglect in conceptual integration. In the midst of rapid refinements of the measurement technology and a growing accumulation of empirical findings, insufficient attention has been paid to the task of theoretical synthesis. Moreover, assumptions about the internal and external validity of laboratory measures have been accepted uncritically, as has the lack of replicability in many instances. Although the major focus of this chapter is to review the range of current physiological assessment techniques, emphasis is also given to issues such as the multifaceted nature of sexual response, the correspondence between objective and subjective measures of arousal, the choice of theoretical models being used to guide laboratory research, gender and individual differences, and the social context of sex research.

Sexual Arousal as a Multi-component Process

There is a well-worn cliche among sex educators that, "The primary sexual organ is the one between the ears." Considering the accumulation of evidence from laboratory studies of sexual response, however, it is apparent that sexual arousal in human beings can best be conceptualized as a complex interaction of cognitive, affective, and somatic processes (e.g., Byrne, 1983; Heiman, 1980; Mosher, 1980). Unfortunately, understanding of the relationship between these response systems has lagged, and a sufficiently broad conceptual view of sexual response has not been proposed despite the considerable technical innovations in laboratory measurement over the past 10 years.

In this regard, Bancroft (1983) has proposed that at least four major components of sexual arousal need to be independently addressed: (a) sexual appetite or drive, including determinants of both motivation and arousability; (b) central arousal, including cognitive or attentional factors that define a given stimulus as sexual; (c) genital responses; and (d) peripheral indices of arousal, encompassing nongenital somatic, and autonomic changes. Bancroft's model does not, however, account for the degrees of involvement of each of these response components or the interaction effects between the different levels of psychophysiological response.

The best example of the complex interactions between physiological and psychological components of arousal is found in the recent experimental literature on the effects of alcohol on sexual arousal (for a complete review of this literature see Leiblum & Rosen, 1984). In brief, although studies have shown that alcohol remains a standard remedy for the sexually inhibited and inept, laboratory research has begun to unravel a complex and multifaceted pattern of effects.

Specifically, following the initial reports of pharmacological impairment of physiological arousal at higher dosage levels in normal males (Farkas & Rosen, 1976; Rubin & Henson, 1976), the focus of research shifted to investigation of the interaction between pharmacological and psychological aspects of alcohol consumption on multiple components of the sexual response (Briddell & Wilson, 1976; Rubin & Henson, 1976). Although both male and female social drinkers show inhibition of physiological responding at higher levels of intoxication (Malatesta, Pollack, Crotty, & Peacock, 1982; Wilson & Lawson, 1978), positive expectancy effects of alcohol have been found to override the pharmacological effect in many instances. Additionally, alcohol's effects on physiological and subjective measures vary widely depending on the dosage level, drinking history of the individual, and situational demands (Leiblum & Rosen, 1984).

In their studies of alcohol and sexual arousal in women, in particular, Wilson and Lawson (1976, 1978) found that although alcohol consumption significantly depressed vaginal engorgement, subjective reports of arousal increased under both conditions of alcohol intake and the belief that alcohol had been consumed. Similarly, studies of female alcoholics have shown that the belief in alcohol's properties for sexual enhancement persist despite longstanding sexual dysfunction associated with chronic abuse (Apter-Marsh, 1983; Covington, 1983). Finally, laboratory studies have also shown an *alcohol disinhibition* effect in males exposed to socially disapproved or aggressive sexual stimuli (Abrams & Wilson, 1983; Briddell et al., 1978).

At this literature suggests, complex interactions of physiological and subjective components of arousal need to be considered in accounting for alcohol's effects on sexual response. Although research on alcohol and sexual response has exemplified the focus of a multicomponent model of arousal, further clarification of the *patterning* of response components is needed in this and other areas. It is not clear whether gender differences observed in the alcohol studies are generalizable to other situations of sexual arousal and whether the powerful expectation effects reported by Wilson and Lawson (1978) could be obtained under nonalcohol arousal conditions. Studies of multiple-response component patterns in sexual dysfunction before and after sex therapy interventions would be especially interesting, given the ambiguous status of studies of treatment efficacy at this time (Everaerd, 1983).

Models of the Sexual Response Cycle

Fundamental assumptions underlying much of the current laboratory research on sexual response are that sexual arousal processes follow a predictable sequence and that a cyclical pattern of physiological responses can be identified. Despite the common-sense appeal of this assumption, the concept of a unitary sexual response cycle, particularly the 4-stage model as described by Masters and Johnson (1966), needs to be critically examined.

Historically, the first explicit depiction of a sexual response cycle was the 2-stage model of Ellis (1906), which was based on the processes of tumescence ("the piling on of the fuel"), and detumescence ("the leaping out of the devouring flame"). For Ellis the terms *tumescence* and *detumescence* were synonymous with the build-up and release of sexual energy, and were applied to the process of sexual arousal in both males and females. Although these terms continue to be widely used, their meaning has become restricted to genital blood flow effects, primarily in the male.

This 2-stage model of Ellis has served as the basis for most subsequent models of the sexual response cycle, and was clearly influential in the development of the 4-stage model of Masters and Johnson (1966).[1] In fact, Masters and Johnson appear to have substituted their "excitement" and "plateau" phases for Ellis' "tumescence" phase, whereas the "orgasm" and "resolution" phases replaced the older notion of "detumescence." This 4-stage model served as the central organizing schema for their observations of sexual response in both sexes, as well as for their subsequent classification of the sexual dysfunctions (Masters & Johnson, 1970).

In recent years, this model has been the target of criticism on both conceptual and empirical grounds. For example, Robinson (1976) particularly has criticised the rationale for distinguishing between the excitement and plateau phases as a "groundless differentiation." He emphasizes that most of the phenomena identified with the excitement phase are observed in the plateau phase and are better described as a progression of events: "Clearly what is being described here . . . is not a two-stage process (excitement/plateau), but a continuous progression, or, if you prefer a musical metaphor, a gradual crescendo" (Robinson, 1976, p. 129).

The Masters and Johnson model has also been criticized as paying insufficient attention to the role of motivational or psychological factors in the process of

---

[1]According to Money (1980), the 4-stage model of sexual response was first proposed by Albert Moll, a German sexologist who lived at the turn of the century.

sexual arousal. In particular, Kaplan (1979) has criticized the field of sex therapy for failing to address the importance of *sexual desire disorders* as a separate clinical entity and has suggested that the sexual response cycle be reconceptualized as consisting of three phases: desire, excitement, and orgasm. The Kaplan *triphasic* model has had its greatest impact on the current clinical classification system, in which "Inhibited Sexual Desire" has emerged as a separate diagnostic category. Although this model has had a major impact on the clinical practice of sex therapy in recent years (e.g., Levine, 1984; Schover & LoPiccolo, 1982), laboratory studies of sexual arousal have not as yet included assessment of this important aspect of the sexual response cycle. In fact, sexual desire has not been adequately operationalized to date, and a suitable methodology has not been developed to measure either the subjective or physiological aspects of desire (Rosen & Leiblum, in press). Overall, future studies in this area need to attend more closely to laboratory assessments of desire.

Clearly, there is a lack of consensus at present concerning the order and sequence of responses to be included in the sexual response cycle. Although the Kaplan model has generally been adopted by clinicians, most researchers continue to draw upon the Masters and Johnson model, albeit with numerous variations. At issue here is the notion of a predictable or inevitable sequence of events, or, as Bancroft (1983) terms it, "a unitary concept of sexual arousal of both an incremental and sequential kind" (p. 48). However appealing, this notion needs to be viewed as little more than a convenient abstraction, which may mask important variations in response sequencing and order from one individual or instance to another.

Gender and Individual Differences in Sexual Response

A central issue in the interpretation of laboratory research on sexual response is the generalizability of findings based on selected samples of male and female subjects. This issue is problematic in two main respects. First, there is an assumption underlying most psychophysiological studies that male and female sexual arousal processes are fundamentally similar. This assumption is again a legacy of the viewpoint provided by Masters and Johnson (1966), who said "The parallels in reaction to effective sexual stimulation emphasize the physiologic similarities in male and female responses rather than the differences. Aside from the obvious anatomic variants, men and women are homogeneous in their physiologic responses to sexual stimuli" (p. 285).

Thus, it is not surprising that subsequent research has emphasized similarities in male and female response in a number of contexts. Examples include studies of male and female arousal patterns to pornography (Heiman, 1975; Osborn & Pollack, 1977; Steinman, Wincze, Sakheim, Barlow, & Mavissakalian, 1981); the effect of continuous subjective monitoring on physiological responses (Wincze, Venditti, Barlow, & Mavissakalian, 1980); applications of biofeedback to sexual arousal (Hatch, 1981); and changes in genital blood flow during REM sleep in both men and women (Abel, Murphy, Becker, & Bitar, 1979; Fisher et al., 1983). A key assumption in these and similar studies is that the processes underlying sexual arousal in the male and female are essentially synonymous.

The emphasis on male and female similarities is likewise reflected in the search for comparability of physiological assessment devices. For example, several studies have recently focused on the use of thermographic assessment of skin temperature as a gender-independent measure of sexual arousal (e.g. Abramson & Pearsall, 1983; Seeley, Abramson, Perry, Rothblatt, & Seeley, 1980). The rationale for this is based, in part, on the belief that a gender-independent physiological measure of arousal can be demonstrated. However, this line of investigation may ultimately obscure important dimensions of difference, as well as indicating possible similarities between the sexes. Future research might indeed focus on clearer differentiation between male and female response patterns rather than attempting to demonstrate further similarities.

A second issue concerning the generalizability of findings is the representativeness of *volunteer subjects* in laboratory investigations. An oft-cited critique of psychophysiological studies of sexual responding is that subject samples may be biased, particularly in regard to sexual attitudes, experience, and perhaps salient demographic features, relative to the general population (Farkas, Sine, & Evans, 1978; Wolchik, Spencer, & Lisi, 1983). The findings of these two studies, in particular, indicate that male volunteers tend to be more sexually experienced, more liberal in attitudes, somewhat older, and more likely to report occasions of erectile failure, compared with nonvolunteers. For females, volunteers were found to have more frequent histories involving sexual trauma, fewer sexual fears, and to have engaged in masturbation more often than nonvolunteers. Although these differences are suggestive of possible subject confounds in this type of research, specific effects on psychophysiological responding warrant further study. Overall, it is clear that gender and individual differences in sexual response have not been adequately addressed to date.

Social Context and Implications of Sex Research

As previously noted, the pioneering studies of Masters and Johnson have paved the way for experimental studies of sexual response. Despite the considerable progress that has been made in the past 2 decades, however, the conduct of research in this area remains a complex and controversial activity. Laboratory sex research continues to pose unique problems of both a conceptual and practical nature. In fact, the availability of a rapidly growing measurement technology has highlighted the need for careful consideration of the social, institutional, and ethical implications of laboratory sex research (e.g., Bohlen, 1980; Masters, Johnson, & Kolodny, 1977).

Although a detailed discussion of these concerns is beyond the scope of this chapter, some attention is given in later sections to the issues involved in the selection and placement of assessment devices, briefing and debriefing of experimental subjects, and other aspects of human subject protection in laboratory sex research. The conduct of sex research has become increasingly more accepted (and acceptable) in recent years. However, it is essential for researchers to remain aware of the special status accorded by this society to both the conduct of sex research and its subject matter. Gagnon (1978) aptly summarizes this state of affairs when he says "Even though social life, which includes the study of social life, has been secularized, sexuality still manages to retain for many people its exemplary status as the observable margin between the sacred and the profane" (p. 225).

Undoubtedly, this "exemplary status" accorded to the study of sexual behavior affects many of the uses and interpretations of findings in sex research, and presents a special challenge to the concerned investigator.

ASSESSMENT OF PHYSIOLOGICAL AROUSAL IN MALES AND FEMALES

Genital Blood Flow Measures in the Male

Among the first and most easily identified of physiological responses associated with sexual arousal in males is erection of the penis (Masters & Johnson, 1966). Moreover, penile tumescence in adult males has been shown to be the only response that *reliably* discriminates sexual arousal from other emotional states (Bancroft & Mathews, 1971; Wenger, Averill, & Smith, 1968; Zuckerman, 1971). Although there is certainly evidence that erections may occur in other (nonsexual) situations (see, for example, Zillman, this volume), no other physiological response is as reliable a predictor of sexual arousal in the human male. The tumescence response is also readily amenable to assessment and quantification in the laboratory. It is not surprising, therefore, that the measurement of erection has been the subject of widespread research interest, as erection measures have been extensively employed in basic and applied research settings (e.g. Geer, 1977; Earls & Marshall, 1983; Rosen & Keefe, 1978).

Physiological Mechanisms of Erection. Penile tumescence is a complex neurovascular process by means of which erection and rigidity of the penis are accomplished. This effect is achieved through vascular engorgement of the cylindrical, sponge-like bodies of erectile tissue in the penis, particularly the *corpora cavernosa,* or two dorsal cylinders. Pressure is thereby maintained against the fibrous *tunica albuginea,* producing the stiffness of erection. Engorgement of the *corpus spongiosum* and glans of the penis also contribute to the process. The penile corpora are composed of many small compartments separated by bands of smooth-muscle tissue, the *trabeculae*. The arterioles supplying blood to these bodies are derived from the internal pudendal arteries, which divide, in turn, into the deep and dorsal arteries of the penis. Multiple anastomotic channels connect the penile arteries throughout the length of the penis (Van Arsdalen, Malloy, & Wein, 1983).

Although it is clear that increased arterial flow is a necessary cause of erection, the mechanism for shunting of blood into the cavernous spaces remains controversial. The traditional view has been to emphasize the role of *polsters,* or specialized arteriolar valves that were believed to facilitate engorgement through their action. The existence of these structures has been brought into question, however, by recent histological studies (e.g., Benson, McConnell, & Schmidt, 1981). These authors suggest that so-called polsters are, in fact, atherosclerotic lesions in various stages of development, which do not contribute to the normal physiology of erection.

Understanding of the role of venous mechanisms in erection has also changed markedly in recent years. For example, Wagner (1981) has described a series of experiments in which decreased venous flow during the onset of erection has been demonstrated. Although most authors still emphasize the primary importance of arterial inflow, it is now recognized that a change in venous drainage may also occur, which could be due to either a reduction in outflow through the normal venous channels or to a switch to an alternative venous drainage mechanism (Van Arsdalen, Malloy, & Wein, 1983).

Some controversy also exists concerning the *neural* mediation of erection. Weiss (1972) described two distinct neurophysiological pathways, the *psychogenic* and the *reflexogenic,* which appear to interact in a synergistic fashion to produce erection. The reflexogenic component, according to Weiss, effects vasodilation by means of parasympathetic sacral outflow via the nervi erigentes. The psychogenic pathway, on the other hand, consists of sympathetic innervation mediated via the thoracolumbar portion of the cord, and appears to facilitate or inhibit the reflexive (parasympathetic) erection mechanism. Despite the long-standing acceptance of the role of the parasympathetic components of erection, Wagner and Brindley (1980) recently reported little effect of *atropine blockade* on erection, thereby questioning the role of cholinergic mediation. The physiological mechanisms responsible for detumescence remain largely unexplored, although it is generally believed that an active arteriolar constriction effect plays an important part in the process (Bancroft, 1983).

The fact that penile tumescence is mediated primarily by the autonomic nervous system has led Masters and Johnson (1970) to assert that "Erections develop just as involuntarily and with just as little effort as breathing. . . . No man can will an erection" (p. 196). Laboratory studies with normal male subjects have indicated, however, that some degree of *voluntary* or instructional control of tumescence is possible (Henson & Rubin, 1971; Laws & Rubin, 1969). Furthermore, the capacity for voluntary control appears to be enhanced through feedback and reward training (Rosen, 1973; Rosen, Shapiro, & Schwartz, 1975). These studies suggest that penile tumescence should not be viewed solely as a reflexive response to exteroceptive stimuli. Although the mechanisms of control are not well understood at present, it appears that most men have the ability to enhance or inhibit erections by means of imagery or other cognitive strategies (Hatch, 1981).

Penile erections have also been observed in association with REM sleep in healthy males. Based upon the results of two classic studies in the mid-1960s (Fisher,Gross, & Zuch, 1965; Karacan, Goodenough, Shapiro, & Starker, 1966), it has been firmly established that about 90% of REM sleep in normal males is associated with full or partial tumescence. Karacan (1970) further demonstrated that measurement of nocturnal penile tumescence (NPT) could be used to distinguish between psychogenic and organic impotence. Since that time, a number of studies have investigated the characteristics of NPT in clinical and non-clinical samples (e.g. Fisher et al., 1979; Marhsall, Surridge, & Delva, 1981; Wasserman, Pollack, Spielman, & Weitzman, 1980).

Despite the utility of NPT testing for the differential diagnosis of organic impotence, certain key questions remain unanswered concerning the underlying physiological mechanisms. For instance, although it is generally assumed that nocturnal erections occur as a result of reflexive physiological processes associated with REM sleep, several authors have reported instances in which psychological factors alone have caused a significant disruption of the sleep erection (Fisher et al., 1979; Jovanovic, 1969; Wasserman et al., 1980).

Another important assumption is that impairment of NPT is an irreversible phenomenon, thus leading to a consideration of penile implant surgery in most instances (Rosen, 1983). This assumption has been brought into question, however, by the report of a reversible loss of NPT in two cases of severe depression (Roose, Glassman, Walsh, & Cullen, 1982). Following treatment with tryclic medication, normal sleep erections were found in both cases. Additionally, Kwan, Greenleaf, Crapo, Mann, and Davidson (1983) have demonstrated reversibility of an NPT impairment in hypogonadal men treated with exogenous testosterone. Finally, Bancroft (1983) has questioned the assumption that the same vascular mechanisms are involved in both sleep and waking erections, and has suggested that NPT may be more directly influenced by the venous mechanisms discussed above. Clearly, more research is needed in each of these areas.

Laboratory Measures of Penile Tumescence.   The first report of a simple electromechanical transducer for objective measurement of erections was described by German researchers, Ohlmeyer, Brilmayer, and Hullstrung (1947). Their device consisted of a contact ring that could be fitted around the subject's penis, and was used to provide a simple binary signal of the presence or absence of erection. The authors used this method for monitoring sleep erections in their

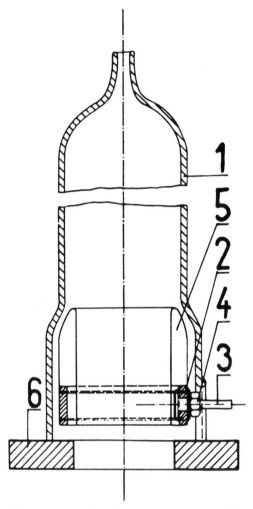

FIG. 3.1.   The Freund volumetric plethysmograph: (1) glass cylinder; (2) plastic
ring; (3) metal tube with threads; (4) locknut; (5) rubber cuff; (6) flat soft sponge
rubber ring (Freund et al., 1965; copyright 1965 by the Society for the Experimental Analysis of Behavior, Inc.).

subjects. Despite the obvious significance of this early research, it is surprising
to note that no further research on erection measurement was reported until the
1960s.

Since that time, two principal measurement approaches have been developed
for the quantification of penile tumescence: *volumetric* and *circumferential*.
Techniques for the volumetric measurement of erection were developed independently by Freund (1963) in Czechoslovakia; Fisher et al., (1965) in the United
States; and McConaghy (1967) in Australia. These techniques all embody the

general principles of volumetric plethysmography (e.g. Hyman & Winsor, 1961), in which a limb or body part is enclosed in a sealed container of known volume with fluid displacement capacity. The plethysmograph employed by Fisher et al. relied on water displacement for this purpose, making it extremely bulky and awkward. Freund and McConaghy, however, used air displacement devices that have subsequently been employed in a variety of laboratory studies on male sexual arousal (e.g. Barr & McConaghy, 1971; Freund, 1965; Freund, Langevin, Cibiri, & Zajac, 1973; Langevin & Martin, 1975).

A major problem in the use of volumetric plethysmography is the potential obtrusiveness and reactivity of these devices. The subject's penis needs to be completely enclosed in a glass cylinder (see Fig. 3.1), which must be carefully positioned and calibrated for use. Clearly, this apparatus would not be appropriate for studies involving masturbation or nocturnal erection, for example. However, the volumetric method offers maximum precision in the measurement of tumescence, as it records changes in the entire penile body, as opposed to circumference changes at a given point along the penile shaft.

Measures of penile circumference change have been obtained from both electromechanical strain gauges (Barlow et al., 1970; Johnson & Kitching, 1968) and the more widely used mercury-in-rubber resistance strain gauges (Bancroft, Jones, & Pullan, 1966; Fisher et al., 1965; Karacan, 1969). These circumferential devices are simple to use, reliable, and relatively unobtrusive (Rosen & Keefe, 1978). The mercury-in-rubber gauge (see Fig. 3.2) responds in a linear

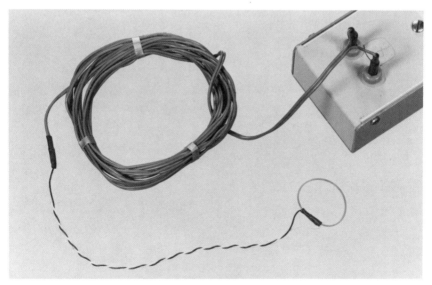

FIG. 3.2.   The mercury-in-rubber strain gauge for measurement of penile circumference. Gauge is shown attached to a resistance bridge, which is attached in turn to a polygraph.

fashion over a wide range of values and has been shown to be reliable with repeated testing (Farkas, Sine, & Evans, 1979). Several technical approaches to response quantification have been recommended, including high- and low-gain DC recording (Rosen, 1973), AC pulse amplitude (Jovanovic, 1967), and measures of maximum circumference and integrated amplitude response (Abel, Blanchard, Murphy, Becker, & Djenderedjian, 1981). Despite the convenience and widespread use of penile circumference measures in laboratory studies of male sexual arousal, several important limitations of this approach have been identified.

First, as noted by a number of investigators, penile circumference appears to show a slight *decrease* at the onset of stimulation (Abel, Blanchard, Barlow, & Mavissakalian, 1975; Earls & Marshall, 1981; Laws & Bow, 1976). This brief reduction in circumference is problematic in that the onset of tumescence may appear as a decrease in responding below basal values. In arguing the case for volumetric measures, McConaghy (1974) pointed out that the penis is a non-isotropic organ, and that changes in volume are not always reflected in circumference changes recorded from a single point. More specifically, Earls and Marshall (1982, 1983) have demonstrated that during the early stages of erection the penis undergoes a substantial increase in length that is typically associated with a simultaneous decrease in circumference. In order to investigate the relationship between penile length and circumference changes, these authors have described the development of a specialized transducer including both open- and closed-ended mercury-in-rubber strain gauges (see Fig. 3.3). Unfortunately, a number of procedural difficulties involving the placement and calibration of this device have not, as yet, been resolved, precluding more widespread use.

Earls and Marshall (1983) have also reported that circumference recordings in their laboratory frequently reach a maximum value some time before subjects report the experience of full erection. This observation suggests a possible non-linear relationship between tumescence and circumference changes at the upper as well as the lower end of the response curve, which may again be related to the nonisotropic characteristics of the penis. This is a potentially serious limitation of circumference measurement as an index of sexual arousal in the male, and warrants further study.

In addition to volumetric and circumference measures, penile tumescence has also been measured by means of *thermistor* assessment of penile surface skin temperature during sexual arousal (Fisher et al., 1965; Solnick & Birren, 1977; Webster & Hammer, 1983). Although this approach offers potential advantages in terms of ease of use and potential comparability to thermistor measures of female genital blood flow, it suffers from at least one major drawback. Skin temperature appears to remain elevated for some time after the peak of sexual arousal, at which time other measures of erection appear to be returning to basal levels (Webster & Hammer, 1983). The measure therefore appears to be unreliable for the assessment of detumescence.

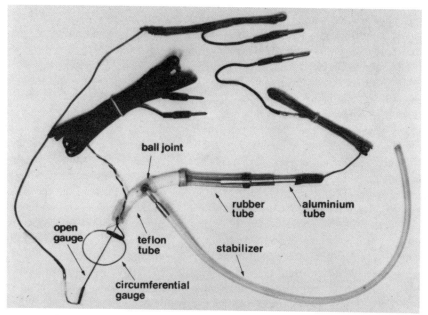

FIG. 3.3.   The Marshall gauge for measurement of length and circumference of the penis (Earls & Marshall, 1982).

Correspondence Between Measures of Erection and Subjective Arousal.   A major concern in assessing the validity of penile tumescence measurement is the correlation between measures of erection and self-report of subjective arousal. Given the prevailing view that penile erection is the most reliable physiological index of sexual arousal in the male (Zuckerman, 1971), a high degree of correspondence with subjective arousal is to be expected. On the other hand, as indicated earlier, sexual arousal can be conceptualized as involving multiple response components, the relationship among which might vary considerably from one individual or situation to another (Bancroft, 1983). Furthermore, current methodology for the assessment of self-report of sexual arousal is problematic in a number of respects, as is discussed.

Several early studies comparing tumescence and subjective arousal to normal and deviant erotic stimuli found a high degree of concordance between penile circumference measures and self-reports of sexual arousal (e.g. Abel, Barlow, Blanchard, & Guild, 1977; Mavissakalian, Blanchard, Abel, & Barlow, 1975). Similarly, studies of the effects of alcohol on sexual arousal in males have reported strong overall correlations between tumescence and subjective arousal (Briddell & Wilson, 1976; Farkas & Rosen, 1976). In each of these studies subjective arousal was measured by means of simple posttest questionnaire responses, assessing sexual arousal in global terms. Although this procedure has generally yielded a high degree of response concordance, at least one recent study found that self-report measures were significantly more responsive than tumescence when the experimental stimuli involved sexually aggressive themes (Malamuth & Check, 1983).

In order to assess the relationship between physiological arousal and self-report on a *continuous* basis, Farkas, Sine, & Evans (1979) described a variable resistance potentiometer dial that was rotated by subjects to indicate varying levels of sexual arousal. The subjects in this study viewed explicit and nonexplicit erotic films under conditions of high- and low-performance demands. Cognitive distraction effects were also assessed by means of a simple counting task. Within-subject correlations between penile circumference and self-report varied widely, while the overall degree of concordance between the measures was positively correlated with the level of physiological arousal. Interestingly, the distraction task was found to have a significant negative effect on tumescence, but not on subjective arousal, whereas the degree of explicitness of the stimuli was found to affect subjective arousal, but not tumescence.

Wincze, Venditti, Barlow, and Mavissakalian (1980) similarly compared strain gauge measures of penile circumference with continuous self-report of subjective arousal as measured by a lever-driven potentiometer. In this study it appeared that use of the so-called cognitive lever resulted in lower levels of physiological arousal. Despite the potential obtrusiveness of the continuous self-report measure, the authors reported an overall correlation between tumescence and subjective arousal of 0.69. Individual correlations were found to be much higher, however, at higher levels of arousal. This study also examined the relationship between objective and subjective measures in female subjects, as is discussed in a later section.

In the most recent study of response concordance in male subjects, Sakheim, Barlow, Beck, and Abrahamson (1984) attempted to control for the effects of visual feedback of erections on ratings of arousal. This was accomplished by the inclusion of an experimental condition in which subjects' genitals were covered by a sheet. Results indicated that at low levels of arousal the availability of visual feedback appeared to inhibit erections, while the opposite result was obtained at high levels of arousal (i.e., subjects showed significantly greater penile responding with visual feedback of their own erections). The authors also examined two different measures of response concordance, namely the agreement between the *direction* and *intensity* of response systems. Surprisingly, response concordance was lowest at high levels of arousal for the intensity comparison. A possible explanation for this finding is that subjects continue to experience greater subjective intensity of arousal beyond the point of full erection. This finding is consistent with the report by Earls and Marshall (1983) of a discontinuity between physiological arousal and self-report at the upper end of the arousal scale.

In summary, studies that have investigated the correspondence between physiological arousal and self-report in males have produced a complex and somewhat inconsistent set of results. Response concordance appears to be generally higher with the more global Likert-type measures, although recent research has tended to favor the continuous assessment approach to subjective arousal. Stronger physiological/subjective correlations have also been obtained at higher levels of arousal, although this relationship appears to depend on which particular measure of concordance is analyzed. Finally, it has been shown that response concordance varies considerably as a function of the experimental set and degree of cognitive distraction available to subjects.

Genital Blood Flow Measures in the Female

The development of physiological measures for the assessment of genital engorgement in women has lagged significantly behind the research on instrumentation for detecting male tumescence. Several factors can account for this. First, devising adequate blood flow measures for the study of female sexual arousal is complicated, in part, by a lack of complete understanding of the underlying physiological mechanisms of vasocongestion and vaginal lubrication. Additionally, technical difficulties related to the need for internal placement have made for problems in transducer design and reliability of measurement. The complicated pattern of interrelationship between female genital blood flow and subjective measures of arousal that has emerged from a number of studies raises fundamental questions concerning the role of these measures in a broader account of female sexual response. Thus, while progress has been somewhat slower in developing an adequate methodology for direct assessment of female genital engorgement, the studies conducted to date have addressed a number of interesting conceptual and technical issues in the measurement of female sexual response.

Physiology of Vaginal Lubrication and Vasocongestion. As outlined by Masters and Johnson (1966), the first physiological index of sexual arousal in the female is vaginal lubrication. In most instances this appears simultaneously with increased blood flow to the internal and external genitalia and is thought to originate from the vaginal epithelium. Content analyses of the vaginal lubricant suggest that it is a modified plasma transudate with an average pH of 4.7 to 4.9. The relationship between the process of vasocongestion and the appearance of vaginal lubrication is not entirely understood, although a hydrostatic mechanism is generally believed to cause increased pressure in the tissue walls, which results in gradual transudation (Masters & Johnson, 1966).

In addition to vaginal lubrication, other physiological signs of arousal include engorgement of the venous plexus, elongation of the vaginal barrel, and vasocongestion of the external genitalia and clitoral body. With increased arousal, the inner portion of the vagina distends and expands upwards. Similarly, the cervix and uterus are raised by increased muscle tone in the parametrial sheath.

In some women, involuntary vaginal contractions begin to occur at higher levels of arousal. Also significant is the apparent retraction of the clitoris, which becomes less prominent while remaining fully engorged. With the approach of orgasm, the so-called "orgasmic platform" is created in the outer third of the vagina, indicating complete genital vasocongestion.

Despite the availability of descriptive data on the various phenomena of female sexual arousal, current understanding of the physiological mechanisms remains incomplete. The role of the specific hemodynamic factors that control vasocongestion, (e.g., the underlying mechanisms of arterial and venous vasomotor action) have been the focus of study for some time (e.g. Danesino & Martella, 1976; Dickinson, 1949). Further understanding of the physiology of vaginal lubrication and engorgement will undoubtedly assist the future development of direct measures of the vasocongestive process. At present, however, all existing measures of female sexual arousal rely upon assessment of correlated physiological changes, such as surface vaginal blood flow and fluctuations in skin temperature.

Measures of Vaginal Vasocongestion.   Whereas physiological measures of sexual arousal in males have focused primarily on penile tumescence, vasocongestion in women affects a variety of changes in both the internal and external genital organs. The range of devices available for the measurement of genital blood flow in women is therefore greater, and the issues of transducer design and response interpretation are more complex. In this section we review the use of photoplethysmography (or *photometry*) in the measurement of vaginal blood flow during sexual arousal, as the most widely used approach at present.

One of the earliest attempts to assess vaginal vasocongestion was reported by Palti and Bercovici (1967). These investigators described the use of a light reflectance photometer attached to a vaginal speculum to measure pulse amplitude during the menstrual cycle (see Fig. 3.4). Despite clear differentiation of responding at different stages of the menstrual cycle, this type of transducer has not been adopted due to the potential obtrusiveness of the speculum.

The next step in the development of vaginal photometry was taken by Sintchak and Geer (1975), who used a light reflectance transducer designed specifically for the laboratory study of female sexual arousal. This device consisted of a tampon-sized acrylic probe containing an incandescent light source and a CdSe photocell (see Fig. 3.5). The method was subsequently improved by Hoon, Wincze, and Hoon (1976), who replaced the incandescent light source with a more efficient and reliable light-emitting diode (LED). Hoon, Murphy, Laughter, & Abel (1984) also replaced the CdSe photocell with a phototransistor detector, thereby reducing a number of recording artifacts, including transient light effects.

Other approaches to vaginal photometry have been developed in recent years. Armon, Weinman, and Weinstein (1978), for example, have described a device

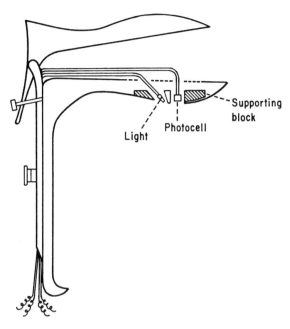

FIG. 3.4.   Vaginal photometer device built into a vaginal speculum (Palti & Bercovici, 1967).

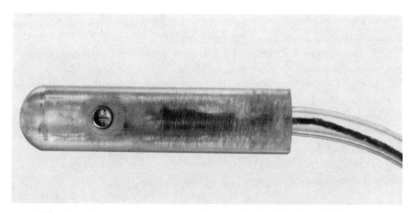

FIG. 3.5.   Vaginal photometer in acrylic tube (Sintchak & Geer, 1975).

consisting of four CdS photoconductive cells and a light reflectance system. The photocells and light source are housed in glass tubing, which is designed to be positioned at the tip of the cervix. Particular attention has been paid in the construction of the instrument to the comfort of the subject and the need for sterilization. A rudimentary calibration system to allow for the adjustment of the illumination has also been described. Only DC measurement is possible with this device, and a preliminary report has indicated the sensitivity of the probe to basal blood volume changes across the menstrual cycle.

Benoit, Borth, and Woolever (1980) have described the development of yet another vaginal photometer device based upon fiber optic methods. Although this approach has not been widely accepted to date, it has proved useful in a study of ovulation-induced changes in vasocongestion (Borth, Benoit, & Woolever, 1980). Further research is needed to determine the validity and reliability of this method, although it is potentially the most sophisticated approach to have been developed thus far.

Vaginal photometry methods generally operate on changes in light backscattered to the photodetector. Because tissue transparency fluctuates as a function of vasocongestion (e.g. Weinman, 1967), increasing vaginal engorgement affects the signal from the phototransducer. When the probe is AC coupled, vaginal pulse amplitude (VPA) is recorded, which is thought to be an indication of the rate of blood flow. Elevated levels of arousal are reflected in greater pulse amplitude. On the other hand, when the photomoter is DC coupled, vaginal blood volume (VBV) is assessed, which is indicative of the overall degree of vasocongestion (Beck, Sakheim, & Barlow, 1983; Hatch, 1979).

Controversy exists concerning the relative merits of these two types of signals for vaginal photometry. The VPA signal has been reported by some authors as the more sensitive index (Geer, Morokoff, & Greenwood, 1974; Heiman, 1977; Osborn & Pollack, 1977), whereas other studies have reported close correspondence between the two indices (e.g. Heiman, 1977). Most investigators currently utilize the VPA signal, owing to its greater ability to discriminate between responding during erotic and non-erotic presentations. Although both approaches lack methods for adequate calibration, the VBV measure also presents difficulties in response quantification. For example, as a DC signal, the choice of an appropriate baseline for VBV is complicated by variability in the resting signal both between and within subjects. In light of these concerns, both VPA and VBV need to be viewed as *relative* measures of response, given the present ambiguity concerning the physiological processes of vasoengorgements.

The issue of which index to use as a measure of arousal is centrally related to validity concerns. One approach to the establishment of validity is to examine correlations between the vaginal blood flow measure and reports of subjective arousal. For example, Heiman (1977) has reported higher correlations between VPA and poststimulus ratings of arousal than between VBV and self-ratings.

However, the issue of correspondence between vaginal blood flow measures and subjective arousal is complex and may not be the ideal method for establishing validity. This issue is discussed in greater depth in a subsequent section. Another approach to determining validity is the assessment of differential responsivity to erotic and non-erotic stimuli. For example, Geer et al., (1974), Heiman (1977), and Osborn and Pollack (1977) have all concluded that the VPA index is more sensitive to the effects of erotic stimulation and also shows a more rapid return to baseline after stimulus offset (Henson, Rubin, & Henson, 1979a). Furthermore, while the VPA index appears to be more sensitive overall, both VPA and VBV are susceptible to artifactual responses during resting or non-erotic conditions, which include movement artifacts and shifts in probe positioning (Heiman & Rowland, 1981).

Regarding reliability, several studies have addressed consistency of response between and within sessions (e.g. Heiman, 1977; Henson, Rubin, & Henson, 1979a). In the latter study, although neither VPA nor VBV showed adequate cross-session reliability, qualitative assessment of the records indicated a consistency in the pattern of individual subjects responding. Although this provides a rough indication of the reliability of the instrument, the consistency of these two signals appears to be quite low. Other investigators have examined the reliability of the probe as well. For example, Beck, Sakheim, & Barlow (1983) investigated signal stability of the DC component in a steady-state environment. These authors reported a distressing lack of stability in this measure over time and between trials, but concluded that this potentially serious reliability problem is less likely to affect the VPA signal, given the use of AC coupling.

Validity and reliability of these indices is also influenced by a number of other important factors. For example, movement artifacts have been shown to interfere markedly with signal recording. Geer and Quartaro (1976) in recording both VPA and VBV during masturbation to orgasm found that the measures were seriously confounded by movement artifacts. This problem was substantial despite the use of highly trained subjects in this study. A similar problem is the potentially confounding effects of probe positioning. While Gillan (1976) has reported marked differences in responsivity from various locations in the vagina, Hoon et al. (1976) failed to find a significant effect of probe placement. Because typical laboratory procedure involves insertion of the device by the subject herself in privacy, determination of relative positioning of the probe across subjects and trials is impossible.

Other potential confounds include possible menstrual cycle effects on vaginal vasocongestion (Schreiner-Engel, Schiavi, & Smith, 1981; Wincze, Hoon, & Hoon, 1976), and the effects of sensitivity to temperature fluctuations (Beck, et al., 1983). Regarding menstrual cycle effects, Wincze et al. found a significant overall correlation ($r = 0.64$) between VBV and day of the menstrual cycle. Despite these findings, few studies have assessed or controlled for the potential influence of menstrual cycle variations. Similarly, the instrument is sensitive to temperature changes, such as occurs during the initial positioning of the device and through the stages of the menstrual cycle.

Applications of Vaginal Photometry.   The vaginal photometer has been used in a number of studies to investigate, for example, biofeedback training of vasocongestion in women (e.g. Hoon, Wincze, & Hoon, 1977a, Zingheim & Sandman, 1978), responsivity to romantic versus erotic stimulus themes (Heiman, 1977; Osborn & Pollack, 1977), the influence of anxiety on sexual responding (Hoon, Wincze, & Hoon, 1977b), and changes in vasocongestions during sleep (Abel, Murphy, Becker, & Bitar, 1979). Although each of these areas can be viewed as interesting and potentially useful applications of the photometry method, a detailed discussion is beyond the scope of the present chapter (see Hatch, 1981; Hoon, 1979 for reviews of these areas).

Of particular interest, however, are a series of studies that have investigated the responses of clinical samples to laboratory stimuli. Heiman (1975), for example, contrasted the responses of anorgasmic women to sexually functional controls and found that the clinical subjects showed significantly lower levels of vasocongestive response to erotic stimuli. A similar finding has been reported by Wincze, Hoon, & Hoon (1976) in a comparison of sexually functional and dysfunctional women. Surprisingly, in the latter study, the two groups reported equivalent levels of subjective arousal, despite the significant differences in vasocongestion. On the other hand, Morokoff and Heiman (1980) found no pretreatment differences in vasocongestion between a sample of dysfunctional women and normal controls.

Several studies have also included vaginal photometry measures as an index of therapeutic change. For example, Wincze, Hoon, and Hoon (1978) reported a multiple-measures analysis of treatment outcome following sex therapy. In contrast with the subjects' reports of increased satisfaction following treatment, these authors failed to find differences in physiological arousal at either posttest or follow-up. Similarly, Morokoff and Heiman (1980) found no differences on objective measures as a result of treatment, although again subjects reported greater satisfaction with sexual functioning following treatment. Given the numerous potential confounds in the photometry method, as well as incomplete understanding of the relationship between subjective arousal, interest and drive levels, and physiological arousability, these findings are intriguing, yet inconclusive.

Other Measures of Genital Blood Flow.   Although most studies of female arousal have utilized vaginal photometry methods, other measures of genital blood flow have been developed. Shapiro, Cohen, Dibianco, and Rosen (1968) describe a thermoconductive vaginal flowmeter that consists of two microthermistors mounted on the ring of a diaphram (see Fig. 3.6). The thermistors are

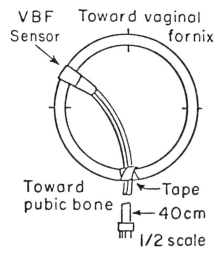

FIG. 3.6.   Thermoconductive flowmeter for detection of vaginal blood flow (Fisher et al., 1983).

held firmly against the lateral vaginal wall by this method. One of the thermistors is heated 5 degrees C. above resting body temperature, while the second thermistor remains at body temperature. The device detects the rate of heat dissipation from the externally heated thermistor, thereby activating a DC amplifier-bridge circuit.

The initial presentation of this approach (Shapiro et al., 1968) described vasocongestion during REM sleep with a single subject. A subsequent report (Cohen & Shapiro, 1970) demonstrated correspondence between vaginal temperature changes and subjective arousal during self-generated sexual fantasies. Recently, Fisher et al. (1983) have extended the use of the device to a study of sleep cycles in 10 normal women. Additionally, comparisons were made between thermoconductive responses during sleep and waking state arousal to erotic stimulation. The results of this study indicated a pattern of cyclical blood flow changes during sleep; however, unlike studies of NPT in males, vaginal engorgement appeared to be less tightly linked to REM sleep and of shorter duration. A more elaborate thermoconductive probe has been developed by Abrams and his colleagues (Frisinger, Abrams, Graichen, & Cassin, 1981; Abrams, Kalna, & Wilcox, 1978; Abrams & Stolwijk, 1972), although its use had been marked by numerous measurement artifacts.

Although this approach is promising as an alternative to the photometer, no direct comparison of the two devices has been conducted to date. More importantly, there is a need for controlled investigation of the reliability and validity of this measure. Other problems include the requirement that subjects be individually fitted and accustomed to the vaginal diaphragm (Geer, 1976), and potential artifacts resulting from slight repositioning of the diaphragm during movement (Semmlow & Lubowsky, 1983).

Temperature changes in the external genitalia have also been assessed by several methods. Jovanovic (1971) described the use of a *clitorograph,* a thermistor for the measurement of clitoral temperature during sexual arousal. Henson, Rubin, Henson, and Williams (1977) devised a system for measuring temperature changes in the *labia minora.* This method consists of a thermistor attached to the labia with a wire clip, as well as reference thermistors on the subject's chest and wall of the experimental chamber. Labial temperature was found to be sensitive to erotic stimulation and moderately correlated ($r = 0.53$) with subjective arousal.

A subsequent study (Henson, Rubin, & Henson, 1979a) demonstrated consistency in response patterns between sessions, although marked variations were noted in the levels of response. Further investigations have indicated considerable variability across individual subjects in correlations between labial temperature and subjective ratings of arousal (e.g., Henson & Rubin, 1978; Henson et al., 1979a, 1979b). Comparisons between the labial thermistor clip and the vaginal photometer suggest high positive correlations between the two measures, although the thermistor has a longer latency for return to baseline following stimulus offset (Henson, Rubin, & Henson, 1979b; Henson, Rubin, & Henson, 1982).

Correspondence Between Vaginal Blood Flow Measures and Subjective Arousal. One of the most pervasive issues in the laboratory study of female sexual response is the relationship between physiological and subjective indices of arousal. As with similar studies of male subjects reviewed earlier, the growing literature on correspondence between objective and subjective measures with females is problematic in a number of respects. Correlations have varied widely depending on the methodology and procedures employed, with a number of explanations being proposed to account for this variability. Moreover, the discordance between measures raises important conceptual issues in the definition of sexual arousal as discussed above.

In one of the earlier studies, Geer et al. (1974) presented erotic and non-erotic films to 20 normal female undergraduates. Response measures included VPA and VBV, as well as global subjective ratings of arousal after the film presentations. Although both vaginal blood flow measures discriminated the effects of the erotic stimulus, neither of these measures were significantly correlated with self-report. This lack of correlation was explained by the authors as possibly resulting from the crudeness of the self-report measures. Other studies with normal female subjects, however, have obtained a range of positive correlations from 0.44 to 0.68 (Heiman, 1977). Henson, Rubin, and Henson (1979b) reported average correlations between subjective ratings and VPA of 0.76, but correspondence between VBV and self-report was only 0.42.

Studies that have compared measures of physiological response with continuous assessment of subjective arousal have shown similar results (Wincze, Hoon, & Hoon, 1978; Wincze, Venditti, Barlow, & Mavissakalian, 1980). Using the same methodology for continuous assessment of subjective arousal as was reported previously for male subjects, Wincze et al. (1977) presented a hierarchy of visual erotic stimuli to 6 normal female subjects. The authors found that use of the continuous lever did not disrupt physiological monitoring. However, correlations between vaginal engorgement and subjective arousal ranged from 0.12 to 0.78. In a further study of the potential obtrusiveness of the continuous lever (Wincze et al., 1980), a comparison was made of physiological arousal with and without concurrent subjective monitoring. Physiological responding was unaffected by the addition of the subjective monitoring task at both high and low levels of arousal, although again correlations between the two measures ranged widely across subjects.

Comparing these findings on response concordance for female subjects with the correlations obtained from male subjects, a number of observations are apparent. First, somewhat paradoxically, the subjective monitoring task was found to have more disruptive effects at low levels of arousal for males than females. This finding contrasts with clinical accounts of the presumed susceptibility of female arousal to external distraction (Barbach, 1975; Masters & Johnson, 1970). Secondly, correlations ranged widely for both sexes, although it appears that response concordance improves at higher levels of arousal for both males and females (e.g. Bancroft & Mathews, 1971; Farkas et al., 1979; Heiman, 1980). Finally, comparisons of response concordance between males and females are confounded by the measurement of different physiological responses, as well as the possibility that males and females may use different criteria in their ratings of subjective arousal.

A study by Korff and Geer (1983) clearly illustrates the effects of different standards for rating subjective arousal on response concordance in women. These authors experimentally manipulated attentional cues for gauging arousal, with one group instructed to focus on specific genital changes, another on overall somatic arousal, and a third with no specific attentional cues. Both forms of attentional directions resulted in substantially higher correlations between vasocongestion and subjective arousal, although no differential effects emerged between these two conditions. These data suggest that in previous studies, subjective arousal ratings may not have been anchored on specific physiological indices of arousal. This investigation does not, however, deliniate the attentional cues that subjects might employ in the absence of specific experimental instructions, an understanding of which would contribute significantly to formulation of the multiple response components of arousal.

The issue of correspondence between vaginal blood flow and self-report measures of arousal is especially salient in comparisons of clinical and nonclinical subjects. Clinical formulations of sexual dysfunction in women have included a strong emphasis on lack of awareness of physiological arousal as an etiological factor in arousal disorders (e.g. Barbach, 1975). In a study of sexual responding with low arousal women and normal controls, Wincze et al. (1976) found that vaginal blood flow measures differentiated between groups, whereas subjective ratings of arousal failed to show differences. In contrast, Heiman (1975) reported that self-reports of arousal were significantly different between functional and dysfunctional groups, whereas vasocongestion measures did not detect group differences. One possible explanation for the discrepancy in these findings is the differences in the age and marital status of the subject groups. However, the lack of concordance between response measures found in both studies is representative of much of the literature in this area and clearly highlights the need for further studies of the relationship between experiential and physiological components of sexual arousal.

Extragenital Measures of Arousal in Males and Females

The detailed description of sexual responding provided by Masters & Johnson (1966) includes mention of a full range of extragenital changes occurring during excitation and orgasm. Some of these changes involve skin coloration in the upper torso (the "sex flush"), elevations in heart rate and blood pressure, increased perspiration, myotonia, and irregularities in respiration. Masters and Johnson have made much of the similarity in males and females of these general body reactions in support of the universality of their 4-stage model of sexual response. Unfortunately, subsequent laboratory investigations have not entirely supported this contention.

A number of studies have attempted to differentiate a generalized pattern of autonomic arousal thought to be associated with sexual arousal in males and females (Bancroft & Mathews; 1971; Sims, 1967; Wenger, Averill, & Smith, 1968). In an influential review of early research in this area, however, Zuckerman (1971) highlighted a number of conceptual and methodological problems associated with this measurement approach. First, extragenital indices are lacking in *stimulus–response specificity*, i.e., they usually fail to differentiate between sexual and nonsexual states of arousal, such as anger or anxiety. Second, the correlations between the genital and extragenital measures of arousal have typically been low, as have been the correlations with subjective arousal. Additionally, the amplitude of measures such as GSR tends to be more closely related to the *novelty* of the experimental stimuli, rather than to the erotic intensity. For these reasons Zuckerman recommended that research on sexual arousal be based on measures of penile tumescence in the male and vaginal engorgement in the female.

Despite these shortcomings, there has been a continuing effort to identify possible extragenital indices of sexual arousal in both sexes. Cardiovascular effects, in particular, have been recorded in a number of studies (Bancroft,

1983). Some investigators have also recorded patterns of electrodermal, respiratory, pupil dilation, and body temperature changes during sexual arousal. Although interesting in their own right, the results of these studies have continued to support Zuckerman's original conclusions concerning the role of extragenital measures. We briefly review recent examples of research in this area, highlighting possible alternative uses of the methodology.

As discussed by Bancroft (1983), sexual arousal in both sexes is typically associated with a wide range of cardiovascular changes such as elevations in systolic and diastolic blood pressure, increased heart rate, and changes in skin temperature. For example, Hoon, Wincze, and Hoon (1976) conducted an extensive investigation of changes in these measures during the presentation of sexually explicit, neutral, and dysphoric stimuli to a sample of normal females. While significant increases in systolic and diastolic blood pressure and in forehead temperature were observed during presentation of the erotic stimuli, these measures were clearly less responsive than concurrent assessments of vaginal blood volume. Furthermore, the specificity of the cardiovascular measures was generally low.

In a study of normal and dysfunctional males, Kockott, Feil, Ferstl, Aldenhoff, and Besinger (1980) contrasted patterns of cardiovascular response in men with primary impotence, secondary psychogenic impotence, organic (diabetic) impotence, premature ejaculation, and an age-matched control group. Surprisingly, the pattern of psychophysiological responses shown by the subjects with secondary psychogenic impotence most closely resembled the responses of the group with diabetes-related dysfunction. Subjects with premature ejaculation, on the other hand, showed response patterns indistinguishable from the normal controls. Although this study did not, unfortunately, include a control condition for assessing autonomic arousal during presentation of nonsexual stimuli, the approach appears useful in differentiating clinical subtypes of sexual dysfunction.

Body temperature changes during sexual responding have received increased attention, owing primarily to technical advances in the field of thermography. Abramson and his colleagues (e.g., Abramson & Pearsall, 1983; Abramson, Perry, Seeley, Seeley, & Rothblatt, 1981; Seeley, Abramson, Perry, Rothblatt, & Seeley, 1980) have investigated the use of thermography for the study of heat generation patterns, and the underlying vascular changes associated with sexual responding in males and females. The results have indicated that sexual arousal in both sexes is accompanied by progressive surface skin cooling in the lower abdomen. An unfortunate drawback of this approach, however, is that thermographic recording cannot be conducted concurrently with other psychophysiological measures due to specific requirements for positioning of the subject.

In an attempt to replicate this finding by means of thermistor recording of surface abdominal temperature, Beck, Barlow, and Sakheim (in press) assessed penile tumescence, subjective arousal and abdominal temperature during erotic presentations to normal males. Although some evidence was found of skin temperature decreases during sexual arousal, the thermistor results did not correlate well with either tumescence or subjective arousal. The authors conclude that while thermographic measures do not appear to be well suited for use in typical sex research paradigms, this approach may be of value in studying basic physiological mechanisms involved in sexual response.

Pupil dilation is another extragenital response that has been viewed as potentially indicative of sexual arousal. In his review of early work in this area, however, Zuckerman (1971) pointed out that pupillometry measures were lacking in specificity and were particularly susceptible to novelty effects. Despite these difficulties, Lucas, Abel, Mittelman, and Becker (1983) have described a method for assessing pupil dilation as a measure of sexual preference in sex offenders. Unfortunately, the pupillometry measure appears to yield only a crude assessment of sexual interest, which does not appear to be comparable to measures of penile erection.

Overall, psychophysiological studies of extragenital responding have yielded sparse and inconclusive results. Although it remains possible that future research will identify additional physiological concomitants of sexual response, none of the variables studied thus far have proved to be reliable predictors of sexual arousal in males or females.

PSYCHOPHYSIOLOGICAL STUDIES OF ORGASM

Throughout the research and literature of modern sexology, orgasm has occupied a central position as one of the most controversial and poorly understood aspects of sexual response. Masters, Johnson, and Kolodny (1982) have emphasized that although orgasm is typically the shortest phase of the sexual response cycle, it is usually associated with the greatest pleasure and subjective satisfaction. Although subjective reactions to orgasm vary widely, one study (Vance & Wagner, 1976) has shown that male and female verbal descriptions of orgasms can not be distinguished by independent raters. Because of its sudden, explosive nature, orgasm has been likened by some authors to a sneeze that involves the entire body (Kinsey, Pomeroy, Martin, & Gebhard, 1953), whereas other authors have compared it to an epileptic seizure (Mosovich & Tallafero, 1954). Much has been written about the *phenomenological* aspects of orgasm, such as D. H. Lawrence's (1928) description of Lady Chatterley's orgasm as "pure deepening whirlpools of sensations swirling through her tissue and consciousness, till she was one perfect concentric fluid of feeling" (p. 128).

The nature of female orgasm has been especially controversial, with much of the debate centered around the existence of distinct "types" of female orgasm. Despite Masters and Johnson's (1966) efforts to establish the equivalence of clitoral and vaginal orgasms, the notion of a typology of female orgasm has continued to find support in the scientific literature (e.g., Bentler & Peeler, 1979; Fisher, 1973; Singer & Singer, 1978). Recently this controversy has focused on the role of the Grafenberg spot and "female ejaculation" in particular (Belzer, 1981; Ladas, Whipple, & Perry, 1982; Sevely & Bennett, 1978; Zilbergeld, 1982). In the only controlled study to date (Goldberg, Whipple, Fishkin, et al., 1983), however, little evidence was found to support these hypotheses. Unfortunately, much of the research in this area has been characterised by the ideological commitment of the investigators rather than the empirical strength of the findings.

From a psychophysiological perspective, orgasm appears to consist of a highly synchronised combination of somatic, autonomic, and subjective responses, which may nevertheless vary considerably. Komisaruk (1982) has described orgasm as an "efferent excitation peak . . . (which) is generated by a process of increasingly synchronous afferent discharge", in which the visceral and somatic systems are "entrained by rhythmical stimulation" (p. 122). This author further attributes the uniquely pleasurable sensory experience of orgasm to this synchronous afferent stimulation. Other authors have placed greater emphasis on the role of peripheral events in general, and myotonia and vasocongestion in particular, as the key determinants of orgasm in both males and females (e.g. Sherfey, 1974; Masters & Johnson, 1966).

The Role of Pelvic Muscle Contractions

According to Masters and Johnson (1966), female orgasm is initiated by involuntary contractions in the orgasmic platform of the outer third of the vagina. For the male, Masters and Johnson described the onset of orgasm as occurring with the testicular contractions noted during the first phase of ejaculation. Similarly, Sherfey (1974) has proposed that orgasm is a spinal reflex that is triggered by pressure on the stretch receptors in the pelvic musculature. Sherfey's model has recently been modified by Mould (1980), who postulates that orgasm consists of clonic contractions of the pelvic and abdominal muscle groups, stimulated by neural impulses in the *alpha fusimotor* system. Much attention has also been paid to the role of the *levator ani* muscles of the pelvic diaphragm, and the *pubococcygeal* muscles in particular. Although research in this area has generally focused on pelvic muscle contractions during orgasm in women, some investigators have also emphasized the importance these responses in males (Bohlen & Held, 1979; Bohlen, Held, & Sanderson, 1980).

Based on his clinical observations of post-partum urinary stress incontinence, Kegel (1952) noted that tonus of the circumvaginal musculature seemed to be important in both the control of bladder function and the maintenance of adequate intravaginal pressure during intercourse. Kegel therefore developed a measuring device, the perineometer, for assessing intravaginal pressure, as well as a set of exercises for strengthening the pubococcygeal (PC) muscles. These exercises have subsequently been adapted by sex therapists for use in the treatment of organic dysfunction (e.g. Barbach, 1980; Kline-Graber & Graber, 1978).

Despite the enthusiasm of many clinicians for PC muscle training, research has not supported either the clinical efficacy of these exercises nor the theory on which they are based. Levitt, Konovsky, Freese, and Thompson (1979) conducted the first normative study of intravaginal pressure in both the resting and contracted state in 142 women. This study unfortunately did not assess the relationship between PC tonus and sexual dysfunction but did reveal a number of methodological problems in the use of the perineometer. The mean resting pressure was found by these authors to be about 5 mm Hg, which was considerably less than the levels previously reported by Kegel (1952).

Graber and Kline-Graber (1979) conducted a retrospective study of the relationship between PC muscle tonus and orgasmic response in 281 female clients in a sex therapy clinic. Although the authors reported significant differences in a measure of sustained contraction pressure between orgasmic and anorgasmic women, these findings are mitigated by the correlational and retrospective nature of the results. In fact, this is the only study to date to have found a relationship between PC muscle tonus and sexual function, and the results may have been confounded by other medical conditions in the subjects, or the lack of control for experimenter expectancy effects.

Several subsequent reports have failed to replicate this relationship. For example, Roughan and Kunst (1981) compared the effects of PC training with relaxation and a no-treatment control group in a study of 46 anorgasmic women. Although the PC training group showed significant increases in muscle tonus after treatment, these effects were unrelated to improvements in orgasmic function. Similarly, Trudel and Saint-Laurent (1983) found no differences in orgasmic ability following treatment with either PC muscle training or a combination of sexual awareness and relaxation exercises.

The strongest disconfirmation of the PC hypothesis can be found in the recent research conducted by Chambless and her associates (Chambless et al., 1982; Chambless et al., 1984). In the first study, Chambless et al., (1982) conducted a correlational study in 102 normal women of pubococcygeal strength, as assessed by the perineometer, and a wide range of measures of sexual responsiveness. Overall, PC strength was not related to either the frequency or intensity of orgasm, nor did women with higher PC tonus report vaginal sensations to be more pleasurable during intercourse. In the second study, Chambless et al. (1984) compared PC muscle training to an attention placebo group in the treatment of secondary orgasmic dysfunction. As in the Roughan and Kunst (1981) study, it was found that increases in PC muscle tonus as a result of treatment were not related to improvements in orgasmic function. Chambless et al. (1984) conclude that while these exercises may be of some value to women who have severely damaged or impaired PC control, they have little relevance to the majority of women.

Regarding the usefulness of the perineometer as a measurement device for the assessment of circumvaginal muscle tonus, a number of methodological problems have emerged from the above studies. For example, Levitt et al. (1979) found that perineometer readings were strongly influenced by the position of the woman's legs or torso, and that the pressure levels could be affected by the use of nonpelvic (e.g., abdominal) muscles. In addition, Chambless et al. (1982) found that test–retest reliability was extremely poor, despite the use of procedures to maximize standardization of measurement across sessions. Perry (1980) has recommended the use of an improved electronic perineometer, or *vaginal myograph*, although reliability problems do not appear to have been resolved (Perry & Whipple, 1981). In view of the repeated failure to demonstrate a relationship between PC muscle tonus and sexual response, however, the value of further methodological improvements in the device is questionable.

A modified perineometer has recently been developed by Bohlen & Held (1979) for the measurement of *anal contractions* during orgasms in males and females. This device consists of a photoplethysmograph and pressure transducer in a closed air chamber located in the neck of the probe (see Fig. 3.7), and is designed to fit comfortably in the anal canal. Signals from the probe are recorded on a polygraph and digitized by means of an analog-to-digital converter.

In a study of 11 normal males, Bohlen, Held, and Sanderson (1980) observed various patterns of anal contractions associated with orgasm. The authors noted, however, that the subjective experiences of orgasm did not always correspond

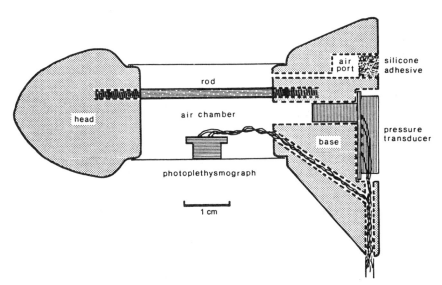

FIG. 3.7.   Anal probe for measurement of blood flow and muscular contractions (Bohlen & Held, 1979).

with the period of anal contractions, which seemed to begin before or after orgasm in several of the subjects. Nor did the contractions correlate with subjective reports of the intensity of arousal or orgasm. Recognizing that anal contractions may not be a primary focus of orgasmic response, the authors nevertheless recommend this site for ease of measurement and potential comparability of male and female response. Potential reactivity problems with this device have not been addressed.

Cardiovascular and Respiratory Changes During Orgasm

Among the physiological changes observed during orgasm, Masters and Johnson (1966) reported particularly dramatic effects in the cardiovascular and respiratory systems. Specifically, they found evidence of high levels of tachycardia in both sexes, with heart rates ranging from 100 to 180+ beats per minute, along with increases in systolic blood pressure of 40–100 mm. Hg. Hyperventilation was also observed as a constant accompaniment to orgasm in both sexes, with respiratory rates as high as 40 breaths per minute.

Similar results were obtained in two single case studies of physiological changes during intercourse (Fox & Fox, 1969). Although marked hyperventilation was observed in association with orgasm in both sexes, the authors also recorded the occurrence of bouts of inspiratory apnea, as measured by a spirometer, prior to orgasm in the female subject. These authors also noted that the sharp rise and fall in systolic blood pressure observed during orgasm may have been mediated by the muscular exertion involved in sexual activity. Furthermore, in a subsequent study of the effects of a beta-blocker (propranolol) on coital physiology, Fox (1970) found that the normal systolic blood pressure rise was markedly attenuated, without any apparent effect on the subjective experience or ease of attainment of orgasm.

Using procedures for continuous recording of blood pressure and heart rate, Littler, Honour, & Sleight (1974) reported further effects of intercourse on cardiovascular function in seven normal subjects. Direct arterial pressure was measured by means of an indwelling catheter attached to a transducer and perfusion pump. Results indicated maximum systolic blood pressure increases of 120 mm.Hg and diastolic pressure increases of 25 to 50 mm.Hg, which the authors attributed to overriding of the baroreceptor regulation of blood pressure at the time of orgasm. Again, it was unclear to what extent these cardiovascular changes were secondary to the effects of muscular exertion.

Studies of cardiovascular function during orgasm are of particular relevance in view of current clinical concerns with the risks of sexual activity for cardiac or hypertensive patients. Research is presently being conducted in our laboratory to assess a wide range of psychophysiological effects of different beta-blocker medications, including the effects of medication on sexual desire and nocturnal tumescence.

EEG Changes During Orgasm

As we have indicated throughout this chapter, laboratory studies of sexual response have tended to focus primarily on peripheral somatic and autonomic events in both sexes. Although useful in some respects, this emphasis on peripheral physiological activity has tended to obscure the importance of CNS phenomena during sexual arousal and orgasm. Phenomenological reports from many sources (e.g., Keiser, 1952) suggest that sexual climax is associated with a unique state of consciousness, involving a brief loss of contact with immediate external reality (or *petite mort*). Fisher (1973) has speculated that this "blurring" of consciousness might elicit fears of object loss, and hence be related to orgasmic difficulties in some individuals. Furthermore, according to Bancroft (1983), these changes in consciousness strongly suggest the mediating role of central neurophysiological events.

Direct evidence for the role of cortical events in sexual arousal comes from a small number of studies in which continuous EEG recordings have been obtained during sexual arousal and orgasm. Mosovich and Tallafero (1954), for example, observed a striking change in the EEG of 6 normal subjects during masturbation to orgasm in the laboratory. Although appropriate quantitative data analysis was not available at that time, visual inspection of the EEG records indicated a generalized slowing of electrical activity with concomitant voltage increases. EEGs from 4 of the 6 subjects were characterized by paroxysmal 3/sec. waves.

In a series of controversial studies, Heath (1972) recorded EEG during sexual activity via deep and surface electrodes in two subjects. Results indicated a striking pattern of spike and slow-wave activity in the septal region during orgasm. With respect to the surface electrode recording, however, the results were obscured by an abundance of muscle artifact. Moreover, the limited sample and severe symptomatology of the subjects limit the generalizability of these findings. Also, Heath found similar patterns of spiking activity in the septal area in conjunction with a number of other nonsexual emotional states, thus raising the question of the specificity of the observed EEG changes.

Research in our own laboratory (Cohen, Rosen, & Goldstein, 1976; Cohen, Rosen, & Goldstein, in press) has fosuced on a specific electrophysiological process, namely patterns of lateral asymmetry in the integrated EEG amplitude obtained during sexual arousal to orgasm. In the first study (Cohen et al., 1976), left and right parietal EEG was continuously recorded while 7 male and female subjects masturbated to orgasm under controlled laboratory conditions. Using an amplitude integration method developed by Goldstein (1975), integrated EEG amplitude ratios (R/L) were computed for all phases of the sexual response cycle. Significant changes in cortical asymmetry were observed, due in large part to a marked increase in amplitude in the nondominant hemisphere, which were attributed to peak levels of sexual excitement. These results were interpreted as indicating a dissociation between the right and left EEG, with a predominant change in the nondominant hemisphere.

Included in this study were experimental tests of two major alternative hypotheses. First, in view of the possible confounding effects of the hand used during masturbation, one subject repeated the experiment with stimulation from the nondominant (left) hand. The subject was able to achieve orgasm in this fashion, and the resulting shift in EEG laterality was consistent with that observed during masturbation with the dominant (right) hand. Secondly, in order to assess the effects of generalized somatic and autonomic exertion on the pattern of cortical activity, a female subject volunteered to produce a "faked" orgasm under laboratory conditions. This "faked" orgasm resulted in the respiratory and cardiovascular changes typically found during orgasm, but without the accompanying shift in EEG laterality.

EEG laterality changes have also been used to distinguish the responses of dysfunctional and normal male subjects to laboratory erotic stimuli (Cohen, Rosen, & Goldstein, in press). In this study 12 normal males were selected as responsive or unresponsive to erotic stimuli, and were compared to an age-matched sample of sexually dysfunctional males. Each subject was exposed to a series of visual and auditory erotic stimuli over two sessions of testing. Response measures included continuous recording of bilateral temporal and occipital EEG amplitude, penile tumescence assessment via a mercury-in-rubber strain gauge, and subjective estimates of arousal. While both the tumescence and EEG laterality measures varied significantly between groups, a more complex pattern was evident in the hemispheric laterality data, particularly in the dysfunctional group. As in the previous study, the highest levels of sexual arousal were associated with significant activation of the right temporal EEG.

Similar findings have also been reported by Tucker (1983), who recorded left and right EEG from a number of cortical sites under conditions of sexual arousal and depression. The subjects were 9 experienced method actors who generated intense feelings of sexual excitement through imagery alone. Based on a spectral analysis of the EEG and coherence analysis of bilateral amplitude relationships, Tucker confirmed that high levels of sexual arousal in normal subjects appear to be associated with greater nondominant hemisphere involvement in right-handed subjects. Consistent with the findings in the Cohen et al., (1976) study, the cerebral asymmetry effect was most striking in the amplitude ratios from the left and right posterior recording sites.

It is interesting to note that an association has also been shown between sleep erections and cerebral lateralization (Hirshkowitz, Ware, Turner, & Karacan, 1979). Specifically, a pattern of cortical asymmetry was observed during REM sleep in 12 male subjects, the onset of which was correlated with the appearance of penile tumescence responses in all subjects. Again, results indicated greater right hemisphere activation during periods of nocturnal penile tumescence.

Taken together the results of the above studies suggest that cortical (EEG) measures may yield important information concerning the role of central events during sexual arousal and orgasm. Measures of lateral brain function have recently been associated with a variety of cognitive and affective states (Tucker,

1981), and more research is clearly needed to determine the specific role of these changes in the experience of sexual arousal and orgasm. These studies are also consistent with a growing interest in the underlying cortical processes involved in sexual response, which Davidson (1980) aptly refers to as "those transformations of consciousness that we label as *sexual*" (p. 126).

CONCLUSION: THEORETICAL AND APPLIED ISSUES IN PSYCHOPHYSIOLOGICAL RESEARCH

The field of sexual psychophysiology has clearly made major strides in the past decade, Notwithstanding the proliferation of measurement techniques and methodologies, however, research in this area has also focused attention on the practical constraints and difficulties inherent in conducting laboratory research, as well as the major task of conceptual integration. As noted by Byrne and Kelley (this volume), the existence of a large and growing body of empirical research in this area is just as remarkable in many ways as the specific findings that have emerged. In concluding this chapter, these general issues are illustrated with some brief discussion of potential uses and abuses of psychophysiological methods in sex research.

Safeguards in Conducting Laboratory Assessments

Generally, institutional concerns for human subjects' protection have increased markedly in recent years; this is especially true in the study of sensitive topics such as sex and aggression. Laboratory assessments of sexual responding raise a number of unique considerations in this regard. One aspect of human subjects' protection concerns the need for careful and thorough briefing and debriefing of all experimental subjects. In a recent review of current laboratory practices, Bohlen (1980) has categorised a wide range of issues involved in the orientation of subjects to experimentation. These include procedures for obtaining informed consent, confidentiality, history taking, physical examination, gender of the experimenter, specification of potential risks and benefits, placement of recording devices, and orientation of the subject to both the methods and physical facilities of the laboratory. Bohlen highlights a number of infrequently cited precautions, such as the need for completely informed and voluntary consent, and the determination of an appropriate risk–benefit balance.

   Assuming adequate preparation of subjects, a number of additional safeguards are also imperative in the conduct of laboratory research. For example, Geer (1980) has emphasized the need for attention to the physical and emotional comfort of the subject throughout. Geer recommends special care and sensitivity in interactions with subjects, and places particular stress on the selection and training of research assistants. Another issue of importance discussed by this author is the need for complete sterilization of genital devices to prevent the accidental transmission of sexually transmitted disease. One approach to sterilization is the immersion of devices in a liquid solution such as activated gluteraldehyde (Cidex 7). On the other hand, we have found that sterilization by means of a gaseous sterilant, ethylene oxide ("Anprolene"), is more effective, safer, and less corrosive to the assessment device.

Careful interviewing at the termination of the procedure is another important aspect of human subjects' protection. Where the experimental procedures involve deception (e.g. Barlow, Sakheim, & Beck, 1983) the need for debriefing is especially salient. Similarly, the use of socially unacceptable stimuli, such as depictions of rape or pedophilia, warrants additional safeguards (Check & Malamouth, 1984; Malamuth & Check, 1984; Sherif, 1980). In fact, Malamuth and Check have described a series of studies investigating the effects of controlled debriefing following presentation of rape stimuli to normal male and female objects. The results of this research indicate that subjects receiving a combination of exposure to rape depictions and subsequent debriefing were less accepting of rape myths following the experiment. Unfortunately, however, few studies in this area have paid as much attention to the importance of complete debriefing.

Issues in the Clinical Application
of Psychophysiological Assessment

In addition to the conceptual and technical issues discussed throughout this chapter, the use of psychophysiological assessment for clinical decision-making poses additional questions. One area of application of psychophysiological assessment that particularly highlights these concerns is the evaluation of sexual deviation. Research in a number of laboratories (e.g., Abel, Barlow, Quinsey 1977; Laws & Osborn, 1983; Blanchard, & Guild, 1977) has examined the use of penile tumescence assessment in determining components of deviant arousal, formulating treatment interventions, and evaluating therapeutic outcome. This research has provided a much needed objective and quantitative approach to clinical assessment, as well as contributing to basic understanding of atypical sexual arousal patterns. A central issue, however, in this area of application is the concern with voluntary control of arousal ("faking") in individuals being assessed for treatment or release from incarceration.

The falsification of sexual arousal responses was first noted by Freund (1963), who observed that exclusively homosexual males were able to produce voluntary erection responses to heterosexual stimuli. Subsequently, Laws and Holmen (1978) have described a number of strategies by means of which pedophilic subjects were able to falsify their assessments. These included cognitive manipulation of imagery content, strategies for attentional distraction, and mechanical manipulation of the penile strain gauge. The authors describe procedures for minimizing the occurrence of faking, but conclude that this is a potentially serious problem that detracts from the use of penile tumescence "as a truly objective measure."

Other researchers in the field of sexual deviation generally concur that voluntary control of arousal is possible, but differ in their view of the implications. For example, Quinsey and Marshall (1983) propose that the problem is limited to a select subgroup of offenders, whose sexual arousal patterns may still be predictive of treatment outcome. These authors further suggest that, "patients who can 'fake' improvement are demonstrating that they have acquired the ability to control their arousal and are therefore good risks" (p. 283). Unfortunately, no empirical evidence is provided to support this controversial claim. Overall, this issue is of major social importance as decisions regarding disposition are increasingly based upon laboratory assessments.

The phenomenon of response faking also represents another instance of discordance between measures of sexual response, an issue that we have discussed throughout this chapter. When a subject voluntarily suppresses his penile erection response to a deviant stimulus, for example, the assumption is typically made that subjective interest in the stimulus is maintained despite the absence of tumescence. Thus, Lucas et al. (1983) have included pupillometry measures in their laboratory assessment protocol in an attempt to detect subjective interest independent of penile tumescence responding. Similarly, research in our own laboratory is investigating the use of EEG hemispheric measures for this purpose. Again, this research raises the key conceptual question of defining sexual arousal in the context of discordance between measures.

Other concerns have also been noted in regard to the use of psychophysiological assessment of deviant arousal. First, it is important to consider the relationship between deviant arousal and the actual commission of deviant sexual acts. Although much of the research in this area is based on Barlow's (1977) assertion that deviant sexual behavior can be broken down into a predictable chain of responses, in which "sexual arousal is a necessary step in the chain leading to the consummation of sexual behavior" (p. 173), there are major exceptions to this rule. For instance, Groth and Birnbaum (1979) have described numerous case histories of violent sex offenders who appeared to be motivated entirely by non-sexual forms of gratification. Conversely, the research of Malamuth and his associates has indicated that sexual arousal to deviant stimuli is common among normal males, most of whom are unlikely to act on their arousal. Secondly, the problem of the external validity of laboratory assessment of offenders has been raised by a number of authors (e.g. Farkas, 1978; Laws & Osborn, 1983). It is unclear at present to what extent deviant arousal in the laboratory is correlated with arousal patterns in a naturalistic setting.

Effects of Psychophysiological Research on Sexual Performance Standards

A final area of concern is the potential misuse of laboratory research results as a basis for the setting of sexual performance standards. Concerns about sexual "normality" are so pervasive in our society that individuals are extremely susceptible to the findings of sex researchers in general. The unfortunate result is that research on topics such as masturbation, sexual fantasy, multiple orgasm, and female ejaculation frequently serves as the basis for prescriptive notions of sexual function. Sex manuals and self-help guides, in particular, all too often oversimplify the results of laboratory research and encourage conformity to ever-changing sexual standards. Our experience as sex therapists has also confirmed that popular coverage of research findings commonly evokes concern in the larger community about "normal" sexual functioning.

The most recent example of this phenomenon is the attention devoted to the Grafenberg spot and female ejaculation as new "discoveries" about female sexuality (Ladas, Whipple, & Perry, 1982). Although individual differences in sexual response patterns in women are clearly a legitimate research topic, most reports of investigations in this area unfortunately have been clearly colored by a prescriptive tone. The novelty of these "discoveries," along with the persuasive rhetoric of the reports, has resulted in many women (and their partners) experiencing pressures to achieve new forms of sexual response.

Despite these potential areas of misuse, the laboratory study of sexual responding holds considerable promise in understanding many facets of male and female sexuality. Toward this goal we have attempted to delineate a range of theoretical and applied issues that need to be considered in conducting research in this area. Considering also that sex research is carried out in the context of an interested and partial society, this review has highlighted potential uses and misuses of psychophysiological studies of sexual arousal. In summation, an attempt has been made to appraise the current status and pinpoint future directions for investigation in this rich and multifaceted field of study.

REFERENCES

Abel, G. G., Barlow, D. H., Blanchard, E. B., & Guild, D. (1977). The components of rapists' sexual arousal. *Archives of General Psychiatry, 34,* 895–903.

Abel, G. G., Blanchard, E. B., Barlow, D. H., & Mavissakalian, M. (1975). Identifying specific erotic cues in sexual deviations by audiotaped descriptions. *Journal of Applied Behavior Analysis, 8,* 247–260.

Abel, G. G., Blanchard, E. B., Murphy, W. D., Becker, J. V., & Djenderedjian, A. (1981). Two methods of measuring penile response *Behavior Therapy, 12,* 320–328.

Abel, G. G., Murphy, W., Becker, J., & Bitar, A. (1979). Women's vaginal responses during REM sleep. *Journal of Sex and Marital Therapy, 5,* 5–14.

Abrams, D. B., & Wilson, G. T. (1983). Alcohol, sexual arousal, and self-control. *Journal of Personality and Social Psychology, 45,* 188–198.

Abrams, R., Kalna, O., & Wilcox, C. (1978). Vaginal blood flow during the menstrual cycle. *American Journal of Obstetrics and Gynecology, 132,* 396–400.

Abrams, R., & Stolwijk, J. (1972). Heat flow device for vaginal blood flow studies. *Journal of Applied Physiology, 23,* 143–146.

Abramson, P. R., Perry, L. B., Seeley, T. T., Seeley, D. M., & Rothblatt, A. B. (1981). Thermographic measurement of sexual arousal: A discriminant validity analysis. *Archives of Sexual Behavior, 10,* 171–176.

Abramson, P. R., & Pearsall, E. H. (1983). Pectoral changes during the sexual response cycle: A thermographic analysis. *Archives of Sexual Behavior, 12*, 357–368.

Apter-Marsh, M. (1983, May). *The sexual behavior of alcoholic women while drinking and during sobriety.* Paper presented at the 6th World Congress of Sexology, Washington, DC.

Armon, H., Weinman, J., & Weinstein, D. (1978). A vaginal photoplethysmographic transducer. *IEEE Transactions on Biomedical Engineering, 25*, 434–440.

Bancroft, J. H. (1983). *Human sexuality and its problems.* New York: Churchill Livingstone.

Bancroft, J. H., Jones, J. G., & Pullan, B. B. (1966). A simple transducer for measuring penile erection with comments on its use in the treatment of sexual disorder. *Behavior Research and Therapy, 4*, 230–241.

Bancroft, J. H., & Mathews, A. (1971). Autonomic correlates of penile erection. *Journal of Psychosomatic Research, 15*, 159–167.

Barbach, L. G. (1975). *For yourself: The fulfillment of female sexuality.* New York: Doubleday.

Barbach, L. G. (1980). *Women discover orgasm.* New York: Free Press.

Barlow, D. H. (1977). Assessment of sexual behavior. In R. A. Ciminero, K. S. Calhoun, & H. E. Adams (Eds.), *Handbook of behavioral assessment* (pp. 461–508). New York: Wiley.

Barlow, D. H., Becker, R., Leitenberg, H., & Agras, W. S. (1970). A mechanical strain gauge for recording penile circumference change. *Journal of Applied Behavior Analysis, 3*, 73–76.

Barlow, D. H., Sakheim, D. K., & Beck, J. G. (1983). Anxiety increases sexual arousal. *Journal of Abnormal Psychology, 92*, 49–54.

Barr, R. F., & McConaghy, N. (1971). Penile volume responses to appetitive and aversive stimuli in relation to sexual orientation and conditioning performance. *British Journal of Psychiatry, 119*, 377–383.

Beck, J. G., Barlow, D. H., & Sakheim, D. K. (1983). The effects of attentional focus and partner arousal on sexual responding in functional and dysfunctional men. *Behavior Research and Therapy, 21*, 1–8.

Beck, J. G., Barlow, D. H., & Sakheim, D. K. (in press). Abdominal temperature changes during male sexual arousal. *Psychophysiology.*

Beck, J. G., Sakheim, D. K., & Barlow, D. H. (1983). Operating characteristics of the vaginal photoplethysmograph: Some implications for its use. *Archives of Sexual Behavior, 12*, 41–58.

Bell, A. P., Weinberg, M. S., & Hammersmith, S. K. (1981). *Sexual preference: Its development in men and women.* Bloomington, IN: Indiana University Press.

Belzer, E. G. (1981). Orgasmic expulsions of women: A review and heuristic inquiry. *Journal of Sex Research, 17*, 1–12.

Benoit, H. J., Borth, R., & Woolever, C. A. (1980). Self-stabilizing system for measuring infrared light back-scattered from vaginal tissue. *Medical and Biological Engineering and Computing, 18*, 265–270.

Benson, G. S., McConnell, J., & Schmidt, W. A. (1981). Penile polsters: Functional structures or atherosclerotic changes? *Journal of Urology, 125*, 800–803.

Bentler, P. M., & Peeler, W. H. (1979). Models of female orgasm. *Archives of Sexual Behavior, 8*, 405–423.

Bohlen, J. G. (1980). A review of subject orientation in articles on sexual physiology research. *The Journal of Sex Research, 16*, 43–53.

Bohlen, J. G., & Held, J. P. (1979). An anal probe for monitoring vascular and muscular events during sexual response. *Psychophysiology, 16*, 318–323.

Bohlen, J. C., Held, J. P., & Sanderson, M. O. (1980). The male orgasm: Pelvic contractions measured by anal probe. *Archives of Sexual Behavior, 9*, 503–521.

Borth, R., Benoit, H. J., & Woolever, C. A. (1980). Detection of the pre-ovulatory period using a vaginal probe in the home. *Contraception, 21*, 41–46.

Briddell, D. W., Rimm, D. C., Caddy, G. R., Krawitz, G., Sholis, D., & Wunderlin, R. J. (1978). Effects of alcohol and cognitive set on sexual arousal to deviant stimuli. *Journal of Abnormal Psychology, 87*, 418–430.

Briddell, D. W., & Wilson, G. T. (1976). The effects of alcohol and expectancy set on male sexual arousal. *Journal of Abnormal Psychology, 85*, 225–234.

Byrne, D. (1983). The antecedents, correlates, and consequents of erotophobia-erotophilia. In C. M. Davis (Ed.), *Challenges in sexual science* (pp. 53–75). Lake Mills, IA: Graphic Publishing.

Chambless, D. L., Stern, T., Sultan, F. E., Williams, A. J., Goldstein, A. J., Lineberger, M. H., Lefshitz, J. L., & Kelly, L. (1982). The pubococcygeus and female orgasm: A correlational study with normal subjects. *Archives of Sexual Behavior, 11*, 479–490.

Chambless, D. L., Sultan, F. E., Stern, T. W., O'Neill, C., Garrison, S., & Jackson, A. (1984). Effect of pubococcygeal exercise on coital orgasm in women. *Journal of Consulting and Clinical Psychology, 52*, 114–118.

Check, J. V., & Malamuth, N. M. (1984). Can there be positive effects of participation in pornography experiments? *The Journal of Sex Research, 20*, 14–31.

Chilman, C. S. (1979). *Adolescent sexuality in a changing American society.* Bethesda, MD: U.S. Department of Health, Education and Welfare.

Cohen, A. S., Rosen, R. C., & Goldstein, L. (in press). EEG hemispheric asymmetry during sexual arousal: Psychophysiological patterns in responsive, unresponsive, and dysfunctional males. *Journal of Abnormal Psychology.*

Cohen, H. D., Rosen, R. C., & Goldstein, L. (1976). Electroencephalographic laterality changes during the human sexual orgasm. *Archives of Sexual Behavior, 5*, 189–199.

Cohen, H., & Shapiro, A. (1970). A method for measuring sexual arousal in the female. *Psychophysiology, 8*, 251.

Covington, S. (1983, May). *Sex and alcohol: What do women tell us.* Paper presented at the 6th World Congress of Sexology, Washington, DC.

Danesino, V., & Martella, E. (1976). Modern conceptions of corpora cavernosa functions in the vagina and clitoris. In T. P. Lowry, & T. S. Lowry (Eds.), *The clitoris* (pp. 75–90). St. Louis: Warren P. Green.

Davidson, J. M. (1980). The psychobiology of sexual experience. In J. M. Davidson & R. M. Davidson (Eds.), *The psychobiology of consciousness* (pp. 124–152). New York: Plenum.

Dickinson, R. L. (1949). *Human sex anatomy.* Baltimore: Williams & Wilkins.

Earls, C. W., & Marshall, W. L. (1981). A limitation of the mercury-in-rubber strain gauge? *Behavioral Assessment, 3*, 3–4.

Earls, C. W., & Marshall, W. L. (1982). The simultaneous and independent measurement of penile circumference and length. *Behavior Research Methods and Instrumentation, 14*, 447–450.

Earls, C. W., & Marshall, W. L. (1983). The current state of technology in the laboratory assessment of sexual arousal patterns. In J. G. Greer & I. R. Stuart (Eds.), *The sexual aggressor* (pp. 336–363). New York: Van Nostrand.

Ellis, H. (1906). *Studies in the psychology of sex.* New York: Random House.

Everaerd, W. (1983). Failure in treating sexual dysfunctions. In B. B. Foa & P. M. G. Emmelkamp (Eds.), *Failures in behavior therapy* (pp. 210–226). New York: Wiley.

Farkas, G. M. (1978). Comments on Levin et al. and Rosen and Kopel: Internal and external validity issues. *Journal of Consulting and Clinical Psychology, 46*, 1515–1516.

Farkas, G. M., & Rosen, R. C. (1976). Effect of alcohol on elicited male sexual response. *Journal of Studies on Alcohol, 37*, 265–272.

Farkas, G. M., Sine, R. F., & Evans, I. M. (1978). The effects of distraction, performance demand, stimulus explicitness, and personality on objective and subjective measures of male sexual arousal. *Behavior Research and Therapy, 17*, 25–32.

Fisher, S. (1973). *The female orgasm.* New York: Basic Books.

Fisher, C., Cohen, J., Schiavi, R., Davis, D., Furman, B., Ward, K., Edwards, A., & Cunningham, J. (1983). Patterns of female sexual arousal during sleep and waking: Vaginal thermo-conductance studies. *Archives of Sexual Behavior, 12*, 97–122.

Fisher, C., Gross, J., & Zuch, J. (1965). Cycle of penile erection synchronous with dreaming (REM) sleep. *Archives of General Psychiatry, 12*, 27–45.

Fisher, C., Schiavi, R. C., Edwards, A., Davis, D. M., Reitman, M., & Fine, J. (1979). Evaluation of nocturnal penile tumescence in the differential diagnosis of sexual impotence. *Archives of General Psychiatry, 36,* 431–437.

Fox, C. A. (1970). Reduction in the rise of systolic blood pressure during human coitus by the beta-adrenergic blocking agent, propranolol. *Journal of Reproduction and Fertility, 22,* 587–590.

Fox, C. A., & Fox, B. (1969). Blood pressure and respiratory patterns during human coitus. *Journal of Reproduction and Fertility, 19,* 405–415.

Freund, K. A. (1963). A laboratory method diagnosing predominance of homo- or hetero-erotic interest in the male. *Behavior Research and Therapy, 1,* 85–93.

Freund, K. (1965). Diagnosing heterosexual pedophilia by means of a test for sexual interest. *Behavior Research and Therapy, 3,* 229–234.

Freund, K., Langevin, R., Cibiri, W., & Zajac, Y. (1973). Heterosexual aversion in homosexual males. *British Journal of Psychiatry, 122,* 163–169.

Freund, K., Sedlacek, F., & Knob, K. (1965). A simple transducer for mechanical plethysmography of the male genital. *Journal of the Experimental Analysis of Behavior, 8,* 169–170.

Frisinger, J. E., Abrams, R. M., Graichen, A. H., & Cassin, S. (1981). New thermal method for evaluating vaginal blood flow. *Gynecology and Obstetrical Investigations, 12,* 71–80.

Gagnon, J. H. (1978). The interaction of gender roles and sexual conduct. In H. Kachadourian (Ed.), *Human sexuality: A comparative and developmental approach* (pp. 158–193). Los Angeles: University of California Press.

Geer, J. H. (1976). Genital measures: Comments on their role in understanding human sexuality. *Journal of Sex and Marital Therapy, 2,* 165–172.

Geer, J. H. (1977). Sexual functioning: Some data and speculations on psychophysiological assessment. In J. D. Cone & R. P. Hawkins (Eds.), *Behavioral assessment: New directions in clinical psychology* (pp. 196–209). New York: Bruner Mazel.

Geer, J. H. (1980). Measurement of genital arousal in human males and females. In I. Martin & P. H. Venables (Eds.), *Techniques in psychophysiology* (pp. 431–459). New York: Wiley.

Geer, J. H., Morokoff, P., & Greenwood, P. (1974). Sexual arousal in women: The development of a measuring device for vaginal blood volume. *Archives of Sexual Behavior, 3,* 559–564.

Geer, J. H., & Quartaro, J. (1976). Vaginal blood volume responses during masturbation. *Archives of Sexual Behavior, 4,* 403–413.

Gillan, P. (1976). Objective measures of female sexual arousal. *Journal of Physiology, 260,* 64–65.

Goldstein, L. (1975). Time domain analysis of the EEG: The integrative method. In G. Dolce & H. Kunkel (Eds.), *C.E.A.N.—Computerized EEG analysis* (pp. 251–270). Stuttgart: Gustav Fischer.

Goldberg, D. C., Whipple, B., Fishkin, R. E., Waxman, H., Fink, P. J., & Weisberg, M. (1983). The Grafenberg spot and female ejaculation: A review of initial hypothesis. *Journal of Sex and Marital Therapy, 9,* 27–37.

Graber, B., & Kline-Graber, G. (1979). Female orgasm: Role of pubococcygeus muscle. *Journal of Clinical Psychiatry, 40,* 348–351.

Greer, J. G., & Stuart, I. R. (1983). *The sexual aggressor.* New York: Van Nostrand.

Groth, A. N., & Birnbaum, H. J. (1979). *Men who rape: The psychology of the offender.* New York: Plenum.

Hatch, J. P. (1979). Vaginal photoplethysmography: Methodological considerations. *Archives of Sexual Behavior, 8,* 357–374.

Hatch, J. P. (1981). Voluntary control of sexual responding in men and women: Implications for the etiology and treatment of sexual dysfunctions. *Biofeedback and Self-Regulation, 6,* 191–205.

Heath, R. G. (1972). Pleasure and brain activity in man. *Journal of Nervous and Mental Disease, 154,* 3–17.

Heiman, J. R. (1975, April). The physiology of erotica. *Psychology Today, 8,* 90–94.

Heiman, J. R. (1977). A psychophysiological exploration of sexual arousal patterns in females and males. *Psychophysiology, 14,* 266–274.

Heiman, J. R. (1980). Female sexual response patterns: Interactions of physiological, affective and contextual cues. *Archives of General Psychiatry, 37*, 1311–1316.

Heiman, J. R., & Rowland, D. L. (1981). Sexual dysfunction from a psychophysiological perspective. *International Journal of Mental Health, 10*, 3–8.

Heiman, J. R., & Rowland, D. L. (1983). Affective and physiological response patterns: The effects of instructions on sexually functional and dysfunctional men. *Journal of Psychosomatic Research, 27*, 105–116.

Henson, D. E., & Rubin, H. B. (1971). Voluntary control of eroticism. *Journal of Applied Behavior Analysis, 4*, 37–47.

Henson, D., & Rubin, H. (1978). A comparison of two objective measures of sexual arousal in women. *Behavior Research and Therapy, 16*, 143–151.

Henson, D., Rubin, H., & Henson, C. (1979a). Analysis of the consistency of objective measures of sexual arousal in women. *Journal of Applied Behavior Analysis, 12*, 701–711.

Henson, D., Rubin, H., & Henson, C. (1979b). Woman's sexual arousal concurrently assessed by three genital measures. *Archives of Sexual Behavior, 8*, 459–469.

Henson, D., Rubin, H., & Henson, C. (1982). Labial and vaginal blood volume responses to visual and tactile stimuli. *Archives of Sexual Behavior, 11*, 23–31.

Henson, D. E., Rubin, H. B., Henson, C., & Williams, J. (1977). Temperature change of the labia minora as an objective measure of human female eroticism. *Journal of Behavior Therapy and Experimental Psychiatry, 8*, 401–410.

Hirshkowitz, M., Ware, J. C., Turner, D., & Karacan, I. (1979). EEG amplitude asymmetry during sleep. *Sleep Research, 8*, 25.

Hoon, P. W., Murphy, W. D., Laughter, J. S., & Abel, G. G. (1984). Infrared vaginal photoplethysmography: Construction, calibration, and sources of artifact. *Behavioral Assessment, 6*, 141–152.

Hoon, P. W., Wincze, J. P., & Hoon, E. F. (1976). Physiological assessment of sexual arousal in women. *Psychophysiology, 13*, 196–204.

Hoon, P. W., Wincze, J. P., & Hoon, E. F. (1977a). The effects of biofeedback and cognitive regulation upon vaginal blood volume. *Behavior Therapy, 8*, 694–702.

Hoon, P. W., Wincze, J. P., & Hoon, E. F. (1977b). A test of reciprocal inhibition: Are anxiety and sexual arousal mutually inhibitory? *Journal of Abnormal Psychology, 86*, 65–74.

Hyman, C., & Winsor, T. (1961). History of plethysmography. *Journal of Cardiovascular Surgery, 2*, 506–510.

Johnson, J., & Kitching, R. (1968). A mechanical transducer for phallography. In *Bio-medical Engineering*. Johnson, J (Ed.) Philadelphia: F. A. Davis.

Jovanovic, U. J. (1967). A new method of phallography. *Confinator Neurologie, 29*, 299–312.

Jovanovic, U. J. (1969). Der effekt der ersten untersuchungsnacht auf die erektionen im schlaf. *Psychotherapy and Psychosomatics, 17*, 295–308.

Karacan, I. (1969). A simple and inexpensive transducer for quantitative measurement of penile erection during sleep. *Behavior Research Methods and Instrumentation, 1*, 251–252.

Karacan, I. (1970). Clinical value of nocturnal erection in the prognosis and diagnosis of impotence. *Medical Aspects of Human Sexuality, 21*–34.

Karacan, I., Goodenough, D. R., Shapiro, A., & Starker, S. (1966). Erection cycle during sleep in relation to dream anxiety. *Archives of General Psychiatry, 15*, 183–189.

Kaplan, H. S. (1979). *Disorders of sexual desire*. New York: Simon & Schuster.

Kegel, A. H. (1952). Sexual functions of the pubococcygeus muscle. *Western Journal of Surgery, 60*, 521–524.

Keiser, S. (1952). Body ego during orgasm. *Psychoanalytic Quarterly, 21*, 153–166.

Kinsey, A. C., Pomeroy, W. B., Martin, C. E., & Gebhard, B. H. (1953). *Sexual behavior in the human female*. Philadelphia: Saunders.

Kline-Graber, G., & Graber, B. (1978). Diagnosis and treatment procedures of pubococcygeus deficiencies in women. In J. LoPiccolo & L. LoPiccolo (Eds.), *Handbook of sex therapy* (pp. 227–241). New York: Plenum.

Kockott, G., Feil, W., Ferstl, R., Aldenhoff, J., & Besinger, U. (1980). Psychophysiological aspects of male sexual inadequacy: Results of an experimental study. *Archives of Sexual Behavior, 9,* 477–493.

Kolodny, R. C., Masters, W. H., & Johnson, V. E. (1979). *Textbook of sexual medicine.* Boston: Little Brown.

Komisaruk, B. R. (1982). Visceral-somatic integration in behavior, cognition, and psychosomatic disease. In *Advances in the study of behavior, Vol. 12* (pp. 1–26). New York: Academic Press.

Korff, J., & Geer, J. H. (1983). The relationship between sexual arousal experience and genital response. *Psychophysiology, 20,* 121–127.

Kwan, M., Greenleaf, W. J., Mann, J., Crapo, L., & Davidson, J. (1983). The nature of androgen action on male sexuality: A combined laboratory self-report study on hypogonadal men. *Journal of Clinical Endocrinology and Metabolism, 57,* 557–562.

Ladas, A. K., Whipple, B., & Perry, J. D. (1982). *The G spot.* New York: Holt, Rinehart & Winston.

Langevin, R., & Martin, M. (1975). Can erotic responses be classically conditioned? *Behavior Therapy, 6,* 45–51.

Lawrence, D. H. (1928). *Lady Chatterly's lover.* New York: Grove.

Laws, D. R., & Bow, R. A. (1976). An improved mechanical strain gauge for recording penile circumference change. *Psychophysiology, 13,* 596–599.

Laws, D. R., & Holmen, M. L. (1978). Sexual response faking by pedophiles. *Criminal Justice and Behavior, 5,* 343–356.

Laws, D. R., & Osborn, C. A. (1983). How to build and operate a behavioral laboratory to evaluate and treat sexual deviance. In J. G. Greer & I. R. Stuart (Eds.), *The sexual aggressor* (pp. 293–335). New York: Van Nostrand.

Laws, D. R., & Rubin, H. B. (1969). Instructional control of an autonomic sexual response. *Journal of Applied Behavior Analysis, 2,* 93–99.

Leiblum, S. R., & Rosen, R. C. (1984). Alcohol and sexual response. *Alcoholism Treatment Quarterly, 1,* 1–16.

Levine, S. B. (1984). An essay on the nature of sexual desire. *Journal of Sex and Marital Therapy, 10,* 83–95.

Levitt, E. E., Konovsky, M., Freese, M. P., & Thompson, J. F. (1979). Intravaginal pressure assessed by the Kegel perineometer. *Archives of Sexual Behavior, 8,* 425–430.

Littler, W. A., Honour, A. J., & Sleight, P. (1974). Direct arterial pressure, heart rate and electrocardiogram during human coitus. *Journal of Reproduction and Fertility, 40,* 321–331.

Lothstein, L. M. (1980). The post-surgical transsexual: Empirical and theoretical considerations. *Archives of Sexual Behavior, 9,* 547–564.

Lucas, L., Abel, G. G., Mittelman, M. S., & Becker, J. V. (1983). *Pupillometry to determine the sexual preferences of paraphiliacs.* Poster presented to the World Congress of Behavior Therapy, Washington, DC.

Malamuth, N. M., & Check, J. V. (1983). Sexual arousal to rape depictions: Individual differences. *Journal of Abnormal Psychology, 92,* 55–67.

Malmuth, N. M., & Check, J. V. (1984). Debriefing effectiveness following exposure to pornographic rape depictions. *Journal of Sex Research, 20,* 1–13.

Malatesta, V. J., Pollack, R. H., Crotty, T. D., & Peacock, L. J. (1982). Acute alcohol intoxication and female orgastic response. *Journal of Sex Research, 18,* 1–17.

Marshall, P., Surridge, D., & Delva, N. (1981). The role of nocturnal penile tumescence in the differentiating between organics and psychogenic impotence: The first stage of validation. *Archives of Sexual Behavior, 10,* 1–10.

Masters, W., & Johnson, V. E. (1966). *Human sexual response.* Boston: Little, Brown.

Masters, W., & Johnson, V. E. (1970). *Human sexual inadequacy.* Boston: Little, Brown.

Masters, W. H., Johnson, V. E., & Kolodny, R. C. (1977). *Ethical issues in sex therapy and research.* Boston: Little, Brown.

Masters, W. H., Johnson, V. E., & Kolodny, R. C. (1982). *Human sexuality.* Boston: Little, Brown.

Mavissakalian, M., BLanchard, E. B., Abel, G. G., & Barlow, D. H. (1975). Responses to complex erotic stimuli in homosexual and heterosexual males. *British Journal of Psychiatry, 126,* 252–257.

McConaghy, N. (1967). Penile volume changes to moving pictures of male and female nudes in heterosexual and homosexual males. *Behavior Research and Therapy, 5,* 43–48.

McConaghy, N. (1974). Measurements of change in penile dimensions. *Archives of Sexual Behavior, 4,* 381–388.

Money, J. (1980). *Love and lovesickness: The science of sex, gender difference, and pair-bonding.* Baltimore: Johns Hopkins University Press.

Morokoff, P., & Heiman, J. (1980). Effects of erotic stimuli on sexually functional and dysfunctional women: Multiple measures before and after sex therapy. *Behaviour Research and Therapy, 18,* 127–137.

Mosher, D. L. (1980). Three dimensions of depth of involvement in human sexual response. *Journal of Sex Research, 16,* 1–42.

Mosovich, A., & Tallafero, A. (1954). Studies of EEG and sex function orgasm. *Diseases of the Nervous System, 15,* 218–220.

Mould, D. E. (1980). Neuromuscular aspects of women's orgasms. *The Journal of Sex Research, 16,* 193–201.

Ohlmeyer, P., Brilmayer, H., & Hullstrung, H. (1944). Periodische vorgange im schlaf. *Pflungers Archive Gestaut Physiologie, 249,* 50–55.

Osborn, C. A., & Pollack, R. H. (1977). The effects of two types of erotic literature on physiological and verbal measures of female sexual arousal. *Journal of Sex Research, 13,* 250–256.

Palti, Y., & Bercovici, B. (1967). Photoplethysmography study of the vaginal blood pulse. *American Journal of Obstetrics and Gynecology, 97,* 143–153.

Perry, J. D. (1980). *Two devices for the physiological measurement of sexual activity.* Paper presented at the meeting of Society for the Scientific Study of Sex, Philadelphia, PA.

Perry, J. D., & Whipple, B. (1981). Pelvic muscle strength of female ejaculators: Evidence in support of a new theory of orgasm. *Journal of Sex Research, 17,* 22–39.

Quinsey, V. L. (1977). The assessment and treatment of child molesters: A review. *Canadian Psychological Review, 18,* 204–220.

Quinsey, V. L., & Marshall, W. L. (1983). Procedures for reducing inappropriate sexual arousal: An evaluation review. In J. G. Greer & I. R. Stuart (Eds.), *The sexual aggressor* (pp. 267–292). New York: Van Nostrand.

Reinisch, J. M., & Rosen, R. C. (1981). The growth and diversity of sex research in the past decade: An introduction to selected topics. *International Journal of Mental Health, 10,* 3–9.

Robinson, P (1976), *The modernization of sex.* New York: Harper & Row.

Roose, S. P., Glassman, A. H., Walsh, B. T., & Cullen, K. (1982). Reversible loss of nocturnal penile tumescence during depression: A preliminary report. *Neuropsychobiology, 8,* 284–288.

Rosen, R. C. (1973). Suppression of penile tumescence by instrumental conditioning. *Psychosomatic Medicine, 35,* 509–513.

Rosen, R. C. (1983). Clinical issues in the assessment and treatment of impotence: A new look at an old problem. *The Behavior Therapist, 6,* 81–85.

Rosen, R. C., & Keefe, F. J. (1978). The measurement of human penile tumescence. *Psychophysiology, 15,* 366–376.

Rosen, R. C., & Leiblum, S. R. Current approaches to the evaluation of sexual desire disorders. *Journal of Sex Research* (in press).

Rosen, R. C., Shapiro, D., & Schwartz, G. E. (1975). Voluntary control of penile tumescence. *Psychosomatic Medicine, 37,* 479–483.

Roughan, P. A., & Kunst, B. A. (1981). Do pelvic floor exercises really improve orgasmic potential? *Journal of Sex and Marital Therapy, 7*, 223–229.

Rubin, H. B., & Henson, D. E. (1976). Effects of alcohol on male sexual responding. *Psychopharmacology, 47*, 123–134.

Sakheim, D. K., Barlow, D. H., Beck, J. G., & Abrahamson, D. J. (1984). The effect of an increased awareness of erectile cues on sexual arousal. *Behavior Research and Therapy, 22*, 151–158.

Schover, L., & LoPiccolo, J. (1982). Effectiveness of treatment for dysfunctions of sex desire. *Journal of Sex and Marital Therapy, 8*, 179–197.

Schreiner-Engel, P., Schiavi, R., & Smith, H. (1981). Female sexual arousal: Relationship between cognitive and genital assessments. *Journal of Sex and Marital Therapy, 7*, 256–267.

Seeley, T. T., Abramson, P. R., Perry, L. B., Rothblatt, A. B., & Seeley, D. M. (1980). Thermographic measurement of sexual arousal: A methodological note. *Archives of Sexual Behavior, 9*, 77–85.

Semmlow, J. L., & Lubowsky, J. (1983). Sexual instrumentation. *IEEE Transactions on Biomedical Engineering, 30*, 309–319.

Sevely, J. L., & Bennett, J. W. (1978). Concerning female ejaculation and the female prostate. *Journal of Sex Research, 14*, 1–20.

Shapiro, A., Cohen, H., Dibianco, P., & Rosen, G. (1968). Vaginal blood flow changes during sleep and sexual arousal. *Psychophysiology, 4*, 394.

Sherfey, M. J. (1974). Some biology of sexuality. *Journal of Sex and Marital Therapy, 1*, 97–109.

Sherif, C. (1980). Comment on ethical issues in Malamuth, Heim & Feshbach's "Sexual responsiveness of college students to rape depictions: Inhibitory and disinhibitory effects." *Journal of Personality and Social Psychology, 38*, 409–412.

Sims, T. M. (1967). Pupillary response to male and female subjects to pupillary differences in male and female picture stimuli. *Perception and Psychophysics, 2*, 553–555.

Singer, J., & Singer, I. (1978). Types of female orgasm. In J. LoPiccolo & L. LoPiccolo (Eds.), *Handbook of sex therapy* (pp. 175–187). New York: Plenum.

Sintchak, G., & Geer, J. (1975). A vaginal plethysmograph system. *Psychophysiology, 12*, 113–115.

Solnick, R. L., & Birren, J. E. (1977). Age and male erectile responsiveness. *Archives of Sexual Behavior, 6*, 1–9.

Steinman, D. L., Wincze, J. P., Sakheim, D. K., Barlow, D. H., & Mavissakalian, M. (1981). A comparison of male and female patterns of sexual arousal. *Archives of Sexual Behavior, 10*, 529–547.

Trudel, G., & Saint-Laurent, S. (1983). A comparison between the effects of Kegel's exercises and a combination of sexual awareness relaxation and breathing on situational orgasmic dysfunction in women. *Journal of Sex and Marital Therapy, 9*, 204–209.

Tucker, D. M. (1981). Lateral brain function, emotion, and conceptualization. *Psychological Bulletin, 89*, 19–46.

Tucker, D. M. (1983). Asymmetries of coherence topography: Structural and dynamic aspects of brain lateralization. In P. Flor-Henry & J. Gruzelier (Eds.), *Laterality and psychopathology* (pp. 158–172). Amsterdam: Elsevier.

Van Arsdalen, K. N., Malloy, T. R., & Wein, A. J. (1983). Erectile physiology, dysfunction and evaluation. *Monographs in Urology, 4*, 137–156.

Vance, E. B., and Wagner, N. W. (1976). Written descriptions of orgasm: A study of sex difference. *Archives of Sexual Behavior, 5*, 87–98.

Wagner, G. (1981). Erection: Physiology and Enocrinology. In G. Wagner & R. Green (Eds.), *Impotence* (pp. 25–36). New York: Plenum.

Wagner, G., & Brindley, G. (1980). The effect of atropine and blockers on human penile erection. In A. Zorgniotti (Ed.), *First International Conference on Vascular Impotence* (pp. 82–97). New York: Charles C. Thomas.

Wasserman, M. D., Pollak, C. P., Spielman, A. J., & Weitzman, E. D. (1980). The differential diagnosis of impotence: The measurement of nocturnal penile tumescence. *Journal of the American Medical Association, 243,* 2038–2042.

Webster, J. S., & Hammer, D. (1983). Thermistor measurement of male sexual arousal. *Psychophysiology, 20,* 111–115.

Weinman, J. (1967). Photoplethysmography. In P. Venables & I. Martin (Eds.), *A manual of psychophysiological methods* (pp. 162–178). Amsterdam: North-Holland.

Weiss, H. D. (1972). The physiology of human erection. *Annals of Internal Medicine, 76,* 793–799.

Wenger, M. A., Averill, J. R., & Smith, D. D. B. (1968). Autonomic activity during sexual arousal. *Psychophysiology, 4,* 460–478.

Wilson, G. T., & Lawson, D. M. (1976). Expectancies, alcohol, and sexual arousal in male social drinkers. *Journal of Abnormal Psychology, 85,* 587–594.

Wilson, G. T., & Lawson, D. M. (1978). Expectancies, alcohol, and sexual arousal in women. *Journal of Abnormal Psychology, 87,* 358–367.

Wincze, J. P., Hoon, E., & Hoon, P. (1976). A comparison of the physiological responsivity of normal and sexually dysfunctional women during exposure to erotic stimuli. *Journal of Psychosomatic Research, 20,* 44–50.

Wincze, J. P., Hoon, E., & Hoon, P. (1978). Multiple measure analysis of women experiencing low sexual arousal. *Behaviour Research and Therapy, 16,* 43–49.

Wincze, J. P., Venditti, E., Barlow, D. H., & Mavissakalian, M. (1980). The effects of a subjective monitoring task in the physiological measure of genital response to erotic stimulation. *Archives of Sexual Behavior, 9,* 533–545.

Wolchik, S. A., Spencer, S. L., & Lisi, I. S. (1983). Volunteer bias in research employing vaginal measures of sexual arousal. *Archives of Sexual Behavior, 12,* 399–408.

Zelnik, M., Kantner, J. F., & Ford, K. (1981). *Sex and pregnancy in adolescence.* Beverly Hills: Sage Publication.

Zilbergeld, B. (1982). Pursuit of the Grafenberg Spot. *Psychology Today, 16,* 82–84.

Zingheim, P., & Sandman, C. (1978). Discriminative control of the vaginal vasomotor response. *Biofeedback and Self-Regulation, 3,* 29–41.

Zuckerman, M. (1971). Physiological measures of sexual arousal in the human. *Psychological Bulletin, 75,* 297–329.

4

Human Sexuality In Cross-Cultural Perspective

Edgar Gregersen
Queens College, CUNY

People everywhere are brought up to regard their own culture as best and their own society as somehow divinely sanctioned, in conformity with the laws of nature, or otherwise cosmically secure.

To believe so is to guarantee ignorance about human nature and the nature of culture. Such an approach is perhaps nowhere as misleading as in speculating about human sexuality because of an additional factor, the confusion of what anthropologists call *ideal culture* with *real culture*. Ideal culture refers to what members of a culture believe their culture should be, as opposed to real culture, which is what the culture is factually and objectively.

Kinsey, Pomeroy, and Martin (1948) and Kinsey, Pomeroy, Martin, and Gebhard (1953) brought out the difference quite clearly—and shockingly, to a great many people. In a society where talking about sex was fundamentally tabu, the statistics these studies offered about condemned behavior (such as adultery, homosexual acts, and even sexual contacts between human beings and animals) constituted a major scandal. Kinsey et al. (1948) and Kinsey et al. (1953) pointed out a significant social problem because of the confusion between the ideal and the real: Because laws were written in conformity with the ideal, the great majority of Americans could be imprisoned if the laws were enforced.

The Kinsey reports also indicated the existence of social class differences with regard to sexual expectations and performance. One could, in fact, talk of the sexual cultures of the college-educated and the noncollege-educated. At the time Kinsey was writing, these cultures differed in areas as diverse as the incidence of nocturnal emissions (college-educated men experienced them earlier and more frequently); premarital intercourse (the noncollege-educated had it more often); masturbation, oral sex, experimentation with copulatory positions, sex in the nude, and interest in pornography (all primarily associated with the college-educated). People from one background when told of the practices of the other would tend to label the other as perverse, degenerate, unnatural; or—from the other side—as uncivilized and just like animals. Needless to say, misunderstandings and false expectations are bound to occur whenever social expectations and practices are misunderstood or even not known.

CULTURAL DIFFERENCES AND THEIR IMPLICATIONS

The subcultural differences brought out by the findings of the Kinsey reports are a small example of what can happen on a worldwide scale. A lack of a cross-cultural perspective inevitably means assuming that one's own very limited cultural experience is representative of all of humanity. Of course, some people persist in theorizing from such a background and justify doing so by dismissing other cultural traditions as dead-ends or in some other way as unworthy of study.

The cross-cultural approach makes a very different assumption. It takes as axiomatic that all cultures are worthy of study because they inevitably represent experiments in survival. It is only by having an insight into the broad spectrum of human sexuality that we can begin to understand that of our own subgroup. Just on an ideological level, we find tremendous variation: societies that encourage premarital promiscuity and those that require nonvirgin brides to be killed, societies that permit polygamy and those that insist on monogamy, societies that make homosexual acts compulsory for all its members and others that condemn all such acts for any members. The very fact of such variation makes unattractive all theories that play up a pan-human framework to the exclusion of variation.

THE STRATEGY OF CROSS-CULTURAL RESEARCH

The strategy of cross-cultural study has been to try to develop a sample of cultures, each of which is relatively independent of other cultures. A very significant problem is actually drawing culture boundaries so that our sample will not include any real repetition. If we were studying monogamy, for example, we would not stack our sample with "cultures" like New York culture, Chicago culture, San Francisco culture, or possibly even societies that have recently adopted monogamy because of intense Christian missionary work. In a sense, all these instances would probably best count as one. The whole question of culture boundaries and its implications for cross-cultural research is known as *Galton's problem*. (Of course, in a study of culture history or culture contact the activities of Christian missionaries would be of potentially great interest.)

The fact of cultural variation with regard to sexual behavior and ideology is of great theoretical importance, as has been mentioned earlier. Indeed, some anthropologists maintain that schools of thought like Freudianism or sociobiology have the underlying flaw of trying to explain enormously varied cultural patterns in terms of universal components of human nature. Whatever the justice of this criticism, not being able to account for such variation in a tenable way would be a serious shortcoming, to say the least.

THE HISTORY OF CROSS-CULTURAL STUDIES OF SEXUALITY

Sexologists such as Havelock Ellis in England and Magnus Hirschfeld in Germany were early pioneers in gathering information from societies through time and across the world. Kinsey felt that most of the work done by anthropologists was of dubious value. He was not against a cross-cultural approach: he felt merely that the information available was basically unreliable. One thing is quite clear: Anthropologists have dealt with rules of sexual conduct, not with actual behavior.

In 1934, Unwin published *Sex and Culture,* a massive cross-cultural study designed to test the relationship between sexual repression and cultural achievement—in reality a test of the Freudian theory of sublimation though not totally Freudian in its formulation. He examined information from about 80 societies and concluded there was a causal relationship. Subsequent research has pointed out errors in Unwin's treatment, but the work is of historical interest; occasionally, an irate letter to *The New York Times* or some other newspaper concerning the dangers of the "sexual revolution" will mention Unwin's book.

The most famous cross-cultural study is *Patterns of Sexual Behavior* (Ford & Beach, 1951). This surveyed information for about 190 societies with regard to a variety of topics such as sexual techniques, varieties of physical attractiveness, frequency of intercourse, attitudes about homosexual acts, as well as cross-species comparisons.

A number of minor studies with a cross-cultural orientation have subsequently appeared considering such topics as severity of punishment for breaking sexual tabus; the relationship of degree of severity of sex roles with acceptability of transvestism; the variety of attitudes about rape; the relationship of social structure to the development of notions varying from modesty to romantic love to the prizing of premarital virginity; the correlation between population pressures, infanticide, and the toleration of homosexual acts; and the like.

In 1982, my own book, *Sexual Practices,* first appeared, which was in part a nontechnical restudy of much of what Ford and Beach considered. Most of the information provided in this chapter is derived from research done for that book.

DISTRIBUTION OF SEXUAL TECHNIQUES AND BEHAVIOR ROUND THE WORLD

Although the general form of intercourse used by mammals and primates other than man is rear entry, this form is seldom reported as the most common or preferred form in any human cultures. However, it is reported as the major form in a few South American Indian groups including the Nambikwara and Apinayé, as well as a few other groups such as the Bushmen of southern Africa. In many of these instances, it seems to be associated with a lack of privacy (because houses are lacking).

The most common human copulatory position throughout the world has both partners laying down, face to face, with the man on top. This is frequently referred to as the "missionary position" because traditionally Christians have seen this as the most "natural" and morally acceptable position: If wives are to be subject to their husbands (as St. Paul and traditional marriage vows maintain), then for a woman to assume, say, the top position could be taken as a symbolic rejection of a woman's subordinate position.

In point of fact, copulation with the woman on top is not reported as the preferred or most common position from any known society, although it is reported as a variant in several and is one of the positions frequently shown in art, both ancient and modern. Interpreting representations of sexual acts found in ancient art is a tricky business. Some sexologists have even believed because of certain artistic motifs not even really sexual, that the ancient Egyptians were a society where coïtus with the woman on top was the preferred or most common position. However, information from texts shows that this is a wrong inference.

A variant of the missionary position has the man squatting or kneeling between the legs of the prone woman. This is frequently referred to as the "Oceanic position" because of its reported frequency throughout the Pacific area. In actual fact, however, the use of this position seems to be getting rarer in these areas although older people sometimes say it is the best way. Probably because of Western influence, the missionary position is becoming more frequent. The Oceanic position is not limited to the Pacific area but can be found elsewhere, e.g., in some African groups such as the Tallensi, as well as in South America among the Karajá, and in Asia among the Santal and Lepcha.

In large parts of black Africa, side by side copulation seems to be the norm. This is frequently acompanied by a left–right symbolism whereby the man is supposed to lie on his right shoulder to keep his left hand free for sexual play. The right hand is in such areas regarded as the hand for eating: using it to touch sex organs—even one's own—leads to ritual contamination. What women do is apparently of lesser importance.

Another primarily black African culture trait is known as "external intercourse" or "pseudo-coïtus". It involves rubbing the penis between the partner's thighs or against the partner's belly; in any event the vagina (or anus) is not to be penetrated. In some African groups such as traditional non-Christian Zulu and Luo it is permitted between unmarried people who could marry (i.e., would not break the rules of incest if they did marry).

Intercourse performed standing is sometimes reported in brief and primarily adulterous relationships. On Hindu temples, where it was formerly the custom to represent sexual acts in reliefs and statues carved on the outside walls, standing copulation is the rule. This seems to be an artistic convention with little reality.

Information about other sexual acts is even less extensive, with the exception of kissing. Although almost universal in highly developed cultures, there are some societies where it is completely unknown, as among the Somali of Africa, the Lepcha of Asia, and the Sirionó of South America.

Other oral acts—cunnilingus and fellation (or fellation)—are less commonly reported but are frequent in highly developed cultures and geographically from parts of Africa and the Pacific. In point of fact, many Polynesian societies including the Mangaians and the Marquesans are very much concerned about sex technique. Polynesian societies are among the only ones in the world where men are generally concerned about whether their female partners have orgasms and where women receive training in techniques to assure that they do reach orgasm.

From the very little information that is available, it seems that fellation is more common than cunnilingus as practiced throughout the world and that cunnilingus is almost never found unless fellation also is, although fellation does occur without cunnilingus.

Information about masturbation is not extensive although generally it seems to be considered worldwide as normal adolescent behavior. However, when practiced by adults it is almost universally frowned upon. The modern Roman Catholic view that masturbation is a serious moral offense, a mortal sin, and the orthodox Jewish view that male masturbation is a "waste of nature" and so the most serious of sexual crimes (which some commentators have said is worthy of death) are unusually severe in cross-cultural perspective.

Possibly only one sexual technique has been developed in the 20th century: the insertion of a hand (or foot) into the vagina or anus. There is no reference to this in writing until the 20th century although there are some depictions of such acts in earlier Japanese art and possibly even in a detail of Michelangelo's *The Last Judgment* in the Sistine Chapel. There is, in fact, not even a respectable term for the act and so I have had to coin one: "gantizing" (from the French *gant* "glove"—the idea being that a body cavity serves as a glove). Although statistically infrequent even in the 20th century, it has nevertheless generated much discussion. It is exceedingly dangerous and deaths have come about because of ruptures of the intestinal wall.

A number of other sexual techniques and coïtal positions are occasionally reported in the studies of anthropologists and travelers. These include copulation in various sitting positions, or various nonvaginal techniques such as inserting the penis between breasts or feet or in armpits. There are no statistics on the frequency of any of these behaviors.

Marriage, Incest, and Other Institutionalized Aspects

Cross-culturally, marriage seems to be the arena where sexual acts most frequently occur. Some societies, such as traditional Christian Western societies, define *marriage* as the only setting for legitimate sexual expression, although this view has often been observed in the breach. Indeed, a double standard and extensive—often legal—prostitution were eloquent counter examples. In particular, the virginity of brides was usually considered highly desirable.

In many societies, however, premarital virginity is not a virtue at all. In fact, in societies that trace descent through females (matrilineal societies, technically), premarital virginity is almost without exception (I know of only two counter examples) never highly regarded. Views about premarital sex vary greatly. Among the Múria Gond of India, boys and girls live together in dormitories and are allowed to sleep together with the proviso that a person not sleep with the same partner more than 3 days in a row. For the most part, even when premarital virginity is not a virtue (as among most groups that live by hunting and gathering rather than by agriculture or animal herding), the age of marriage is much younger than in the industrialized west, often between 12 and 18 for girls. In some societies, such as the Tiwi of Australia and the Zande of Africa, a girl could be legally married in infancy although sexual intercourse would be delayed several years, usually until puberty but often it began at age 8 or 9. Among Hindus there is the traditional belief that every occurrence of menstruation represents murder; girls were traditionally married before the onset of menstruation to avoid ''killings'' of this sort as much as possible.

In societies that trace descent through males (patrilineal societies), premarital virginity in brides is regarded as crucial. Marriage is seen as involving contractual agreements between two families and one of the stipulations for the bride's family is that the bride be handed over to her husband intact. In such societies (and some others) proofs of virginity are established, e.g., a sheet displaying blood shed in the breaking of the hymen during the couple's first intercourse. In rural Egypt, the test requires that the bridegroom insert his cloth bound index finger into the bride's vagina before intercourse. In rural Greece, it is said to be the bride's mother-in-law who performs. In the Middle East traditionally, a bride who did not prove to be a virgin brought her family into profound disgrace and could be killed by stoning, sometimes even by her own father and brothers. This is, in fact, the biblical custom as set down in Deuteronomy 22.

To prevent such a disgrace some societies have gone to great lengths, involving hiding the body and even face behind veils, enforcing a chaperone system, and in some areas (primarily in the Sudan and the Horn of Africa) a genital operation called infibulation, in which the opening to a girl's vagina is sewn together so that intercourse is impossible. On the day of a girl's marriage a midwife comes by and cuts her open with a razor. Another mutilation performed for similar reasons involves partial or total removal of the clitoris. This is found in many Islamic groups, among the Falashas (black Jews) of Ethiopia, and several other African groups. Clitoridectomy is almost never found unless males are also circumcised, but male circumcision is found in many societies that do not practice genital mutilations on women.

The most commonly approved form of marriage cross-culturally is for a man to have more than one wife at a time. This is a form of polygamy (literally, "many marriages") known technically as *polygyny* (literally, "many wives"). In reality, however, even in societies that consider polygyny to be ideal, the great majority of marriages are monogamous either because a man cannot afford many wives or because the sex ratio does not allow otherwise.

Monogamy is associated with most Christian groups and western Jews but there is no biblical rule about monogamy.

For a woman to be permitted several husbands at one time is very rare. It is a form of polygamy known technically as *polyandry*. This has been most common in Tibet and neighboring areas, where it usually meant that a woman would marry a number of brothers. Although women are seldom allowed several husbands anywhere in the world they might have sexual access to a number of men other than their husbands, and sometimes they might even be forced to have sex with another man by their own husbands. One such custom, which is called "wife-lending," requires men who are friends or trading partners to exchange wives. The expression "sex hospitality" is more inclusive and means that guests are provided not only with food and shelter but also with the sexual services of women of the host's household (not necessarily the host's wife). Such customs are known from the Eskimo and Australian aborigines. Some scholars believe that sex hospitality existed among the ancient Hebrews: Details from the story of the destruction of Sodom (Genesis 19) are hard to understand unless something like this was practiced.

There is also a custom of "seed-raising" whereby a man who cannot sire children for one reason or another gets another man to impregnate his wife.

Homosexual Acts

Homosexual acts of all sorts have traditionally been condemned in the western Christian world. In other cultures, markedly different attitudes have existed. The Navaho accept sex between a man and another man who is a transvestite, but otherwise believe that homosexual acts lead to madness. Various New Guinea groups require all boys to experience extensive homosexual contacts with older men as part of the standard life cycle. Among the Étoro this is combined with extensive prohibitions on heterosexual intercourse (forbidden on more than 150 days of the year; ritually correct homosexual contacts are never forbidden). Homosexual marriage is recognized in at least 15–20 societies.

Several mode or styles of homosexual interest are reported—at least for males; virtually nothing has been reported cross-culturally about females. Four modes are frequently discussed in the cross-cultural literature: (a) adolescent experimentation (often associated with a lack of appropriate heterosexual partners); (b) pederasty (where there is a culturally significant age difference between the partners); (c) pathicism (where one of the partners is a transvestite); and (d) homophilia (where people of the same age status, who are not transvestites, are attracted to each other). The first three types are found in cross-cultural reports. The fourth, homophilia, has become the predominant mode only in the western world—and that only within the past 200 years.

Homosexual techniques are seldom reported. Generally, it is assumed that anal foration (anal intercourse) is the most common technique in primitive societies, but this may not be true. Anal foration seems to be common in some societies, but among the Ojibwa Indians it is reportedly nonexistent among homosexuals, and is practiced only among heterosexuals. Only interfemoral foration (rubbing the penis between the partner's thighs) was permitted among the Zande and seems to have been the custom among the ancient Greeks. Fellation is the custom among several New Guinea groups who require the transfer of semen from men to boys, but sometimes this is accomplished through anal foration and even masturbation.

Even less is known of lesbian techniques, although the use of a dildoe (penis substitute) is reported from a few societies.

Paraphilias and Other Topics

Paraphilias have been defined as statistically infrequent sexual interests. Perhaps a better definition is that they are sexual interests independent of sexual orientation (e.g., heterosexuality, homosexuality) or technique, that play up nongenital stimuli. For example, sexual arousal from shoes or pain or a dead body (because it is dead) would all count as paraphilias. The boundaries between paraphile and nonparaphile interests are sometimes difficult to draw. A man who is attracted only to redheads would hardly be labeled as having a paraphilia. But if he is attracted only to redheads who are 6' tall, dressed in black leather clothes and stiletto-heeled shoes, and carrying a whip—he would be.

By and large, paraphilias are male interests. What is more important for this discussion is that they are generally found only in advanced societies, particularly the west. This fact may be a function of reporting. However, in small homogeneous "primitive" societies such interests would hardly go unnoticed.

The major paraphilias include: (a) fetishes (interest in inanimate objects, particularly articles of clothing such as gloves, underwear, or shoes and frequently associated with special materials such as leather); (b) partialisms (intense interest in body parts other than the genitals, e.g., feet or breasts); (c) sadomasochism (interest in giving or receiving pain, humiliation, discipline); (d) exhibitionism (interest in exposing oneself to others); and (e) voyeurism (interest in seeing other people naked or performing sexually). Of these, only partialisms are sometimes reported for technologically simple societies and then in a sense that strains at the definition: Frequently, long labia minora are regarded as highly attractive and they may, in fact, be stretched to several inches in length. This partialism (if, in fact, it can count as a true partialism) is reported from many southern African societies as well as from Easter Island in the Pacific.

Some partialisms are centered on age. The best known is paedophilia, a sexual interest in children. In the west, the great majority of paedophiles are heterosexual—unlike a common stereotype of homosexuals. It is not clear to what extent this paraphilia and another at the opposite end of the age scale—gerontophilia, a sexual interest in the old—actually occur in the world's cultures. Some societies permit or require child or even infant marriage. For example, among the Tiwi of Australia and Zande of Africa, girls were married virtually from birth. Paraphilias in such instances were apparently not involved but we cannot be sure. Although actual sexual relations did not occur until much later, they might occur when the girl was still quite young, at age 8 or 9. It is not reported what effects, if any, such sexual contacts had on the psychological development of the girls. Possibly the fact that they occurred with cultural sanctioning made their efforts significantly different from what would happen in western society in cases of child molestation.

There are other sexually related interests and acts that do not fall under the rubric of paraphilia. Sexual contacts with animals are occasionally reported and, in fact, rituals involving such contacts have sometimes been developed. They seem not to be motivated by genuine sexual passion for animals (zoöphilia) but more often than not by absence of suitable human partners.

Transvestism is sometimes, but not invariably, accompanied by clothing fetishes. In the western world, transvestism is more frequent among heterosexuals than homosexuals despite stereotypic notions about the matter. It is not clear whether the same holds true in other societies. Possibly, reports of transvestism have been generally associated with homosexuality because of mistaken conceptions by western reporters. But at least many instances are known where both interests are definitely combined. A clothing interest that seems to be limited to the west is cisvestism, which involves dressing in a way that is culturally inappropriate from the point of view of age or occupation (but staying within the clothing options of one's own sex). For example, adults want to dress up in diapers, others in military or other uniforms. These desires are frequently associated with very specific sadomasochistic scenarios. The most famous instance of cisvestism is modern motorcycle drag, found in certain male homosexual circles (associated with so-called leather bars).

PARALLEL DEVELOPMENTS OF SEXUAL CUSTOMS

Despite the variation in sexual morality and practices that occurs throughout the world, presumably as responses to particular settings, there is considerable similarity as well. For example, as has been said before, the missionary position is the most common one found in the world.

How similarities should be accounted for is sometimes difficult to say. One possibility is shared inheritance from some common ancestral tradition (which may be true of the basic sexual techniques). Another is that practices have been borrowed by one or more groups from another (which was the case when traditionally polygamous societies took over monogamy because of Christian influence). Yet another is the independent but parallel development of the same or similar customs. This last category is very difficult to give examples for, to everyone's satisfaction. I suggest the following (among others):

1. Value placed on virginity. Not all societies place value on premarital virginity and the societies that do could not all have been in direct association with each other, e.g., the Plains Indians of North America and the ancient Near East.

2. An intact hymen taken as proof of virginity. Some societies do not even know that there is such a thing as the hymen, so the presence of one intact as proof of virginity is not so obvious as it might seem. This notion is commonplace in Africa, Europe, and Asia. The Apache is the only society in all of North and South America that developed it independently.

3. The belief that sex with a virgin is dangerous. Although many western men have had a mania for deflowering virgins, in several parts of the world there is a great fear of doing so—presumably because virgins are believed to possess special powers and so are dangerous. Such a belief is found in a number of Siberian groups and also among the Kágaba of South America. If the *droit du seigneur* actually existed in Europe—that is, the right of a feudal lord to copulate with any woman on his estate on the first night of her marriage—then it very likely developed for similar reasons.

4. The belief that intercourse causes the onset of menstruation. At least 12 societies are known to have held this erroneous belief, including the Tepoztecans of Mexico, the Lepcha of Sikkim, the Tupinambá of Brazil, and the Murngin of Australia.

5. The belief that men can get pregnant. This belief has been held by the Ila of Africa, who forbid homosexual intercourse precisely because it can bring about pregnancy, and the Kéraki of New Guinea, who give contraceptive drinks to boys playing the passive role in ritualized homosexual encounters. Remarkably enough, a report exists that some people in the United States also believe this (John Money, the eminent sexologist, and Geoffrey Hostra report that some black male homosexuals insist that they have themselves been pregnant but they all had miscarriages. Money & Hosta, 1968).

6. The development of ritual sexual acts associated with agriculture. Because agriculture was itself independently developed in several parts of the world—most notably for our purposes, the ancient Near East and Central America—any sex rituals associated with these different traditions must also be independent developments. Some American Indian groups required that sexual acts take place before planting; others that people abstain from sex at these periods. Among the

ancient Sumerians of the Near East, ritual sexual intercourse was performed by a priest and priestess to ensure fertility.

7. Prostitution. Native prostitution is found, apparently as independent developments, both in the Old World and the New. American Indian groups said to have had prostitution before European contacts include the high culture of the Aztecs, Maya, and Inca, as well as the Kwakiútl, Bororó, and Araucanicans.

8. Genital mutilations. Some Australian aborigine groups and a single non-Australian group, the Samburu of east Africa, make a cut on the ventral side of the penis from one end to the other. This operation is known as subincision. There are some reports that circumcision was practiced by a few American Indian groups before European contact but some of these reports are unclear or unconvincing. Only two South American groups developed female genital mutilations. The Pano of Ecuador developed clitoridectomy, common in black Africa and among certain Islamic groups. The Conibo of Perú seem to have developed a kind of infibulation, found mostly in northeastern Africa from southern Egypt to the Horn of Africa.

Other possible parallel developments reported from different parts of the world include penis enlargement techniques, genital preservation, chastity garments, priestly chastity, and possibly even Victorian-like senses of modesty.

CULTURE AREAS OF SEX

Certain sexual customs, beliefs, and practices tend to cluster geographically. The following paragraphs will try to indicate the boundaries of some fairly general (and tentative) sex culture areas.

Black Africa

Polygyny is the cultural ideal virtually everywhere. A common form for intercourse is side by side, with a left–right symbolism mentioned earlier. Generally there is a tabu on having sex outside of a house or during daylight hours. Circumcision is widely found among men; clitoridectomy, though common, is less so for women. Beliefs in various forms of adultery detection magic occur all over the continent; one form insures that an adulterous couple will not be able to be physically separated (a wife's lover might actually discover that his penis will stretch to great lengths in trying to get separated but it will still be stuck inside her vagina).

When homosexuality is reported it is described as occurring in either pederastic and pathic forms, not both. Reactions are very different in different societies.

Among Bantu-speaking peoples and their neighbors the following (which may also be found elsewhere in Africa but reports are usually silent about them) is found: A wife is required to wipe her husband's genitals after intercourse, using a special cloth (which must be carefully protected because it is especially vulnerable to use in black magic). Semen testing occurs before marriage: a woman will try to collect some from a man she has intercourse with to determine from its color and consistency what sort of husband he might make and whether he will be able to sire many children.

Middle East

At present, the Middle East is predominantly Muslim with an almost universal acceptance of the sexual laws recorded in the Koran. Virginity in women before marriage is traditionally stressed, as is faithfulness during marriage. Polygyny is permitted (but only up to four wives at a time according to the orthodox rules), and there has traditionally been a separation of the sexes in various customs known as purdah, which includes the veiling of women, and generally preventing the social mixing of the sexes when marriage or kinship is not involved. Marriage with first cousins is permitted but not marriage with a person who has drunk milk from one's wet-nurse (I call this tabu "milk incest"). Homosexual acts are forbidden by the religion but a folk distinction is made between active and passive roles—only the passive partner being contemptible.

India and Southeast Asia

Throughout most of the area there is *de facto* monogamy. This is the area where life-long chastity was first thought to be a virtue, being incorporated in the Buddhist and Jain religions. On the other hand, until recently, sacred prostitutes were commonly found in various Hindu temples; it was believed that having sex with them was a pious act (some sacred prostitutes are still found, particularly in southern India).

In much of the area, it is felt that women should marry early and conceive often. But abstinence for men is highly prized because the belief is strong that by saving semen (which can be stored in a special organ in the brain) a man can develop superhuman powers.

Although this is an area where elaborate sexual manuals such as the *Kaama Suutra* have existed for centuries, there seems to be little interest in varieties of sexual technique on the traditional rural level.

Far East

Among the Chinese, polygyny and concubinage were formerly common at least among the rich. The Japanese and Koreans, despite significant influences from the Chinese, were monogamous. Among Tibetans and neighboring Himalayan groups, polyandry was practiced—usually with a group of brothers sharing the same wife.

The Chinese are said to be the first to invent sex manuals of any sort, and also developed erotica extensively. The Chinese are particularly unusual for having created in imperial times an extensive class of eunuchs (castrated men)—indeed, the civil service was largely staffed with eunuchs. Binding the feet of women, which must have started out as a fashion to indicate that upper-class women would not (indeed, could not) work like peasants, became a national partialism: Chinese erotic paintings often depict women naked except for socks over tiny crippled feet.

As in India, the Chinese also feared semen loss, and this fear was related to philosophical notions of maintaining a balance between yin and yang "essences." Adherents of this philosophy often went to great lengths to learn to delay or prevent ejaculation during intercourse.

Information about actual sexual behavior is rare for this area, but some studies have been made of Japanese sexual practices. A notable feature of the Japanese is the frequent occurrence of sadomasochistic themes (primarily bondage) in their erotica.

When homosexuality is reported, it is often pederastic or pathic or a combination of the two.

Aboriginal Australia

Australia represents a distinct area because of three fairly unusual practices. The first involves highly complicated marriage rules found in many groups, associated with special marriage classes. The second is uncommon genital mutilations; in many parts of the continent men are subincized and women undergo introcision (slitting the perineaum—essentially the episiotomy women in the west undergo during labor to prevent irregular and difficult to heal tears). The third is the tradition of fertility ceremonials involving group sex to a degree seldom reported from anywhere else in the world, and certainly not from other hunting and gathering groups on other continents.

Institutionalized homosexual pederastic practices are reported from some parts of Australia, which may relate this area with the next.

New Guinea

Many parts of New Guinea have been described as having an extreme form of male–female hostility based on fears of pollution from menstrual blood. It is said that because of this fear, men are often unaggressive sexually and it is the women who actively pressure men. Another consequence of this fear is the tabu of having sex inside a house (the opposite of a common African tabu mentioned earlier).

One of the distinctive characteristics of the area is a fairly common (though by no means universal) institution of ritual pederasty. Boys in several groups are required to get semen from older men. Boys play a passive homosexual role for several years until they themselves become semen-givers. All other forms of homosexual activity are tabu, and roles are clearly age-graded.

Polynesia

This huge geographical area is the only place where reports regularly suggest a great emphasis on sex technique and variety among everyday people. It is also an area where men are concerned about whether their female partners are sexually satisfied—very rare in the accounts we have.

A considerable interest in genital cleanliness exists for both men and women. No female genital mutilations are performed but various cleaning techniques are sometimes begun in childhood, as well as the use of astringents to keep the vaginal canal tight. Males are frequently supracized (a cut is made in the top of the foreskin, which is not, however, removed); this is sometimes justified because it facilitates thorough cleaning. Genital tatooing is also reported from the area.

There are reports from this area of prodigious sexual activity including the story of a Marquesan man who copulated 31 times in a single night. The reliability of such reports is not clear.

A practice reported from Polynesia and much of Oceania as a whole is that of night-crawling (also known as sleep-crawling) whereby a man steals into a room to have intercourse with a woman without her prior consent. The room may, in fact, be filled with the woman's parents and other relatives. This act is sometimes accompanied by the fantasy that a man can copulate with a sleeping woman without waking her.

When homosexuality is reported it is almost invariably in the pathic mode.

Aboriginal Americas

Information about both North and South America is meager. But enough information exists to point to tremendous differences, from the near Victorian prudery of the Kuna of South America to the bawdiness of the Hopi, who make use of simulated sex in religious rituals and create place names that impress a speaker of English as abscene.

The Plains Indians of North America and the Inca of South America both developed interest in female virginity. Seldom did any Indian groups develop this interest to the same degree as that of the Middle East. In many places marital and sexual arrangements are quite loose, as shown in the group marriage of the Kaingáng and the wide sexual options of the Aleút and Eskimo.

Apart from the extraordinary erotic pots from pre-Columbian Perú, there is no evidence of much interest in elaborate sexual technique anywhere on the two continents.

When homosexuality is reported it is almost always associated with pathicism in North America. In fact, transvestites seem to have held high status in several societies. In South America, reported homosexuality seems mostly to involve adolescent experimentation or deprivation (lack of appropriate partners of the opposite sex).

Europe and America

This is the area we have most information from about actual sexual activity. In this section, however, rather than focus on the behavior of industrialized groups, I discuss folk customs and traditional norms.

These traditions actually reflect the major religious boundaries within Christianity. But they all share a basic Christian tradition of monogamy and the belief that certain forms of sexual behavior are intolerable because inherently sinful, such as masturbation and homosexual acts.

The Eastern Orthodox groups of eastern Europe and the Balkans have preserved notions of sexual pollution given up several centuries ago in the rest of Europe. Menstruating women may not participate in various religious activities. Crucifixes and holy pictures may not be kept in the bedrooms of married couples. Nocturnal emissions must be atoned for. Formerly (and in some very rural areas still today), proofs of virginity were important. Milk incest (as in the Middle East) is tabu.

Roman Catholics in southern Europe and Protestants in the north have none of these rules. But they differ among themselves. Catholics do not permit divorce or contraception. Protestants (for the most part nowadays) permit both. In northern Europe the virginity of a bride was traditionally not of consequence among peasants, where it was more important that a woman prove her fecundity.

Interestingly, it is from northern European Protestant areas and among their descendants in the Americas that we find the most elaborate development of the various paraphilias, particularly fetishes and sadomasochism. Also it is this cultural group where homophilia seems to have developed as a significant social phenomenon. It continues to be the major homophile area of the world although homophilia is itself largely condemned or at most ignored.

This last area of Europe and America is of special importance in the history of human sexual customs because it has for many centuries tried to force its own notions of sexual morality on the rest of the world in the process of Christianization or imperialism. The process continues in part if only because of extensive efforts to disseminate contraception on a massive scale.

REFERENCES

Ford, C. S., and Beach, F. A. (1951). *Patterns of sexual behavior.* New York: Harper.

Gregersen, E. (1982). *Sexual practices: the story of human sexuality.* London: Mitchell Beazley; New York: Franklin Watts.

Kinsey, A. C., Pomeroy, W. B., and Martin, C. E. (1948). *Sexual behavior in the human male.* Philadelphia & London: W. B. Saunders.

Kinsey, A. C., Pomeroy, W. B., Martin, C. E., and Gebhard, P. H. (1953). *Sexual behavior in the human female.* Philadelphia & London: W. B. Saunders.

Money, J., and Hosta, G. (1968). Negro folklore of male pregnancy. *The Journal of Sex Research,* 4:34–50.

Unwin, J. D. (1934). *Sex and culture.* London: Oxford University Press.

5 The Sociological Approach to Human Sexuality

Kathleen McKinney
Oklahoma State University

INTRODUCTION

The purpose of this chapter is to describe and illustrate the sociological approach to human sexuality. No attempt is made to review all the relevant literature. Rather, this chapter consists of a discussion of what constitutes a sociological approach in the area of human sexuality. In the discussion, selected opinions, theories, and examples of research by sociologists are cited.

To the extent that disciplines frequently overlap, the boundaries of the sociological perspective are somewhat ambiguous. Some sociologists consider both the learning and cross-cultural approaches to be a part of, or at least related to, the sociological viewpoint. However, because there are individual chapters on these two approaches in this volume, they are not stressed here. Furthermore, because I am a sociological social psychologist, who sees social psychology as a part of sociology, consideration of a social psychological approach is included.

This chapter, then, attempts to answer three questions: What is a sociological approach to human sexuality?; What problems exist with the sociological approach?; Where do we go from here?

WHAT IS A SOCIOLOGICAL APPROACH TO HUMAN SEXUALITY?

There are several ways to answer the question of what constitutes a sociological approach to human sexuality. Basically, the issue focuses on how scientific disciplines differ or what defines a discipline. There are at least three ways in which disciplines differ and can, therefore, be defined. First, what topics are studied? What questions are asked? Second, what theoretical models or perspectives are emphasized? Third, what research methods are most often used?

Issues Studied and Questions Asked

Levels of Analysis

There are certain issues and questions related to human sexuality and utilizing different levels of analysis, that are dealt with primarily by sociologists. Many writers agree on what these general emphases are. For example, Beach (1977) states that a sociological perspective looks at "the ways in which each society structures male and female sexuality. . .and the significance of sex with respect to the total fabric of a society's organization" (p. 7).

DeLamater and MacCorquodale (1979) argue that social control is one important aspect of the sociological emphasis, that is, "from a sociological viewpoint, sexual activity is ordered or patterned by norms, including laws, and these norms are reinforced by social control: rewards for conformity to and punishments for deviation from them" (p. 3). Such regulation of sexuality by society is stressed by several writers. Edwards (1972) says "sex, too, is patterned and learned behavior. It's mode of expression, timing, the type of partner it is engaged in with, and the imagery associated with it are all culturally conditioned and socially regulated" (p. 5). Similarly, Gagnon and Simon (1973) point out that "our laws embody our felt margin between those acts that are natural and those that are crimes against nature, delineating a narrow definition of *de jure* legitimacy by constraining the age, gender, legal, and kin relationships between sexual actors, as well as setting limits on the sites of behavior and the connections between organs" (p. 4).

Sociologists, then, emphasize three levels of analysis in their approach to human sexuality, the macro level (influences of society and culture on sexual attitudes and behavior), the subcultural level (the influences of class, gender, ethnicity, etc. on sexuality), and the interpersonal/group level (the influence of our membership in small groups and of other people on our sexual lives).

There are many examples in the extant literature of these emphases; a few are mentioned here. The classic examples of research on frequencies of behavior and subcultural differences in our society are, of course, the Kinsey studies (Kinsey, Pomeroy, & Martin, 1953; Kinsey, Pomeroy, Martin & Gebhard, 1948). Although the research by Kinsey suffered from some methodological problems, notably poor sampling, this research was the first attempt at a wide scale study of sexual behavior, and of the differences by gender and class, in our society. Kinsey made use of a methodology which is frequently used in the sociological approach—interviews.

Studies by Kantner and Zelnik (1972, 1973; Zelnik & Kantner, 1977) also provide an example of interview research focusing on group differences and the influence of social forces on human sexuality. Their research has dealt with the sexual and contraceptive behavior of young women. Using large, national probability samples, they have focused on differences in sexual behavior by race, class, and religion.

A third example, of all three levels of analysis, is the interview study of premarital sexuality by DeLamater and MacCorquodale (1979). Using a large random sample of college students and a systematic probability sample of 18 to 23-year-old nonstudents in the same city, DeLamater and MacCorquodale attempted to integrate the macro and social psychological orientations toward human sexuality. Their results focused on group differences (male vs. female; student vs. nonstudent) in premarital sexuality, and social background and interpersonal (partner, peers) influences on premarital sexual attitudes and behavior.

Blumstein and Schwartz (1983) make use of both questionnaires and face-to-face interviews in a study of American couples, their lifestyles and sexuality. The focus on the couple and on power differentials within the relationship reflects the interpersonal orientation. Their comparisons of men and women, spouses and cohabitors, and gays and straights reflect the subgroup and macro perspectives.

Another example is the work of Bartell (1970). He chose participant observation as a methodology for a study of mate-swapping or swinging. He studied many aspects of and influences on swinging behavior, including group differences (age, social class, ethnicity), and the interpersonal influences (partner influence and the negotiation of sexual exchanges).

Demographic research into fertility rates and fertility decision-making is another type of sociological research dealing with human sexuality. Researchers, such as Westoff and Bumpass (1973) have studied group differences and trends in contraception and fertility.

Ideas and Concepts

The emphasis on macro, subcultural, and interpersonal influences on human sexuality leads to special attention to certain ideas and concepts. These ideas and concepts include socialization, social control, laws and norms, scripts, roles, and the life-cycle approach. These concepts are not independent of one another, but rather, are all related. Each concept is briefly discussed and its application to the study of human sexuality is illustrated.

Socialization. Socialization is the process of teaching and encouraging the development of an understanding of the appropriate ways to think and behave within a particular society. Human beings must become aware of the norms, laws, manners, language, social skills, and values of their culture in order to adequately relate to others. Socialization, then, is also a form of social control. Teaching a particular value or norm guides and limits a person's beliefs and behavior.

One major area of socialization is sexual socialization. The socializing agents in the area of sexuality are, primarily, parents, siblings, spouse, peers, media, church, school, and the legal system. The content of sexual socialization includes sexual attitudes, values, behavioral norms, and gender roles. Sexual socialization focuses on gender roles and sex differences during childhood, gender roles, sexual knowledge and attitudes during adolescence, sexual knowledge, sexual experience and intimate relationships for young adults, marital and parental behavior for adults, and adjustment toward decreased sexuality during old age. The techniques of sexual socialization include observation and modeling, role-playing, rewards and punishments, dependency and power, and anticipatory socialization (imagining, fantasizing and practicing for the future). Sexual socialization varies across time and place.

Sociologists frequently study these various aspects of sexual socialization. For example, studies of the content and development of gender roles abound, including research on how they are influenced by social institutions (church, school, media) and other people (parents, peers), and how they affect behavior including sexual attitudes and behavior (see for example, Adams, 1973; Atkin, 1982; Bem, 1975; Block, 1976; Dweck, 1975; Gagnon, 1977; Spence, Helmreich, & Stapp, 1975; Tavris, 1977). Other studies assess the interpersonal, subcultural, and societal influences on our sexual attitudes. Such studies usually focus on attitudes about specific sexual behaviors such as homosexuality (MacDonald & Games, 1979), premarital sexuality (DeLamater & MacCorquodale, 1979; Reiss, 1960, 1967, 1968) or attitudes toward contraception (Jaccard & Davidson, 1972; McKinney & DeLamater, 1983).

Norms, Laws, Social Control. A major part of the content of our sexual socialization deals with sexual norms. Such norms, which provide behavioral standards, include both prescriptions (we're supposed to marry, and have sex and children with our spouse) and proscriptions (it is inappropriate to have premarital and extramarital sex, sex with relatives or children). Using Murdock's (1949) typology, we can classify sexual norms into: (a) prohibitive norms that specify inappropriate behaviors; (b) permissive norms that cover behaviors that are acceptable but not required; and (c) obligatory norms about behaviors you are expected to engage in.

Behavioral norms in the area of sexuality are learned from and sanctioned by, primarily, the family, peers, and religion. Norms about sexuality and intimate relationships not only specify appropriate and inappropriate behaviors, but also have a powerful impact on our sexuality by specifying who we may date or marry, and when in our lives these behaviors are expected. Furthermore, sexual norms not only vary across time and culture, but even within a particular culture;

subcultures may differ in their teaching of or emphasis on certain sexual norms (Ellis, 1962).

Many of our norms about sexuality become formalized into laws. The sociological approach to human sexuality includes the study of the origin of laws related to sexuality, their content, their enforcement, and their consequences (see for example, Boggan, Haft, Lister, & Rupp, 1975; Packer, 1968; Rosenbleet & Pariente, 1973; Slovenko, 1965). If there is one conclusion that can be drawn from such research it is that despite a large number of laws prohibiting certain sexual behaviors, "Americans commonly and regularly engage in sexual practices which are technically forbidden by law" (Slovenko, 1965, p. 5).

According to DeLora, Warren, and Ellison (1981) laws about sexuality focus on behaviors where force is involved and where consent of the partner is questionable (sex with animals, minors, people under the influence of drugs). Many laws also prohibit sexual behavior between consenting adults. These laws may attempt to regulate behavior that is seen as offensive to others or a threat to morality.

Related to the focus on norms, laws, and other mechanisms of social control is the fact that sociologists frequently study not only *normative* sexuality, but also *deviant* sexuality. Many sociological studies of human sexuality, perhaps a disproportionate number, deal with sexual deviance, such as studies on homosexuality (Humphreys, 1970; Jay & Young, 1979) and transsexualism (Driscoll, 1971; Green, 1975; Raymond, 1979).

Norms and laws are, of course, but two types of social control that others use to constrain our sexual behavior. According to DeLamater (1981), institutions in our society (religion, family) are sources of both norms and general perspectives that control our sexuality. These institutions support certain perspectives about sexuality, such as sex is only legitimate for purposes of reproduction, which then contribute to the existence of particular norms. In a review of this literature, DeLamater (1981) concludes that in general, religion and parents have a conservative effect on one's sexuality; whereas peers have a more permissive influence on our sexual attitudes and behavior. Furthermore, the emotional quality (intimacy or satisfaction) of the heterosexual relationship is positively related to the frequency of sexual activity.

Scripts.   Sexual scripts also control our sexuality and guide our sexual behavior. Gagnon and Simon (1973) argue that a script "defines the situation, names the actors, and plots the behavior. . .Scripts are involved in learning the meaning of internal states, organizing the sequences of specifically sexual acts, decoding novel situations, setting the limits on sexual responses, and linking meanings from nonsexual aspects of life to specifically sexual experience" (p. 19). Scripts, then, fulfill an extremely useful function for people, allowing us to utilize our past experience and other learning to structure our behavior in both novel and familiar situations involving various others. The concept of script takes into account both social/normative influences on sexuality, as well as the interpersonal/negotiation aspect of sexual interactions.

Nass, Libby, and Fisher (1981) offer a typology of sexual scripts. Each of these scripts may influence a person's sexual behavior, possibly in conflicting ways. The five scripts are the traditional religious script, the romantic script, the sexual friendship script, the casual/mutual horniness script, and the utilitarian/predatory script. Nass et al. point out that although scripts are functional, their usefulness has limitations. For example, we may lack a relevant script for a particular situation, scripts may conflict with each other, and scripts may be too rigid or may ignore individual needs. Interesting and detailed examples of the impact of scripts on female sexuality are provided by Laws and Schwartz (1977). DeLamater (1982) discusses gender differences in sexual scripts and their impact on male and female sexuality.

Roles.   No sociological analysis of sexuality would be complete without the consideration of roles—norms, behaviors, rights, and duties associated with a particular position. Roles can be ascribed (assigned) such as one's kinship relationships or achieved (earned), such as occupational or educational roles. Roles related to sexuality often have components of both an ascribed and achieved status (gender roles). As previously mentioned, gender roles—their content, measurement, development, and effect on sexuality—are frequently studied by sociologists, often in the context of socialization. There are studies of sexual role-playing by individuals in various stages of heterosexual (Rainwater, 1965) or homosexual (Califia, 1979) relationships. The occupational role of prostitute (Pittman, 1971; Sheehy, 1973; Winnick & Kinsie, 1973) has also been examined.

Roles can influence our sexual attitudes and behavior in several ways. Directly, as part of a gender role or marital role, we may be taught that it is our duty and/or right to engage in certain sexual behaviors, but not others. Indirectly, nonsexual traits/aspects of gender roles, marital roles, courtship roles, or parental roles may encourage or inhibit certain sexual attitudes and behaviors. For example, acceptance of passivity as part of a woman's role and/or belief in the male's right to dominate his wife can contribute to a woman who never initiates sex and is a candidate for spouse abuse. Beliefs about one's obligations as a parent may affect sexual expression in front of one's children, and may encourage or inhibit sexual communication with children. Peplau, Rubin, and Hill (1977), and Blumstein and Schwartz (1983) report findings on the relationship between gender, roles, attitudes, and sexuality for spouses, cohabitors, and homosexual couples.

Life Cycle.   A final concept that is stressed by many of those doing sociological analysis of human sexuality is the life-cycle approach. Such an approach takes a longitudinal, rather than a cross-sectional, view of sexuality. The life-cycle approach involves the study of the development of, and changes in, sexual attitudes, behavior, and physiological processes. Sociology is, of course, not the only perspective utilizing the life-cycle approach. The perspective is also common in biology and developmental psychology. A life-cycle strategy gives us a broader perspective on sexuality and illuminates the changes in and relationships among biological, interpersonal, and cultural influences on sexuality over the life span from infancy to old age.

Kirkendall and Rubin (1970) summarize the life-cycle approach in this way, "Throughout the life cycle, physiological, emotional, social, and cultural forces condition sexuality in intricate and important ways, most especially during early and late childhood. As individuals age, these influences may result in a widening range of possible sexual attitudes and expressions" (p. 152). Much research has focused on adolescence and adulthood, under the assumption that sexuality is most important in these life-cycle stages. However, with increased recognition of childhood sexuality (Elias & Gebhard, 1969; Ford & Beach, 1951) and sexuality in the elderly (Weg, 1983), research on sexuality at all ages is increasing.

True longitudinal studies of sexuality across the life cycle are rare due to the amount of time and the costs involved. In addition, survey or observational research of children's sexuality is limited by ethical concerns. Most research then, focuses on one stage of the life cycle, especially adolescence (Kantner & Zelnick, 1972, 1973) or young adulthood (DeLamater & McCorquodale, 1979). A second strategy is retrospective, that is, to ask adults about not only their current sexuality, but also their childhood sexuality. This latter strategy was utilized by Kinsey et al. (1948, 1953) and Bell, Weinberg, & Hammersmith (1981), and invites measurement error due to respondent bias and memory problems.

This section has briefly summarized a few of the most common concepts or ideas that are utilized by individuals taking a sociological approach to human sexuality. A second way in which we can answer the question "What is a sociological approach to human sexuality?" is to consider which theoretical perspectives are utilized.

Theoretical Perspectives

No attempt is made to cover all the theoretical perspectives involved in the sociological approach, rather, several commonly used sociological theories and how they relate to human sexuality are briefly summarized here.

Learning Theory

Given the emphasis on socialization in the sociological approach, learning theory is one popular theoretical perspective. Because there is a chapter in this volume on learning to be sexual, it is only pointed out here that this perspective is a very important part of the sociological approach. Sociology, with its emphasis on macro, subcultural, and interpersonal influences on sexuality argues that much of human sexuality is learned. This is not to deny the importance of biology, but given the cross-cultural, subcultural and individual differences in human sexual attitudes, norms and behaviors, differential learning is necessary to explain such variation. Rewards, punishments, role models, role playing, observation, vicarious experience, persuasion, and conditioning are all techniques that produce this differential learning that affects our sexual attitudes and behavior.

Some specific examples can be used to illustrate the importance of learning in human sexuality. For instance, sexual arousal is a result, not only of physiological processes, but also of the way in which potentially arousing stimuli are labeled and interpreted (Berscheid & Walster, 1974; Dutton & Aron, 1974). A nude body or other stimuli is only arousing for some people in certain situations. The ability of a stimulus to elicit arousal is a result of learning. Furthermore, sexual attitudes, stereotypes and myths, about rape (Burt, 1980) or homosexuality (Smith, 1973) for example, are learned and mediate our sexual responses. The earlier discussion of socialization, social control, and scripts also points to the crucial role of learning in human sexuality. Learning theories, then, present assumptions about and analysis of the content of learning, and the techniques or processes by which learning operates, including operant and classical conditioning, role modeling, and the more complex Social Learning Theory (Bandura, 1969).

Functionalism

Functionalism offers another sociological perspective on human sexuality. Functionalists assume there are certain values held in agreement by members of a society. These values lead to the formation of norms and other social controls that support these core values. Society is viewed as consisting of various groups and institutions that are interrelated. Institutions, groups, and individual behaviors exist, presumably because they serve a function (support the core values) for society. Furthermore, behaviors are evaluated in terms of how they relate to (support or threaten) the core values of society.

Davis (1937) provides an interesting statement of this viewpoint. He argues that the attitudes toward and social control of sexual behaviors, such as premarital and extramarital sex, will depend on their relationship to the core values of society. More specifically, prostitution is illegal and negatively evaluated because it is seen as a threat to the value we place on monogamy and the family. Yet, prostitution serves a positive function for society (and no serious attempts have been made to eliminate it) because it allows a form of casual, low commitment sexual release that is less of a threat to marriage and parenting (core values) than, for example, a serious, emotionally involved extramarital affair. Benjamin and Masters (1964) propose a similar argument about prostitution.

Labeling Theory

Labeling theory is essentially a theory of social control, concerned with how/why certain behaviors/individuals are labeled negatively (deviant), and with the consequences of such labeling to the individuals involved. Labeling theory posits that whether an individual is labeled sick, deviant, or criminal depends, to a substantial degree on his or her characteristics or place in the social structure (age, race, gender, status) and partly on perceived qualities of the act (public or private, victims involved). Individuals who lack power and status, and whose act was public and involved victims are more likely to be negatively labeled and sanctioned, especially if the audience (labelers) can gain from labeling the actor. According to the theory there are severe, negative consequences of being labeled. Rather than deterring the behavior, labeling presumably leads to negative treatment by others, restriction of legitimate or normative opportunities, the acceptance of a negative or deviant self-concept, and the self-fulfilling prophecy—the individual comes to behave in accordance with the label and the expectations of those around him or her.

Labeling theory can be used to explain deviant sexuality; however, it cannot explain the initial or primary deviance, only the deviance that occurs after the label has been applied (secondary deviance). To the extent that society has negative evaluations, norms and laws about various types of sexual behavior, certain individuals are likely to be labeled and stigmatized (homosexual, prostitute, child molester). Labeling theorists believe that such labeling will only serve to increase the deviant sexual behavior. One proposed solution is to decriminalize or legalize all sexual behavior between consenting adults in an effort to reduce the labeling and stigma of these behaviors. Examples of studies of sexual behavior using a labeling approach or aspects of a labeling approach include, an analysis of male hustlers (Reiss, 1961), a study of lesbians (Kelly, 1979), and research on homosexuals in the military (Williams & Weinberg, 1971).

Conflict Theory

Conflict theory is especially concerned with power differences in society and the imposition of certain values and definitions of behavior over others. Many conflict analyses focus on the development and passage of laws. In general, the elites or groups with the power in society are seen as capable of dictating which behaviors will be illegal. Their own values and behaviors are supported by the political and legal system, whereas the values and behaviors of minorities and less powerful groups in society will become deviant and criminalized. Such theoretical reasoning accurately predicts laws against homosexual behaviors, for example. Furthermore, it helps deal with issues such as why certain laws have special formal or informal exclusions (husbands "cannot rape" their wives; wife abuse is "not assault").

Szasz (1980) uses aspects of conflict theory in his critique of sexual therapy and sex education in our society. Szasz argues that certain groups, in particular the medical profession, use their power to label or define certain sexual attitudes and behavior as deviant, diseased or problematic, and, therefore, in need of therapy and treatments that the medical profession can provide for a price. Furthermore, he questions government and tax-sponsored sex education that imposes certain "facts" (biases and values represented as fact) on less powerful members of society (children, poor). Finally, feminist critiques of society's definitions and treatment of transsexuals provides another example of conflict theory applied to human sexuality (Billings & Urban, 1982; Raymond, 1979).

Symbolic Interactionism

Symbolic interactionism is another widely used perspective in sociology. Labeling theory, in fact, is related to symbolic interactionism. Symbolic interactionism focuses on roles and identities. Roles are the result of a process of negotiation between individuals in a social context. There are universal aspects of roles as prescribed by society, but there are also idiosyncratic aspects to roles that are negotiated by the participants.

Learning to take the role or perspective of other people and role-playing are important parts of learning appropriate social behavior, including sexual behavior. Our self-concept, including our body image and sexual self are assumed to be a result of our interactions and negotiations with others. Even how we come to define behaviors (sexual or not; immoral or moral) is a result of these processes.

The concept of scripts is a component of symbolic interactionism. Scripts, through the use of situational cues that are agreed upon symbols, guide people's behavior through interactions. Scripts include a definition of the situation and clarification of the actors' roles. For example, most women and their gynecologists have a script that defines genital contact during a gynecological exam as nonsexual. Scripts, including sexual scripts, help us define the situations we face (Gagnon & Simon, 1973). An off-shoot of symbolic interactionism is ethnomethodology that emphasizes the social construction of objective reality. An example of this approach is Kessler and McKenna's (1978) work on the attribution of gender.

Symbolic interactionism, by focusing on how we negotiate, define, give meaning to, and play our roles, identities, and relationships with other people stresses, primarily, interpersonal influences on our sexual attitudes and behavior. Studies of sexuality using a symbolic interactionist perspective include Humphreys' (1970) study of homosexual behavior, Victor's (1978) analysis of sexual arousal, and aspects of Feinbloom's (1976) research on transvestites and transsexuals.

Exchange Theory

Another theoretical perspective used in the sociological approach to human sexuality, and in particular to intimate relationships, is exchange theory. Human relationships are seen as partially structured in terms of exchanges. We fulfill the needs of others in return for fulfillment of our own needs, including affection, financial support, sex, emotional support, and so on. We also evaluate relationships in terms of the fairness or equity of the exchanges. Are we getting enough out of the relationship relative to our investments and to our partner's outcomes? Gouldner (1960) argues that there is an informal norm of reciprocity, such that we believe exchanges will be reciprocated over the long run of a relationship.

Predictions about satisfaction within a particular relationship and termination of a relationship can be made using exchange theory. For example, a popular, current perspective on divorce stems from exchange theory. Divorce becomes more likely, according to this view, when the costs of maintaining the marriage are high and the rewards from it are low relative to the costs and rewards of being alone or in some other relationship (Levinger, 1976; Nye, 1982). Premarital and extramarital sexuality have also been analyzed using equity theory, a special version of exhange theory (Hatfield, Traupmann, Walster, 1979; Walster (Hatfield), Walster, & Traupmann, 1978).

Typologies

Although not a theoretical perspective per se, the use of typologies as a theoretical tool is fairly common in the sociological approach to human sexuality. Based on case studies and observational or survey research, types or categories of individuals in certain sexual groups or who engage in certain sexual behaviors are identified. Such typologies then serve a descriptive function, as well as provide clues for explanations of the sexual behaviors and for future research. Examples of this theoretical tool in the area of human sexuality include typologies of homosexuals (Bell & Weinberg, 1978; Humphreys, 1970) and rapists (Cohen, Garofalo, Boucher, & Seghorn, 1971; Groth & Birnbaum, 1979).

In sum, classic and current sociological theories can be and have been successfully applied to human sexuality. These theories provide ways to understand the social influences on sexual learning, attitudes and behavior.

Research Strategies

A third way to answer the question "What is a sociological approach to human sexuality?" is to consider which research methods are preferred.

Gebhard (1969) identifies five fields of sex research: (a) clinical/medical (sexual problems and pathologies); (b) legal/forensic (laws governing sexuality); (c) reproductive/population (fertility and contraception); (d) sex education (sexual knowledge and control through teaching); and (e) basic research (parameters and variables affecting sexual attitudes and behavior). Although sociologists may be involved in research in all five categories, they are most commonly concerned with legal/forensic, reproductive/population, and basic research.

Because many fields or disciplines use the same few research strategies, one cannot delineate an approach solely on this basis. Virtually every research methodology imaginable has been used by sociologists and others to study human sexuality, including case studies, comparative studies, historical analysis, content analysis, observation, participant observation, interviews, questionnaires, and laboratory and field experiements. However, individuals using different approaches to human sexuality do prefer or are forced by the nature of their questions and subject matter to utilize certain methods more frequently. The sociological approach to human sexuality commonly uses several research methods.

Occasionally, researchers using the sociological approach have used historical analysis or content analysis. Much more common strategies for the sociological approach are case studies, experiments (used primarily by social psychologists), observation, and survey research (interviews and questionnaires).

Case Studies

Case studies involve the detailed, descriptive analysis of one or a small number of persons or groups. Case studies are often utilized for exploratory research and when accessability to a large number of subjects/respondents is difficult. Therefore, they frequently involve studies of "deviant" sexuality. The data obtained in a case study often involves in-depth interviews, observations, and analysis of records. Although case studies provide rich, detailed information, their interpretation is rather subjective and their most serious limitation is, of course, lack of generalizability. Examples of this research strategy include case studies of transsexuals (Bogdan, 1974), sex offenders (Parker, 1972), prostitutes (Greenwald, 1958, 1970), and sexual behavior in a singles' apartment complex (Proulx, 1973).

Experiments

The experimental method is highly valued for its methodological control and ability to provide us with information on causal relationships. Due primarily to ethical constraints, lack of realism, and the questions being studied, the experimental method is of limited use in the sociological approach to human sexuality. However, some sociologists, especially social psychologists, use experiments to study aspects of interpersonal relationships such as, attraction, sexual arousal, sexual communication, and other topics relevant to human sexuality. Definitions of a "true" experiment vary, but most researchers include the following components: experimental and control groups, random assignment of subjects and/or pretests along with the posttest, and independent and dependent variables where the categories of the independent variables occur naturally or are manipulated by the researcher.

Experimental research then, rather than focusing specifically on sexual behavior, usually involves studies of attitudes or behavior relevant to sexuality. Research on the correlates and causes of interpersonal attraction has relied primarily on field and laboratory experiments (Harvey, Christensen, & McClintock, 1983; Huston, 1974). Studies of social and physical factors affecting sexual arousal have also used the experimental method (Briddell & Wilson, 1976; Dutton & Aron, 1974; Wilson & Lawson, 1976). Two final examples would be the many experiments on sexual and aggressive responses to pornography (Donnerstein & Berkowitz, 1981) and experiments on perceptions and attributions of rape and rape victims (Cann, Calhoun, & Selby, 1979; Krulewitz & Payne, 1978; Shotland & Goodstein, 1983).

Observational Research

A method used more frequently than case studies and experiments by researchers with a sociological approach to human sexuality is observational research. This category includes various types of observational studies, the most general being participant (the researcher is simultaneously an observer and a participant of the group or in the behavior being studied) and nonparticipant (the researcher is in the observer role only) observation. Observational research usually occurs in the field and may involve note taking, structured coding schemes, and audio or video taping. Observational research is generally high in validity and may be the only way to study some aspects of human sexuality. However, observer bias, especially in participant observation, and reactivity by the subjects are both limitations. Generalizability is dependent on the quality of the sample observed.

Masters and Johnson's (1966) research on sexual response and physiology, although less relevant to sociology, is the classic example of observational research in the laboratory. Social aspects of human sexuality, however, are better observed in naturalistic settings. Three frequently cited studies utilized participant observation. Humphreys (1970) studied the casual, homosexual behavior of men in a public restroom by playing the role of ''lookout.'' Bartell (1970) and Palson and Palson (1972) contacted and/or joined ''swinging'' groups in order to study this extramarital phenomenon. Nonparticipant observational research (sometimes with interviews) includes, for example, Warren's (1974) studies of the gay community, Sheehy's work on prostitution (1973) and Silverman's (1971) observational study of physical attractiveness and courtship in bars.

Survey Research

Probably the most common methodology used in the sociological approach to human sexuality is survey research, including both face-to-face interviews and self-administered questionnaires. The greatest advantage of survey research is the ability to obtain large, probability samples of respondents, increasing external validity or generalizability. However, it should be pointed out that simply doing a survey is no guarantee of a quality sample. In fact, several of the often cited surveys on sexual behavior have serious sampling limitations (Athanasiou,

Shaver, & Tavris, 1970; Hunt, 1974; Levin & Levin, 1975). Survey research on sexuality has focused on attitudes and behavior of the adult population, as well as of more specific groups within the population. Questionnaires provide for respondent anonymity and are usually less costly than interviews. However, interviews allow respondents to develop rapport and to clarify questions and language with the interviewer. Survey research, by definition because it does not involve direct observation of sexuality, relies on the respondent's self-reports of their attitudes and behaviors. Self-reports may be biased by memory problems and concern with social desirability.

A tremendous amount of our information on human sexual behavior, including attitudes about normal and deviant sexuality, prevalence, incidence and frequency of involvement in normal and deviant sexuality, group differences in these attitudes and behaviors, and correlates of these attitudes and behaviors comes from surveys (longitudinal research may also assess some causal relationships). Interviews have been used to study, for instance, prostitution (Bryan, 1965), massage parlors (Velarde & Warlick, 1973), sexual preference (Bell, Weinberg, & Hammersmith, 1981), premarital sexuality (DeLamater & Mac-Corquodale, 1979), contraceptive attitudes and behavior (McKinney, Sprecher, & DeLamater, 1984) and sexual behavior in men and women (Kinsey et al., 1948, 1953). In addition, researchers have made use of questionnaires to study sexuality in dating relationships (Peplau, Rubin, & Hill, 1977), cohabitation among college students (Macklin, 1974), sexuality in men and women (Athanasiou et al., 1970; Hunt, 1974; Levin & Levin, 1975), sexual and contraceptive behavior of teenage women (Kantner & Zelnick, 1972, 1973), and verbal, physical, and sexual violence in dating relationships (Laner, 1982; Makepeace, 1981; McKinney & Welch, 1983).

Related to the use of questionnaires, several self-administered scales have been designed for use in the area of human sexuality, usually to assess attitudes that are then related to behavior. These include scales to assess homophobia (Mosher & O'Grady, 1979; Smith, 1973), acceptance of rape myths (Burt, 1980), attitudes toward courtship violence (McKinney & Welch, 1983), attitudes toward women in society (Spence, Helmreich, & Stapp, 1973), gender roles (Bem, 1974; Spence, Helmrich, & Stapp, 1975), loving and liking (Rubin, 1970; Hatfield & Sprecher, in review), and premarital sexual standards (Reiss, 1960, 1967).

In conclusion, although a variety of research methods are used in the sociological approach to human sexuality, the most common strategies are survey research, including both interviews (quantitative and qualitative) and questionnaires, and observational studies.

In answer to the question "What is a sociological approach to human sexuality?", the particular questions asked, and the concepts, theoretical perspectives and research methods used by researchers with a sociological viewpoint have been discussed. In summary, the sociological approach focuses on macro, sub-

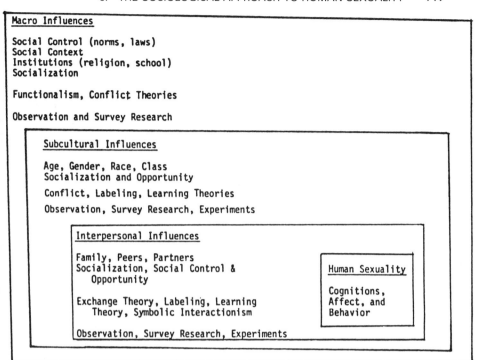

FIG. 5.1. Graphic representation of the sociological approach to human sexuality.

cultural, and interpersonal influences on human sexuality utilizing ideas such as, socialization, social control (norms, laws), scripts, roles and the life-cycle perspective. Common theoretical perspectives in this approach focus on the structure and relationships of institutions and groups in society and the negotiation of interpersonal relationships, and include learning theory, functionalism, labeling, conflict theory, symbolic interactionism, and exchange theory. Finally, sociological research on human sexuality relies most frequently on survey methods (interviews, scales, and questionnaires) and observational studies. (See Fig. 5.1 for a representation of the sociological approach to human sexuality.)

ISSUES IN THE SOCIOLOGICAL APPROACH TO HUMAN SEXUALITY

There are several problems and issues that must be faced in the study of human sexuality. Although, these issues are discussed in the context of the sociological approach, it must be emphasized that these concerns are *not* unique to this approach. Versions of these same problems and issues are found to varying degrees in all approaches to sexual behavior. These issues can be categorized into ethical and methodological issues.

Ethical Issues

When studying any form of human behavior, ethical concerns are paramount. This statement may be even more true for studies of human sexuality because of the topic's highly personal, salient, and perhaps threatening nature. Concern has been expressed by the public and by legislators about human sexuality research. It is important, then, that we consider to what extent ethical concerns are a problem in sociological research on human sexuality. Several commonly discussed ethical criteria have been related to research in the area of human sexuality.

Informed Consent

One standard of ethical research is informed consent. This criterion emphasizes the importance of both accurately informing your subject or respondent as to the nature of the research and what will happen to him or her, and obtaining his or her verbal or written consent to participate after he or she has been so informed. Coersion is not to be used to force participation and subjects may terminate their involvement in the research at any time. There are many possible violations of this standard. Researchers may be hesitant to inform participants that their study is about sexuality for fear of high rates of refusal. So, misrepresentation may be used when describing the topic of the study. Researchers may also misrepresent what is expected of the subject, for example, by indicating that they will privately interview the respondent, but then later requesting the respondent fill out a long, detailed questionnaire or when deception is used in an experimental design. Covert research also violates the informed consent standard because subjects are unaware that they are being studied. This is frequently a problem with observational research. The dilemma for the researcher of course, is to weigh the ethical violation against the belief that certain types of human sexual behavior cannot be studied if informed consent is utilized.

Informed consent creates special problems with certain populations. For example, studies of the sexuality of children are limited by the concern that children may be cognitively and emotionally unable to give informed consent. Furthermore, studies of sexuality within institutions (prisons, mental hospitals) or of criminal sexual behavior using inmates as subjects raises questions of coersion. Although participation may be described as voluntary, members of such populations may feel that it is not. They may believe instead that they will be rewarded for participation and punished for refusing. Although there are problems obtaining fully informed consent, most research is clearly voluntary and consent is requested prior to or after the data is gathered.

Right to Privacy

A second criterion involves the subject's right to privacy. Given the highly personal nature of sexuality and society's tremendous concern with the social control of sexuality, the right to privacy is a very salient ethical concern for research in this area. Individuals may risk losing their jobs, having family difficulties, or being ostracized by peers if certain facets of their sexual lives are revealed. This is especially true for individuals involved in sexual behavior categorized as deviant (homosexuality, transvestism, etc.). Violations of right to privacy occur when researchers identify members of certain groups they have studied, release or share an individual's data or responses, violate a promise of anonymity or confidentiality, or covertly observe sexual behavior. Again, the issue arises as to whether there are legitimate exceptions to this rule when it is the only way to obtain information about an area of human sexual behavior and when the risks of negative outcomes stemming from the ethical violation are low. In most cases, right to privacy is easily maintained by the sociological researcher. In survey research, self-administered questionnaires can be totally anonymous and interviews can be kept confidential. In case and observational studies the identity of the person or group studied can be disguised in any reports or publications. In all the research methods (except case studies), analysis and reporting of data should be at the group or aggregate level, not the individual level.

Protection From Harm

A final ethical standard (in which some writers incorporate the right to privacy) is protection from harm. Harm may include emotional or psychological distress, as well as physical harm. The latter is not very common in sociological research. It is more likely to be found in physiological or medical studies (assessing the affects of drugs on sexual arousal or testing new contraceptive methods, for example). Potential for harm also varies by research method; it is more likely in experimental studies where the researcher manipulates or does something to the subject than it is in observational or survey research. Emotional distress, however, is a possibility in sociological studies of human sexuality. Respondents may be asked questions that elicit anxiety, dredge up unpleasant memories or cause them to critically evaluate themselves. Attention has focused on reducing the potential for distress during a study by using anonymous, self-administered questionnaires, well-trained interviewers and carefully worded questions. Little attention has yet been given to dealing with such distress in the long run by following up respondents or providing counseling.

All three ethical criteria, including protection from harm, are quite subjective. Violations may be excused or justified if it can be argued that the harm to the subject or respondent is outweighed by the benefit to them or to society. The issue here, of course, is who makes that critical decision. Usually, such decisions are made by the researcher and often a screening committee that deals with ethical concerns. Most researchers have been able to follow these ethical guidelines. Attempts by researchers using the sociological approach to human sexuality to follow these ethical standards may, however, contribute to several of the methodological problems of this approach.

Methodological Issues

There are several methodological problems that arise when studying human sexuality using the sociological approach. The ethical constraints just discussed contribute to some of these methodological limitations. Several authors, including Comfort (1950) and Shope (1975) have recognized these methodological problems. Most of the concerns discussed in this section deal with problems faced when using the two most common methodological strategies of the sociological approach—observational and survey research.

Sampling

Due to the controversial, salient, and personal nature of the topic of human sexuality, and to the emphasis on the rigorous study of macro, subcultural, and interpersonal influences on sexuality of the sociological approach, sampling becomes a crucial issue and often a problem in such research. A major goal of the sociological approach is to learn something about human sexuality from a sample of people so that we can draw conclusions about the whole population. Of course, such conclusions cannot be made unless the sample is representative of the population. Probability sampling (random, systematic, etc.) is necessary to draw such conclusions. However, these sampling techniques require some type of sampling frame. If our interest is in the general population we can utilize common sampling frames (phone books, voter lists, college registrar lists). For example, DeLamater and MacCorquodale (1979) utilized random and systematic sampling in their study of premarital sexuality. Zelnik and Kantner (1977) used a national probability sample of 15 to 19-year-old women in their studies of sexual behavior and contraception. Westoff (1974) has also drawn national probability samples of women for his fertility studies. But where do we get a sampling frame for homosexuals, or transsexuals, or rapists? For special subpopulations, in particular those populations of individuals engaging in deviant, rare, or illegal sexuality, we will be unable to utilize probability sampling.

Along with the nature of the population, resource limitations can contribute to sampling difficulties. Due to negative attitudes by some legislators, funding agencies, and academic colleagues, research on human sexuality may be unfunded or underfunded. Properly executed probability sampling can be expensive.

A final difficulty with sampling, per se, focuses on the types of people we study. Social science is frequently criticized for our use of college students (often undergraduates in sociology and psychology) in survey research and especially in experimental studies. This criticism centers on whether information obtained on human sexuality and interpersonal relationships from college students is informative, accurate, nontrivial, and generalizable.

Because of these limitations on sampling, sociological studies of human sexuality often rely on nonprobability samples, such as haphazard, convenience, volunteer, and snowball samples. Such techniques limit our ability to do statistical analyses and to generalize the results to the population of interest (Athanasiou et al., 1970; Kinsey et al., 1948, 1953; Levin & Levin, 1975).

Nonresponse

A problem related to sampling is that of nonresponse. This can occur at two levels, refusal to participate in a study and refusal to answer certain questions on a questionnaire or in an interview. Refusals may be a special problem in studies of sexuality due to the personal and moral aspects of the topic. Nonresponse, of course, contributes to volunteer bias and can ruin a probability sample. The problem is that those who refuse may be dissimilar in some relevant ways to those who do participate. There are studies that suggest that individuals who volunteer to participate in sex research have higher self-esteem, are more politically liberal, and more sexually experienced than those who refuse (Kaats & Davis, 1971; Maslow & Sakoda, 1952). These results have not been consistently found, however (Barker & Perlman, 1975; Bauman, 1973).

Not all researchers unquestioningly accept the notion that studies of sexuality, due to the sensitive topic, will have higher refusal rates. Johnson and DeLamater (1976) argue that, frequently, response rates in surveys related to sexuality are equivalent to the response rates for studies of other topics using similar methodology. In fact, the evidence they reviewed supported the idea that nonresponse in sexuality surveys is primarily the result, not of the topic, but of practical problems common to all survey research. Furthermore, in studying nonresponse of items within a survey on sexuality, they conclude that such refusals cannot be generally explained by the sensitive nature of the topic. Finally, they summarize several strategies used to increase response rates for research on potentially sensitive topics, including: (a) mailing letters of introduction to prepare the respondent for the study; (b) making a personal (phone or face-to-face) contact with respondents prior to the study; and (c) beginning interviews on sexuality with a general, nonthreatening statement of the study's purpose. This latter strategy, however, raises the ethical issue of informed consent.

DeLamater and McKinney (1982) reviewed the literature on nonresponse and response effects due to question content in survey interviews. The four aspects of question content that affect responses are all relevant to the topic of sexuality. These four aspects are: (a) the degree to which the topic arouses anxiety; (b) the degree to which a topic arouses a concern with social desirability; (c) the salience of the topic; and (d) the wording of the question. In terms of the refusal to paticipate in research, DeLamater and McKinney conclude that ''there is no consistent evidence that refusals by adults to participate in surveys are related to the topics covered'' (p. 15). Studies of adolescent sexuality, however, do have high rates of refusal by both parents and potential respondents. Finally, reviewing studies on refusals to particular questions in a survey, it was concluded that questions about sexuality are refused by less than 10% of respondents.

Response Effects

Simply obtaining a response is, of course, no guarantee of the reliability or validity of the answers. It has been generally assumed that a variety of response biases or errors occur in studies of sexual behavior. Such response effects may include purposeful distortion such as concealment (underreporting) and enlargement (overreporting), concern with social desirability, memory problems, inaccurate estimates, and misunderstanding of words or questions.

Although several authors report that questions dealing with presumably threatening topics with strong social desirability components (sexual behavior, drug use, illegal behavior) do not, necessarily, elicit nonreponse, these questions may contribute to underreporting of those behaviors (DeLamater & McKinney, 1982; Sudman, 1976). On the other hand, Nowakowska (1973) found that responses to anxiety-arousing items were actually more stable (reliable) over a 2-week period than were responses to neutral items.

Sexuality is not only considered to be a sensitive topic, but also a relevant or salient topic. Generally, research has shown that items dealing with salient topics elicit more reliable responses (Nowakowska, 1973; Sudman & Bradburn, 1974). Finally, studies indicate that variations in survey strategy (interview vs. self-administered), placement of sexual questions in the survey (early vs. late), order of certain questions (own current behavior vs. past behavior vs. peer's behavior), and terminology used in sexuality studies have no substantial effects on reported sexual attitudes or behavior (DeLamater, 1974; DeLamater & MacCorquodale, 1975).

Generalizability

The issue of external validity or generalizability has repeatedly surfaced in this discussion as a problem in sociological studies of human sexuality. As mentioned previously, our ability to generalize from our sample to the population of interest is limited by lack of sampling frames, inability to draw probability samples, refusals or nonresponse, small samples, and overuse of certain subjects/respondents, such as college students. Finally, inability to generalize is more of a problem with certain research methodologies, such as case studies and observational research.

Establishing Causal Relationships

A final concern that is methodological and also has theoretical implications is the issue of assessing causal relationships rather than or in addition to correlational relationships. Establishing causal relationships is a major goal of all research. As a result of ethical and methodological limitations on studies of human sexuality, it is often difficult to conduct research designed to provide unambiguous information about causal relationships. Longitudinal research and the experimental method can provide such data. In the area of human sexuality, ethical and practical concerns often prohibit the use of experiments. Limited time and resources, and attrition complicate longitudinal studies. Although writers will infer causal relationships from other types of studies (cross-sectional, retrospective), one must be very critical in accepting such conclusions.

In summary, there are several ethical and methodological limitations and problems with the sociological approach to human sexuality. Ethical constraints, sampling, nonresponse, and generalizability are especially problematic. There is less agreement on the issue of response effects.

However, these problems are not unique to the sociological approach, but rather are common to most attempts to study human behavior and human sexuality specifically. Furthermore, despite these limiations, research on human sexuality is feasible and vital. Sexual issues permeate the lives of human beings and must be studied. Much of the research manages to overcome the ethical and methodological problems. Most researchers treat these problems with concern and creativity. Even research that suffers from some of these limiations provides us with needed information. Such research is legitimate as long as readers are careful to critically evaluate and interpret these studies.

CONCLUSIONS

The purpose of this chapter has been to define, delineate, and provide examples of the sociological approach, thereby differentiating it from other approaches to human sexuality.

As outlined in Fig. 5.1, the sociological approach focuses on three levels of analysis: the macro-societal level, the subcultural level, and the interpersonal level. Sociologists are interested in institutional influences such as laws, religion, and school on human sexuality, differences in human sexuality based on membership in gender, age, race, and class categories, and the impact of family, peers, and partners on our sexuality.

These levels of analysis are reflected in the theories and concepts utilized by researchers using the sociological approach. Causes and correlates of human sexuality, and the processes by which these causes operate, include macro, group, and interpersonal level constructs, such as labeling, exchange, learning and socialization, laws, norms and social control, symbols, scripts, roles and negotiation, and values and functions.

The research methods utilized by individuals with a sociological approach do not necessarily distinguish this approach from others. Sociologists rely on a wide range of research techniques, but especially on observational methods and survey research. Social psychologists also use experiments. Furthermore, the ethical and methodological problems discussed, including informed consent, right to privacy, protection from harm, sampling, nonresponse, response effects, generalizability, and causality are *not* unique to the sociological approach, but are problems for much of the research on human sexuality. Finally, these problems can be and are frequently overcome by researchers. The sociological approach is crucial to the study of human sexuality. As Comfort (1950) argues, "any attempt to isolate sexual behavior from the other factors in a social pattern is bound to hinder our comprehension of it and lead to false emphases" (p. 43).

Where does the sociological approach to human sexuality go from here? There are several general suggestions that can be summarized. First, we must continue to maintain high ethical standards in our research. Many professional organizations offer ethical guidelines that can be used to judge one's research and avoid ethical violations and harm to our subjects/respondents. Ethical standards become increasingly important as our technological skills advance into new areas with unknown consequences (e.g., genetic engineering, invitro fertilization, surrogate mothers, new contraceptive techniques). Recognition of ethical issues in research may also include some consideration of the applied or practical implications of our results. Much sociological research on human sexuality is basic research, yet the topic has obvious and important applications.

Second, as DeLamater (1981) points out, the sociological approach to human sexuality lacks an integrated perspective and an integration of diverse empirical results. .Because theories are never proven correct, we must engage in theory development and integration that leads to theories with falsifiable hypotheses that can be clearly tested. If our concern is to more accurately and completely explain and predict human sexual behavior, it is important to avoid reductionism, whether it is sociological, psychological, or biological reductionism. Therefore, integration of theories and an interdisciplinary approach are essential for a better understanding of human sexuality.

Third, we must strive to improve our methodological rigor. Samples must be improved, with increasing reliance on probability sampling. Furthermore, understudied groups can be given additional consideration such as in studies of the contraceptive behavior of men, and sexuality in the elderly and ethnic/racial minorities. In order to assess causal relationships and increase prediction of sexual attitudes and behavior, more experiments and longitudinal surveys must be conducted. These methods should create interesting ethical and practical challenges for the sociological researcher. Finally, studies need to more explicitly test specific hypotheses and assumptions directly stemming from our sociological theories of human sexuality. All too often, studies are merely descriptive and exploratory, or indirectly test hypotheses that are related post hoc to our theories. More research is also needed on some of the current topics such as AIDs, the "G" spot and courtship violence, not because such topics are inherently more important than older ones, but because of the media attention (and often inaccurate information) about such topics.

Finally, it is necessary to continue to integrate theory and methodology in our research on human sexuality. As pointed out by Harvey, Christensen, and Mc-Clintock (1983) in a detailed discussion of research issues in the study of close relationships, "theory and method are not independent. Theoretical development often generates new methodological strategies for studying relationships. And methodologies often produce new information which stimulates theoretical development" (p. 58).

ACKNOWLEDGMENTS

I wish to thank John DeLamater, Susan Sprecher, and Robert Graham for their valuable time and useful comments on a draft of this chapter.

REFERENCES

Adams, J. (1973). *Understanding adolescence.* Boston: Allyn & Bacon.

Athanasiou, R., Shaver, P., & Tavris, C. (1970, July). Sex. *Psychology Today,* pp. 39–52.

Atkin, C. (1982). Changing male and female roles. In M. Schwarz (Ed.), *TV and teens: Experts look at the issues* (pp. 66–70). Reading, MA: Addison-Wesley.

Bandura, A. (1969). *Principles of behavior modification.* New York: Holt, Rinehart & Winston.

Barker, W. J., & Perlman, D. (1975). Volunteer bias and personality traits in sexual standards research. *Archives of Sexual Behavior, 4,* 161–171.

Bartell, G. D. (1970). Group sex among the mid-Americans. *Journal of Sex Research, 6,* 113–130.

Bauman, K. (1973). Volunteer bias in a study of sexual knowledge, attitudes and behavior. *Journal of Marriage and the Family, 35,* 27–31.

Beach, F. A. (Ed.). (1977). *Human Sexuality in four perspectives.* Baltimore: Johns Hopkins Press.

Bell, A. P., & Weinberg, M. S. (1978). *Homosexualities: A study of diversity among men and women.* New York: Simon & Schuster.

Bell, A. P., Weinberg, M. S., & Hammersmith, S. K. (1981). *Sexual preference: Its development in men and women.* Bloomington, IL: Indiana University Press.

Bem, S. (1975). Sex-role adaptability: One consequence of psychological androgyny. *Journal of Personality and Social Psychology, 31,* 634–643.

Benjamin, H., & Masters, R. E. L. (1964). *Prostitution and morality.* New York: Julian Press.

Berscheid, E., & Walster (Hatfield), E. (1974). A bit about love. In T. Huston (Ed.), *Foundations of interpersonal attraction* (pp. 355–381). New York: Academic Press.

Billings, D. B., & Urban, T. (1982). The socio-medical construction of transsexualism: An interpretation and critique. *Social Problems, 29,* 266–282.

Block, J. (1976). Issues, problems and pitfalls in assessing sex differences. *Merill-Palmer Quarterly, 22,* 283–308.

Blumstein, P., & Schwartz, P. (1983). *American couples.* New York: William Morrow.

Bogdan, R. (1974). *Being different: The autobiography of Jane Fry.* New York: Wiley.

Boggan, E. C., Haft, M. G. Lister, C., & Rupp, J. P. (1975). *The rights of gay people.* New York: Discus Books Avon.

Briddell, D., & Wilson, G. (1976). Effects of alcohol and expectancy set on male sexual arousal. *Journal of Abnormal Psychology, 85,* 225–234.

Bryan, J. H. (1965). Apprenticeships in prostitution. *Social Problems, 12,* 278–297.

Burt, M. P. (1980). Cultural myths and support for rapes. *Journal of Personality and Social Psychology, 38,* 217–230.

Califia, P. (1979). Lesbian sexuality. *Journal of Homosexuality, 4,* 255–266.

Cann, A., Calhoun, L., & Selby, J. (1979). Attributing responsibility to the victim of rape: Influence of information regarding past sexual experience. *Human Relations, 32,* 57–67.

Cohen, M. L., Garofalo, R., Boucher, R., & Seghorn, T. (1971). The psychology of rapists. *Seminars in Psychiatry, 3,* 307–327.

Comfort, A. (1950). *Sexual behavior in society.* New York: Viking.

Davis, K. (1937). The sociology of prostitution. *American Sociological Review, 2,* 744–755.

DeLamater, J. (1974). Methodological issues in the study of premarital sexuality. *Sociological Methods and Research, 3,* 30–61.

DeLamater, J. (1981). The social control of human sexuality. *Annual Review of Sociology, 7,* 263–290.

DeLamater, J. (1982, September). *Gender differences in sexual scripts.* Paper presented at the American Sociological Association meetings, San Francisco, CA.

DeLamater, J., & MacCorquodale, P. (1975). The effects of interview schedule variations on reported sexual behavior. *Sociological Methods and Research, 4,* 215–236.

DeLamater, J. & MacCorquodale, P. (1979). *Premarital sexuality: Attitudes, relationships, behavior.* Madison, WI: University of Wisconsin Press.

DeLamater, J., & McKinney, K. (1982). Response-effects of question content. In W. Dijkstra & J. van der Zouwen (Eds.), *Response behavior in the survey interview* (pp. 13–48). London: Academic Press.

DeLora, J. S., Warren, C. A. B., & Ellison, C. R. (1981). *Understanding sexual interaction.* Boston: Houghton Mifflin.

Donnerstein, E., & Berkowitz, L. (1981). Victim reactions in aggressive erotic films as a factor in violence against women. *Journal of Personality and Social Psychology, 41,* 710–724.

Driscoll, J. P. (1971, March–April). Transsexuals. *Transaction,* pp. 28–31.

Dutton, D., & Aron, A. (1974). Some evidence for heightened sexual attraction under conditions of high anxiety. *Journal of Personality and Social Psychology, 30,* 510–517.

Dweck, C. (1975, April). *Sex differences in the meaning of negative evaluation in achievement settings.* Paper presented at the meeting of the Society for Research in Child Development, Denver, CO.

Edwards, J. N. (Ed.). (1972). *Sex & society.* Chicago: Markham Publishing.

Elias, J., & Gebhard, P. (1969). Sexuality & sexual learning in childhood. *Phi Delta Kappan, 50,* 401–405.

Ellis, A. (1962). What is 'normal' sex behavior? *Sexology, 28,* 364–369.

Feinbloom, D. H. (1976). *Transvestites and transsexuals.* New York: Dell.

Ford, C. S., & Beach, F. A. (1951). *Patterns of sexual behavior.* New York: Harper & Row.

Gagnon, J. (1977). *Human sexualities.* Glenview, IL: Scott, Foresman.

Gagnon, J., & Simon, W. (1973). *Sexual conduct.* Chicago: Aldine.

Gebhard, P. H. (1969). Human sex behavior research In M. Diamond (Ed.), *Perspectives in reproduction and sexual behavior* (pp. 391–410). Bloomington, IN: Indiana University Press.

Gouldner, A. W. (1960). The norm of reciprocity: A preliminary statement. *American Sociological Review, 25,* 161–179.

Green, R. (1975). Adults who want to change sex: adolescents who cross-dress; and children called 'sissy' and 'tomboy'. In R. Green (Ed.), *Human sexuality: A health practioner's text* (pp. 83–95). Baltimore: Williams & Williams.

Greenwald, H. (1958). *The call girl.* New York: Ballantine.

Greenwald, H. (1970). *The elegant prostitute: A social and psychoanalytic study.* New York: Walken.

Groth, A. N., & Birnbaum, H. J. (1979). *Men who rape: The psychology of the offender.* New York: Plenum.

Harvey, J. H., Christensen, A., & McClintock, E. (1983). Research methods. In H. H. Kelley, E. Bersheid, A. Christensen, J. H. Harvey, T. L. Huston, G. Levinger, E. McClintock, L. A. Peplau, & D. R. Peterson (Eds.), *Close relationships* (pp. 1–58). San Francisco: Freeman.

Hatfield, E., & Sprecher, S. (in review). Measuring passionate love. *Journal of Personality and Social Psychology.*

Hatfield, E., Traupmann, J., & Walster, G. W. (1979). Equity and extramarital sex. In M. Cook & G. Wilson (Eds.), *Love and attraction: An international conference* (pp. 309–321). Oxford: Pergamon Press.

Humphreys, L. (1970). *Tearoom trade: Impersonal sex in public places.* Chicago: Aldine.

Hunt, M. (1974). *Sexual behavior in the 1970's.* Chicago: Playboy Press.

Huston, T. L. (Ed.). (1974). *Foundations of interpersonal attraction.* New York: Academic Press.

Jaccard, J. J., & Davidson, A. R. (1972). Toward an understanding of family planning behaviors. An initial investigation. *Journal of Applied Social Psychology, 2,* 228–235.

Jay, K., & Young, A. (1979). *The gay report.* New York: Summit Books.

Johnson, W. T., & DeLamater, J. (1976). Response effects in sex surveys. *Public Opinion Quarterly, 40,* 165–181.

Kaats, G., & Davis, K. (1971). Effects of volunteer biases in studies of sexual behavior and attitudes. *Journal of Sex Research, 7,* 26–34.

Kantner, J. F., & Zelnick, M. (1972). Sexual experience of young unmarried women in the United States. *Family Planning Perspectives, 4,* 9–18.

Kantner, J. F., & Zelnick, M. (1973). Contraception and pregnancy: Experience of young unmarried women in the United States. *Family Planning Perspectives, 5,* 21–35.

Kelly, D. H. (1979). The structuring and maintenance of a deviant identity: An analysis of lesbian activity. In D. H. Kelley (Ed.), *Deviant behavior: Readings in the sociology of deviance* (pp. 592–603). New York: St. Martin's Press.

Kessler, S. J., & McKenna, W. (1978). *Gender: An ethnomethodological approach.* New York: Wiley.

Kinsey, A. C. Pomeroy, W. B., & Martin, C. E. (1953). *Sexual behavior in the human female.* Philadelphia: Saunders.

Kinsey, A. C., Pomeroy, W. B., Martin, C. E., & Gebhard, P. H. (1948). *Sexual behavior in the human male.* Philadelphia: Saunders.

Kirkendall, L. A. & Rubin, I. (1970). Sexuality and the lifecycle: A broad concept of sexuality. *Sexuality and Man.* New York: Scribner's.

Krulewitz, J., & Payne, E. J. (1978). Attributions about rape: Effects of rapist force, observer sex and sex role attitudes. *Journal of Applied Social Psychology, 8,* 291–305.

Laner, M. R. (1982). Courtship abuse and aggression: Contextual aspects. *Sociological Spectrum, 3,* 69–83.

Laws, J. L., & Schwartz, P. (1977). *Sexual scripts: The social construction of female sexuality.* Hinsdale, IL: Dryden Press.

Levin, R. J., & Levin, A. (1975, September). Sexual pleasure: the surprising preferences of 100,000 women. *Redbook,* pp. 51–58.

Levinger, G. (1976). A social psychological perspective in divorce. *Journal of Social Issues, 32,* 21–47.

MacDonald, A. P., & Games, R. (1979). Some characteristics of those who hold positive and negative attitudes toward homosexuality. *Journal of Homosexuality, 4,* 9–27.

Macklin, E. (1974, November). Cohabitation in college: Going very steady. *Psychology Today,* pp. 53–59.

Makepeace, J. M. (1981). Courtship violence among college students. *Family Relations, 30,* 97–102.

Maslow, A., & Sakoda, J. (1952). Volunteer-error in the Kinsey study. *Journal of Abnormal and Social Psychology, 47,* 259–267.

Masters, W., & Johnson, V. (1966). *Human sexual response.* Boston: Little, Brown.

McKinney, K., Sprecher, S., & DeLamater, J. (1984). Self images and contraceptive behavior. *Basic and Applied Social Psychology, 5,* 37–57.

McKinney, K., & Welch, J. A. (1983). [Courtship violence]. Unpublished raw data.

Mosher, D. L., & O'Grady, K. E. (1979). Homosexual threat, negative attitudes toward masturbation, sex guilt, and males' sexual and affective reactions to explicit sexual films. *Journal of Consulting and Clinical Psychology, 47,* 860–873.

Murdock, G. P., (1949). *Social structure.* New York: MacMillan.

Nass, G. D., Libby, R. W., & Fisher, M. P. (1981). *Sexual choices.* Monterey, CA: Wadsworth.

Nowakowska, M. (1973). Perceptions of questions and variability of answers. *Behavioral Science, 18,* 99–108.

Nye, F. I. (1982). *Family relationships: Rewards and Costs.* Beverly Hills, CA: Sage.

Packer, H. L. (1968). *The limits of the criminal sanction.* Stanford, CA: Stanford University Press.

Palson, C., & Palson, R. (1972). Swinging in wedlock. *Society, 9,* 43–48.

Parker, T. (1972). *The hidden world of sex offenders.* Indianapolis, IN: Bobbs-Merrill.

Peplau, L. A., Rubin, Z., & Hill, C. T. (1977). Sexual intimacy in dating relationships. *Journal of Social Issues, 33,* 86–109.

Pittman, D. J. (1971). The male house of prostitution. *Transaction, 8.*

Proulx, C. (1973, April). Sex as athletics in the singles complex. *Saturday Review,* pp. 60–62.

Rainwater, L. (1965). *Family design.* Chicago: Aldine.

Raymond, J. G. (1979). *The transsexual empire: The making of the she-male.* Boston: Beacon Press.

Reiss, A. J. (1961). The social integration of queers and peers. *Social Problems, 9,* 102–120.

Reiss, I. (1960). *Premarital sexual standards in America.* New York: Free Press.

Reiss, I. (1967). *The sexual context of premarital sexual permissiveness.* New York: Irving.

Reiss, I. (1968). How and why America's sex standards are changing. *Transaction, 5,* 26–32.

Rosenbleet, C., & Pariente, B. J. (1973). The prostitution of the criminal law. *American Criminal Law Review, 11,* 373–427.

Rubin, Z. (1970). Measurement of romantic love. *Journal of Personality and Social Psychology, 16,* 265–273.

Sheehy, G. (1973). *Hustling: Prostitution in our wide open society.* New York: Delacorte Press.

Shope, D. F. (1975). *Interpersonal sexuality.* Philadelphia: W. B. Saunders.

Shotland, R. L., & Goodstein, L. (1983). Just because she doesn't want to doesn't mean it's rape: An experimentally based causal model of the perception of rape in a dating situation. *Social Psychology Quarterly, 46,* 220–232.

Silverman, I. (1971). Physical attractiveness and courtship. *Sexual Behavior, 1,* 22–25.

Slovenko, R. (1965). *Sexual behavior and the law.* Springfield, IL: Charles C. Thomas.

Smith, K. (1973). The homophobic scale. In G. Weinberg (Ed.), *Society and the healthy homosexual,* (pp. 132–136). New York: Anchor.

Spence, J., Helmreich, R., & Stapp, J. (1973). A short version of the attitudes toward women scale (AWS). *Bulletin of Psychonomic Society, 2,* 219–220.

Spence, J., Helmreich, R., & Stapp, J. (1975). Ratings of self and peers on sex role attributes and their relation to self-esteem and conceptions of masculinity and feminity. *Journal of Personality and Social Psychology, 32,* 29–39.

Sudman, S. (1976). Sample surveys. In A. Inkeles, J. Coleman, & N. Smelser (Eds.), *Annual Review of Sociology, 2,* 107–120.

Sudman, S., & Bradburn, N. M. (1974). *Response effects in surveys.* Chicago: Aldine.

Szasz, T. (1980). *Sex by prescription.* New York: Penguin Books.

Tavris, C. (1977, January). Men and women report their views on masculinity. *Psychology Today,* pp. 35–38; 42; 82.

Velarde, A. J., & Warlick, M. (1973). Massage parlors: The sensuality business. *Society, 11,* 63–74.

Victor, J. S. (1978). The social psychology of sexual arousal: A symbolic interactionist approach. In

N. K. Denzin (Ed.), *Studies in symbolic interaction: Vol. 1.* (pp. 147–180). Greenwich, CT: JAI Press.

Walster (Hatfield), E., Walster, G., & Traupmann, J. (1978). Equity and premarital sex. *Journal of Personality and Social Psychology, 36,* 82–92.

Warren, C. (1974). *Identity and community in the gay world.* New York: Wiley.

Weg, R. B. (Ed.). (1983). *Sexuality in the later years: Roles and behavior.* New York: Academic Press.

Westoff, C. (1974). Coital frequency and contraception. *Family Planning Perspectives, 6,* 136–141.

Westoff, C., & Bumpass, C. (1973). The revolution in birth control practices of U.S. Roman Catholics. *Science, 179,* 41–44.

Williams, C. J., & Weinberg, M. S. (1971). *Homosexuals and the military: A study no less than honorable discharge.* New York: Harper & Row.

Wilson, G., & Lawson, D. (1976). Effects of alcohol on sexual arousal in women. *Journal of Abnormal Psychology, 85,* 489–497.

Winnick, C., & Kinsie, P. M. (1973, January). Prostitution. *Sexual Behavior.*

Zelnick, M., & Kantner, J. F. (1977). Sexual and contraceptive experience of young unmarried women in the United States, 1976, and 1981. *Family Planning Perspectives, 9,* 55–71.

6

A Psychological Approach to Human Sexuality: The Sexual Behavior Sequence

William A. Fisher
University of Western Ontario

INTRODUCTION

This chapter discusses a psychological approach to human sexuality. In principle, psychological approaches could focus on clinical issues (e.g., LoPiccolo, 1977), physiological bases (e.g., Davidson, 1980), or developmental (e.g., Freud, 1959), personality (e.g., Fisher, Byrne, White, & Kelley, 1984), or social (e.g., Byrne, 1977a) psychological analyses of human sexuality, among other possible perspectives. What follows is an attempt to identify some generally relevant issues from among this diversity in order to form the basis of a psychological approach (but certainly not *the* psychological approach) to human sexuality.

As psychologists, we are concerned with understanding the causes of an individual's sexual behavior: What are the relevant external stimuli and internal mediating processes that determine an individual's sexual output? The present psychological approach is conceptualized as merely one part of a macro- to micro-level analysis of human sexual behavior (toward the micro end of this analysis), and as such should complement rather than compete with the evolutionary, anthropological, and sociological perspectives discussed elsewhere in this volume. In particular, it is likely that many of the effects of evolution and culture work through an individual's mind to affect his or her sexual behavior. The psychological approach tries to understand the way in which these and other external influences may affect an individual's internal processes and result in distinctive patterns of sexual behavior.

In this discussion, the focus is on an individual's arousal, affective, and cognitive processes because they appear to be the key mediators of human behavior, sexual or otherwise (see, for example, Byrne, 1971; Clark & Fiske,

131

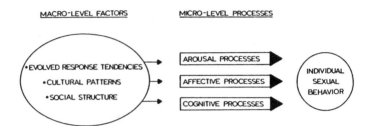

FIG. 6.1.   The place of a psychological approach in a macro- to micro-level analysis of human sexual behavior.

1982; Fishbein & Ajzen, 1975; Lazarus, 1984; Zajonc, 1980, 1984; Zillmann, 1979). On one hand, it is believed that arousal, affect, and cognition are affected by macro-level forces (i.e., naturally selected response tendencies, cultural norms, social structure); on the other hand, arousal, affect, and cognition are thought to motivate and guide an individual's sexual behavior. Thus, evolutionary and cultural factors are viewed as distal variables that affect internal arousal, affective, and cognitive processes that are in turn the immediate causes of sexual behavior. These general relationships are depicted in Fig. 6.1.

THE SEXUAL BEHAVIOR SEQUENCE

A number of psycholgical theories are relevant to our interest in arousal, affective and cognitive determinants of sexual behavior (cf. Byrne, 1971; Fishbein & Ajzen, 1975; Zillmann, 1979). Most existing models, however, deal with only *some* of these constructs, and do not provide a general enough framework for investigating the joint effects of these variables on sexual behavior. One exception to this generality is the Sexual Behavior Sequence (Byrne, 1977a, 1983; Byrne & Kelley, 1981; see also Byrne, this volume), a model that was developed specifically for the study of human sexuality and that deals with the roles of arousal, affect, and cognition as determinants of sexual behavior. For this reason, the Sexual Behavior Sequence is used as the basis for discussion of this psychological approach to human sexuality.

   The present rendering of the Sexual Behavior Sequence may be seen in Fig. 6.2. From left to right, the model suggests that human beings respond to both unlearned (Unconditioned Erotic Stimuli) and learned (Conditioned Erotic Stimuli) erotic cues. These cues may elicit sexual arousal (Physiological Sexual Arousal), affective responses (Affective and Evaluative Responses) and cognitive responses (Informational, Expectative, and Imaginative Responses). Arousal, affect and cognition may motivate and guide instrumental acts (Preparatory Sexual Behavior) that increase the likelihood of an overt Sexual Behavior. This behavior may be linked with hedonically positive or negative conse-

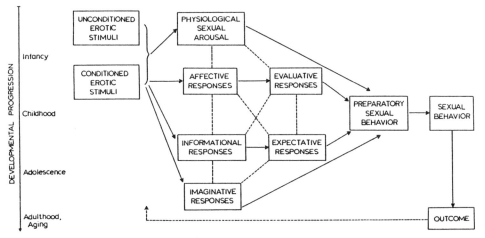

FIG. 6.2.   The Sexual Behavior Sequence (after Byrne, 1977a, 1983; Byrne & Kelley, 1981). The boxes indicate constructs in the model, the arrows indicate proposed antecedent-consequent relationships, broken lines indicate secondary relationships among constructs, and the broken line at the bottom of the figure indicates a feedback system whereby the positive or negative outcome of a sexual behavior influences the future probability of responses that led to that behavior. The developmental progression scale to the left suggests that certain constructs are phased into the model at earlier or later points in development.

quences (Outcome) that will influence the future probability of the responses that led to the behavior in question. A Developmental Progression arrow indicates that the topmost constructs are thought to be prominent somewhat earlier in the life span, whereas lower constructs come to the fore at later points in development.

It may be noted that the mediating constructs in the Sexual Behavior Sequence are simply specifications of the arousal, affective and cognitive processes depicted in Fig. 6.1. As such, the mediating constructs of the Sexual Behavior Sequence are presumed to be influenced by macro-level factors and to influence in turn individual sexual behavior. The remainder of this discussion considers how arousal, affective, and cognitive responses are learned, how they mediate sexual behavior, how they unfold developmentally, and how macro-level factors may work through the system to affect individual sexual behavior.

SEXUAL STIMULI—AROUSAL—BEHAVIOR

According to the Sexual Behavior Sequence, human beings respond to certain cues—unconditioned erotic stimuli—with unlearned sexual–physiological responses. For human beings, unconditioned erotic stimuli involve tactile stimulation of the genitals or erogenous zones (Masters & Johnson, 1966), and possibly chemical secretions call *pheromones* that act as sexual attractants (Comfort, 1971; Doty, Ford, Preti, & Huggins, 1975; Michael, Bonsall, & Warner, 1974). The physiological sexual arousal evoked by unconditioned erotic stimuli includes pelvic vasocongestion, heart and respiration rate increases, and myotonia (Masters & Johnson, 1966; see Rosen & Beck, this volume).

Human beings who experience physiological sexual arousal of sufficient intensity and duration ordinarily desire to reduce this arousal in some way. Thus, physiological sexual arousal may motivate the individual to enact preparatory sexual behaviors (e.g., retiring to one's room alone and locking the door; scanning the crowd at a single's bar in search of a suitable partner) that result in overt sexual behaviors (e.g., matsturbation, coitus). The relationship between sexual arousal and preparatory sexual behavior has been investigated in a series of studies by Griffitt and his colleagues. In the first such investigation, Griffitt, May, and Veitch (1974) found that aroused (vs. unaroused) persons attended visually more to opposite (vs. same) sex others in an interpersonal setting. Subsequent research (Griffitt, 1979a, 1979b; Weidner, Istvan, & Griffitt, 1979) examined whether sexual arousal may result in another important form of preparatory sexual activity: increased sensitivity to, and biased evaluation of, the sexual characteristics of others. In this research, aroused and unaroused subjects were asked to rate the sexual attractiveness of opposite sex targets. Results showed that aroused subjects rated an unattractive target as particularly unattractive, but they rated an attractive target as significantly more sexually attractive than did nonaroused subjects. Hence, sexual arousal appears to elicit preparatory sexual behavior in terms of identifying the most—and least—appealing sexual possibilities in one's environment. Presumably, such preparatory behaviors may initiate a sequence of acts that ultimately result in overt sexual behavior.

Assuming that preparatory sexual behaviors have been successful in producing an overt sexual behavior, the outcome of this behavior may be experienced as hedonically positive, neutral, or negative, and this outcome is believed to feed back into the system to increase or diminish the future likelihood of the responses that led to the outcome. Although it might be imagined that the nature of sexual outcomes is obvious (sex acts that result in orgasm are positive, sex acts that do not are negative), this may not be the case when higher order variables in the system (affect, cognition) come into play. For example, for a person with strong religious beliefs, masturbation resulting in orgasm may be extremely guilt provoking and hedonically negative, whereas for a nonreligious person masturbation with orgasm may provoke little guilt and be experienced as a positive outcome.

Beyond this unconditioned stimulus—arousal—sexual behavior chain, it is clear that human beings *learn* to be aroused by a vast array of stimuli. According to the model, classical conditioning may occur such that virtually any stimulus, after repeated pairings with an unconditioned erotic stimulus, can become a conditioned erotic stimulus that is capable of eliciting components of sexual–

physiological arousal. Rachman (1966) has demonstrated experimentally in males the ease with which sexual arousal may be conditioned to previously nonarousing stimuli. In this case, sexual arousal was paired with depiction of black knee length boots that themselves soon became capable of eliciting sexual arousal, recorded on a penile plethysmograph. These arousal responses generalized from the original conditioned stimulus to other related stimuli (black high heels, black low heels, but not to brown sandals), and the responses extinguished and then spontaneously recovered in accord with the familiar classical conditioning pattern. In addition to this experimental demonstration, it might be noted that practitioners who engage in orgasmic reconditioning procedures (introducing new, adaptive stimuli in place of prior, maladaptive stimuli for arousal; Marquis, 1970) are utilizing the same classical conditioning process that is thought to underlie human learning of arousal responses to diverse and often idiosyncratic conditioned erotic stimuli.

AFFECTIVE PROCESSES

Affective Determinants of Sexual Behavior

The Sexual Behavior Sequence proposes that individuals learn affective responses to sexual cues. These affective responses are thought to be conditioned by social influences, and to serve as mediators of individual sexual behavior. In general, to the extent that a person has learned positive emotional responses to sex, he or she should show approach responses to sexuality, such as engaging in preparatory and actual sexual behavior and experiencing positive sexual outcomes. In contrast, an individual who has learned negative emotional responses to sex should show avoidance responses to sexuality, eschewing preparatory and actual sexual behavior and experiencing negative sexual outcomes. In discussing sex-related emotions, I consider the learning of affective responses to sexuality and the role these responses play in mediating sexual behavior.

Learning Affective–Evaluative Responses to Sexuality. Judging by the joyous sexual self-stimulation that many small children engage in, human beings are probably all born with *erotophilic* or positive emotional responses to sex, and it is only due to later learning that some degree of *erotophobia* or negative affective response to sex is acquired. How does an individual learn negative (erotophobic) or positive (erotophilic) emotional responses to sexuality? According to the Sexual Behavior Sequence, such learning involves the pairing of sexual cues (or what will come to be defined as sexual cues) with emotion-producing punishment or reward. After repeated pairings of punishment or reward with cues that society defines as sexual, an individual will learn a habitual and generalized disposition to respond to a class of sexual stimuli with negative-to-positive affect, or the trait of erotophobia–erotophilia. A simple, 21-item scale, the Sexual Opinion Survey, has been developed and used rather extensively to assess individual differences in erotophobia–erotophilia (cf., Fisher, Byrne, & White, 1983).

An erotophobic or erotophilic disposition is regarded as a self-reinforcing, self-maintaining system that is somewhat resistant to change. For example, a highly erotophobic person should either avoid sexual situations (leaving the original disposition intact), or react to enforced or accidental contact with sexuality with strong negative affect (which involves another pairing of sex with punishment, that is, an additional learning trial for erotophobia). A highly erotophilic person, in contrast, should seek out sexual situations and respond to them with positive emotions, and this will ensure continued reinforced learning trials for erotophilia (Fisher et al., 1984). A person in the middle range of erotophobia–erotophilia should ordinarily learn to become more erotophilic across time, assuming that intrinsically rewarding sexual experiences occur to condition increased emotional positivity to sex.

Beyond focus on trait erotophobia–erotophilia, it is important to note that specific situations can elicit strong negative or positive affective states that may overpower the trait disposition for the moment (e.g., an erotophobic person may experience an overwhelmingly positive orgasm; an erotophilic person may discover that his or her partner has herpes). To the extent that affective states that are inconsistent with trait affect may accumulate, the original trait should eventually change in the direction of the inconsistent sex-related affective states, and this principle is one basis for therapeutic interventions to alter maladaptive sexual affect.

In addition to emotional responses per se, individuals also make evaluative responses to sexual stimuli. Specifically, it has been suggested that an individual may make self-justificatory evaluations of a stimulus, to explain or justify how the stimulus makes one feel (Byrne, 1971; Byrne, Fisher, Lamberth, & Mitchell, 1974). Thus, a person who is disgusted and angered by a picture of fellatio may evaluate that stimulus negatively—as pornographic and obscene—in order to justify his or her emotional response to the stimulus. An individual who reacts to the same stimulus with positive affect—say, curiosity and delight—should make positive but still self-justificatory evaluations of the stimulus (e.g., evaluate it as educational and enlightening). In fact, experimental evidence—where affect is independently varied and evaluations are assessed—has verified this link between affective and evaluative responses (see, for example, Byrne, 1971; Griffitt & Veitch, 1971; Sachs & Byrne, 1970), albeit with affect and evaluations concerning nonsexual stimuli.

In the sexual domain, considerable correlational evidence is available linking sex-related affect and evaluations. For example, it would be expected that trait erotophobic and erotophilic persons would make consistently negative or positive evaluations of sexual stimuli, and precisely this effect has been observed. Erotophobic (vs. erotophilic) men and women evaluate more negatively a diversity of sexual topics including erotica, homosexuality, and contraception

(Fisher, Byrne, & White, 1983; Fisher, Byrne, White, & Kelley, 1984). Similarly, affective states should mediate evaluations of the sexual stimuli that elicited them, and correlational evidence confirms this assumption. For example, Fisher and Byrne (1978a) found that affective responses to an erotic movie were correlated with evaluations of this stimulus as pornographic or nonpornographic (see also Byrne, Fisher, Lamberth, & Mitchell, 1974, for related findings), and Fisher, Fisher and Byrne (1977) found that men's emotional responses to buying condoms were related to their evaluations of condoms, the pharmacist who sold them the condoms, and even tended to be related to the men's evaluations of the drugstore where the condoms were purchased! Because negative or positive affect seems generally to be accompanied by negative-to-positive evaluations, the Sexual Behavior Sequence treats these constructs as a single affective–evaluative response subsystem.

Learning Affective–Evaluative Responses to Sex: Parental Influences.   It is believed that parents are critically important in conditioning children's affective–evaluative responses to sex. Parents are the earliest and (at least for the first part of life) the most powerful influences on children's sexuality. Parents interpret the culture's values and define for children what is sexual, and systematically reward or punish such sexual behavior. Moreover, these early influences occur when children and young adolescents are exposed to relatively few other influences on their sexuality and when they are much less cognitively sophisticated than their parents. Because children and young adolescents lack resources (i.e., alternate sources of influence, cognitive abilities) to resist, parents' influence on how their children feel about sex may be especially profound. And, as mentioned earlier, affective–evaluative responses to sex may be self-reinforcing and resistant to change. Therefore, childhood patterns of emotional response to sex may have long term significance.

Based on these assumptions, a very simple model has been developed concerning the role of parents in conditioning children's affective–evaluative responses to sex or trait erotophobia–erotophilia (see Fig. 6.3). The model proposes that erotophobic (or erotophilic) parents will be systematically punishing (or rewarding) of their children's sexual expression. Systematic sex-related punishment or reward, in turn, should condition relatively erotophobic (or erotophilic) children. The model takes things full circle by assuming that erotophobic (or erotophilic) children will become erotophobic (or erotophilic) parents who will systematically punish (or reward) *their* children's sexuality, and so on (see Byrne, 1965, for a related developmental model in the area of authoritarianism). Keeping in mind that these assumptions are obviously oversimplified and that data concerning the model are somewhat fragmentary, let us consider research support for this conceptualization.

Parental Erotophobia–Erotophilia and Selective Reinforcement of Children's Sexuality.   A number of findings suggest that erotophobic and erotophilic

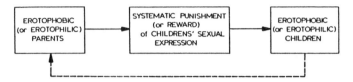

FIG. 6.3. A model of the development of affective–evaluative responses to sexuality (erotophobia–erotophilia).

parents are selectively punishing or accepting of their children's sexuality. In an interview study of parents of preschool children, for example, Yarber and Whitehill (1981) found a correlation of .49 ($p < .01$) between fathers' erotophobia–erotophilia and their scores on the "Are you an askable parent?" questionnaire (Gordon, 1977). Erotophobic fathers reported that they would be less likely than erotophilic fathers to give candid answers to their children's questions about sex. For instance, if asked by a 4-year-old where babies come from, 17.4% of the erotophobic fathers—but none of the erotophilic fathers—reported that they would dismiss the child's questions by saying, "When you get older I'll tell you about that." In a related study of parent–child communication about sex, Lemery (1983) found a correlation of .42 ($p < .05$) between mothers' erotophobia–erotophilia and their reports of how much information about sex they had given to their 6- to 9-year-old children, such that erotophobic mothers had provided their children with less sexual information. In still another study that may be regarded as laboratory analogue research on parental reinforcement of children's sexuality, Mendelsohn and Mosher (1979) examined the link between sex guilt (a construct that is related to erotophobia–erotophilia) and moral acceptance or condemnation of premarital coitus. In role-playing a sexual advice dialogue, high (vs. low) sex guilt women showed significantly greater moral condemnation of a role-played friend's first coitus. Thus, evidence suggests that erotophobic parents are relatively rejecting of their children's sexuality (they provide their children with less sexual information and fewer candid answers to sexual questions, and they may be morally condemning of their children's sexuality as well), whereas erotophilic parents seem to be more accepting of their children's sexuality along each of these dimensions.

A related set of findings also seem to shed light on the conditioning of erotophobia–erotophilia in the family context. Three independent studies have shown moderately strong correlations ($r = .52 - .59, p < .01$) of husbands' and wives' erotophobia–erotophilia (Byrne, Becker, & Przybyla, 1984; Fisher & Gray, 1983; Lemery, 1983; see also Byrne, Cherry, Lamberth, & Mitchell, 1973 for related findings). This degree of husband–wife similarity equals or exceeds spousal correlations on such dimensions as authoritarianism (husband–wife correlation of .30, Byrne, 1965), dogmatism (husband–wife correlation of .31, Byrne & Blaylock, 1963), and agreement on marital goals (husband–wife correlation of .44, Levinger & Breedlove, 1966), and it is probably particularly functional for spouses to agree on relative enjoyment or abhorrence of sex. In the present context, these findings show that there is a signifcant probability that children will grow up with two erotophobic parents who are relatively nonaccepting of sex, or two erotophilic parents who are relatively accepting of sex. Such consistent parental responses to children's sexuality are assumed to contribute to the conditioning of erotophobic or erotophilic children.

Selective Reinforcement of Sexuality and Development of Erotophobia–Erotophilia.   Evidence suggests that erotophobic and erotophilic parents may be consistently rejecting or accepting of their children's sexuality. The question remains, however, as to whether such selective reinforcement actually conditions erotophobia–erotophilia in children who are so reinforced. Findings from retrospective surveys—as problematic as such data may be— may be informative in this regard. For example, in a study reported by Fisher et al. (1984), 274 undergraduate men and women responded to a measure of erotophobia–erotophilia and to a questionnaire about their sexual socialization. In line with our assumptions about the conditioning of erotophobia–erotophilia, erotophobic subjects reported that their sexuality had been inhibited (during childhood or adolescence) by such things as fear of parent's reaction, guilt, "morals," "knowledge that it was wrong," fear of social disapproval, fear of harming themselves physically, and other concerns that were almost certainly communicated in part by parents. Although these findings are consistent with the view that parental reinforcement may condition children's erotophobia–erotophilia, however, other of the survey's results are not so clearly understood. Specifically, despite the catalogue of sex-related fears, guilt, and so on that erotophobic subjects reported, they also indicated that they were relatively happy with their sexual upbringing, that their parents had not been embarrassed to discuss sex with them, nor had made them feel guilty about sex, and so on. Thus, the parents of erotophobic respondents—who reportedly orchestrated a quite restrictive sexual socialization for their children—were also reported to be somewhat idealized sex educators. One explanation for this puzzling finding is to note that erotophobic subjects' rosy views sound much like authoritarian persons' tendency to idealize their parents (Adorno, Frenkel-Brunswick, Levinson, & Sanford, 1950), and research has in fact shown a positive correlation (in the .30 - .36 range) between erotophobia–erotophilia and authoritarianism–equalitarianism (Fisher et al., 1984).

A second line of evidence linking parental reinforcement of sexuality and children's erotophobia–erotophilia comes from cross-cultural research conducted by Bose, DasGupta, and Burman (1978). These researchers examined erotophobia–erotophilia among two groups of students in Calcutta, India that were known to have differed in their socialization to sex. One group consisted of traditional, orthodox Bengalee-Hindus who—according to reports of parents and guardians—were raised in homes where the parents were rigid, punishing, and conservative about their children's sexuality. The second group came from a more liberal, mixed Bengalee-Hindu community where parents and guardians reported that the children were raised in a much less religious and less sexually restrictive context. Results showed that the students who were raised by sexually restrictive parents were relatively erotophobic, whereas students who were raised by more sexually liberal parents were significantly more erotophilic. This finding, incidentally, provides an interesting example of how macro-level factors (here, culture) may enter the system to affect sex-related internal process (erotophobia–erotophilia).

In summary, then, support has been adduced for the developmental model that suggests that erotophobic and erotophilic parents differentially reinforce their children's sexuality, and that such differential reinforcement may condition children's erotophobia–erotophilia. Presumably, many of these erotophobic and erotophilic children grow up and marry similarly erotophobic or erotophilic partners (and spousal correlations on this characteristic are substantial) and begin the conditioning of erotophobia–erotophilia anew for the next generation. Obviously, these relationships need to be the subject of further research, but a beginning has been made in understanding the acquisition of affective–evaluative responses to sexuality that have been identified by the Sexual Behavior Sequence as important mediators of sexual behavior. Discussion now turns to some of the consequences of affective–evaluative responses to sexuality.

Affective–Evaluative Responses and Sexual Behavior

Affective–Evaluative Responses and Preparatory Sexual Behavior.   According-ing to the Sexual Behavior Sequence, affective–evaluative responses may influence whether an individual will engage in preparatory sexual behaviors that increase the likelihood of an overt sexual act. Negative or positive affective responses are expected to mediate avoidance or approach of preparatory sexual behavior, respectively, and a number of studies have confirmed this supposition. In a laboratory investigation, for example, Griffitt and Kaiser (1978) showed erotic stimuli to subjects and assessed their affective responses to these stimuli. Subjects who experienced highly positive affective reactions to the erotica "learned and performed instrumental acts that were effective in *increasing* or at least maintaining their opportunities to view the erotic stimuli. In contrast, those whose affective responses were negative or minimally positive engaged in instrumental behaviors that served to *reduce* their exposure to erotic stimuli" (p. 856). Thus, affective responses were found to mediate the sort of approach or avoidance of sexual stimuli that is the hallmark of preparatory sexual behavior.

Beyond these findings, it appears that affective–evaluative responses are also related to preparatory sexual behavior in an interpersonal context. Griffitt, May, and Veitch (1974) exposed subjects to sexually explicit slides, assessed their affective responses to these stimuli, and then examined subjects' gazing behavior and interpersonal distance in relation to same- and opposite-sex others. Results indicated that subjects who experienced more positive affective responses to the erotica gazed more at opposite- (vs. same-) sex others, whereas subjects who responded to the sexual stimuli with more negative affect maintained greater interpersonal distance from opposite- (vs. same-) sex others. Further data bearing on the relation of affective and preparatory sexual responses come from research by Fisher and his colleagues (Fisher et al., 1983; Fisher, Miller, Byrne, & White, 1980). These researchers examined the link between dispositional affec-tive–evaluative responses to sexuality (erotophobia–erotophilia) and a variety of preparatory sexual behaviors including planning to have sexual intercourse, reac-tions to talking openly about sex, and the acquisition of contraceptives prior to sexual activity. Results showed that erotophobic persons were less likely to plan on having sexual intercourse in the future, they had more negative reactions to talking openly about sex, and they failed to acquire contraceptives prior to sexual activity, compared to erotophilic persons. Thus, data from a variety of sources confirm the proposed link between negative-to-positive affective responses to sexuality and avoidance or approach of preparatory sexual acts.

Affective–Evaluative Responses and Overt Sexual Behavior.   The Sexual Behavior Sequence proposes that affective responses to sexual cues (via their effect on preparatory sexual behavior) will influence performance of overt sexual behaviors. Persons who are sexually stimulated and who find this experience to be hedonically negative should discontinue contact with the sexual stimulus and an overt sexual act will be unlikely to occur. In contrast, persons who experience sexual stimulation as a positive event should continue contact with the stimulus and this will more likely result in preparatory and overt sexual behaviors.

Research on affective–evaluative responses and overt sexual behavior has confirmed this reasoning. For example, Fisher et al. (1983) found that erot-ophobic men and women masturbated less frequently, and had fewer premarital partners, than did their erotophilic counterparts. (See also research by Mosher & Cross, 1971, for related findings.) In another study—this time of pregnant and postpartum women's sexuality—Fisher and Gray (1983) found that erotophobic (compared to erotophilic) women masturbated less frequently during pregnancy and they had fewer manual-genital or oral-genital contacts and less frequent intercourse during this time. During the postpartum period, erotophobic women reported less frequent masturbation and they also waited longer before resuming sexual intercourse than did erotophilic women. Thus, data confirm the link between affective responses to sex and overt sexual behavior.

Affective–Evaluative Responses and the Outcome of Sexual Behavior.   From the standpoint of the Sexual Behavior Sequence, affective responses may influ-ence the outcome of sexual behaviors. If a sexual act (performed for whatever reason) elicits negative affect, the outcome will likely be negative and future such behaviors will be less frequent. If an individual responds to a sexual act with positive affect, the outcome will ordinarily be positive and will feed back into the system so that in the future such behaviors occur more often.

Research in general is consistent with the notion that affective–evaluative responses influence outcomes. For example, Fisher et al. (1983) found that erotophobic (vs. erotophilic) men and women indicated that masturbation had (or would) make them feel more guilty. Similarly, in the study of sexual behavior during pregnancy and postpartum (Fisher & Gray, 1983) erotophobic women reported less satisfaction with their sexual relationships during pregnancy. And, with respect to another form of negative outcome—complaints of sexual dysfunction—Barlow (Personal communication, October 23, 1984) reported that males with erectile dysfunction scored almost a standard deviation more erotophobic than did a matched sample of functional males (see, however, Byrne, Przybyla, & Grasley, 1982, for findings that erotophobes report fewer sexual dysfunctions overall, possibly because of their lower base rate of sexual behavior). Taken together, these studies suggest that dispositional affective–evaluative responses to sex may help determine the negative or positive outcome of overt sexual behavior.

COGNITIVE PROCESSES

Cognitive Determinants of Sexual Behavior

According to the Sexual Behavior Sequence, human beings learn certain types of cognitive responses to erotic stimuli, and these responses are assumed to mediate sexual behavior. The cognitive responses in question include informational responses, expectative responses, and imaginative responses to sexual cues. Informational responses involve beliefs about the attributes of some sexual phenomenon (Fishbein & Ajzen, 1975) that may or may not objectively be correct (e.g., the belief that one can or cannot conceive at midcycle). Informational responses are often associated with expectative responses (probabilistic notions about the likely outcome of a sexual event; Fishbein & Ajzen, 1975), such as the expectancy that if one engaged in unprotected coitus at midcycle, one would have a 0% or a 50% chance of conceiving. Informational and expectative responses may exist in single pairs or small groups, or assemblies of beliefs and expectancies may merge to form sexually relevant belief systems or ideologies (E. R. Allgeier, 1983) such as sexual liberalism or conservatism. Finally, sex-related imaginative or fantasy responses involve internal, imagery based representations of sexual events. In our discussion of cognitive determinants of sexual behavior, I consider the acquisition and effects of sex-related informational, expectative, and fantasy responses.

Learning Sexual Information, Expectancy, and Fantasy. We are all born with the capacity to acquire, store, and retrieve sexual and other cognitions, and sexual information, expectancies, and fantasy may be input into the system in several ways. First, it appears that exposure to direct tuition is an effective means of acquiring sexual information (A. R. Allgeier, 1983). Lectures, self-instruction, and audiovisual presentations have all produced significant gains in sexual knowledge (Watts, 1977); knowledge gains as the result of such instruction have been demonstrated in both university (Zuckerman, Tushup, & Finner, 1976) and high school (West, 1976) settings, and a review of the sex education literature has concluded that sex education students "...regardless of population membership, showed gains in sexual knowledge..." (Kilmann, Wanlass, Sabalis, & Sullivan, 1981, p. 201). Such increases in sexual knowledge involve modifications in informational responses (e.g., "I now know that spermicides are not a very effective form of contraception") and related expectancies (e.g., "There is a 15%-25% chance I'll get pregnant if I use a spermicide") and in fantasy responses as well (e.g., imagining the possible ramifications of a pregnancy, imagining other contraceptive options). Of course, it is important to note that not all direct instruction about sexuality comes in formal sex education settings. In fact, a number of surveys suggest that same-sex peers (rather than formal sex education) are the modal source of adolescents' sexual information (Abelson, Cohen, Heaton, & Suder, 1971; Athanasiou, Shaver, & Tavris, 1970; Gebhard, 1977). It seems fair to assume that although the sexual knowledge of same-sex peers may be astoundingly inaccurate (Fisher, 1980; Kantner & Zelnik, 1973), it is likely as impactful on informational, expectative, and fantasy responses as are the more accurate data conveyed in formal sex education settings. As long as an individual is convinced of the accuracy of sexual information (independent of its actual accuracy) it will tend to guide behavior (cf. Byrne, 1977a).

Beyond these effects of direct instruction, the process of observational learning (Bandura, 1971) may also influence sex-related cognitive responses. In essence, merely observing a model engaging in sexual behavior (on film, in written material, or wherever) may affect our sexual beliefs, expectancies, and fantasies. For example, a reader of violent pornography may acquire the (abhorrent) belief that women "need" physical abuse to enjoy sex. Observing the model's outcome (the benefits or losses incurred as a result of the model's behavior) may also affect the individual's expectancies. For example, an observer of violent pornography may discover that violence is surprisingly effective in obtaining sex and is never punished, and may form expectancies ("If I tried that, it would work for me too") based on the modeled behavior. And, because observing behavior modeled in some context may provide a rich array of imagery (i.e., sights, sounds, etc.), observation of modeled sexual behavior may be a particularly important source of sexual fantasy.

Recent research on the effects of violent pornography (Malamuth & Donnerstein, 1982) confirms that observational learning may affect beliefs, expectancies, and fantasy in the sexual domain. For example, Malamuth and Check (1981a) exposed subjects to violent pornography or to neutral material. Several days later, male subjects who had seen the violent pornography had stronger beliefs favoring violence against women than did control males. Observation of violent pornography has also been found to influence expectancies. In this regard, Malamuth and Check (1981b) exposed males to audiotapes that depicted a rape that had "positive" consequence (the victim became sexually aroused) or negative consequences (the victim's abhorrence was highlighted). Males who were exposed to the rape/positive consequences depiction estimated that approximately 23% of women would actually enjoy being raped, whereas those who heard the rape/victim abhorrence stimulus expected that fewer women (11%) would enjoy such a fate. Finally, as proposed earlier, observation of models may affect fantasy responses. In a study on this topic, Malamuth (1981) found that 56% of the male subjects who were exposed to rape stimuli created fantasies about rape, compared to 0% of control subjects. Thus, evidence suggests that the process of observational learning may help account for the acquisition and modification of sex-related beliefs, expectancies, and fantasy.

In addition to the effects of instruction and observation of models, it seems clear that direct experience with sexual behavior may also influence cognitive responses to sexuality. Although most research has been concerned with sex-related cognitions as causes of behavior, it can be speculated that the relationship is a reciprocal one such that behavior also influences our beliefs, expectancies, and fantasy (see Bem, 1972, for a related rationale bearing on behavior as a cause of attitudes). Thus, the strong relationship between beliefs about the acceptability of premarital coitus, and actually engaging in this behavior (DeLamater & MacCorquodale, 1979; Reiss, 1967) can be interpreted to suggest that sexual behavior may influence beliefs about the acceptability of that behavior. Moreover, experience with specific sexual behaviors (e.g., woman-on-top coitus) is likely to be informative about attributes of these behaviors (e.g., "I can control the tempo of thrusting in this position") and hence may modify beliefs about the act in question. Experiencing sexual behaviors also seems to help shape relevant expectancies; for example, persons in stable (vs. unstable) relationships are more effective users of contraception (Fisher, Byrne, Edmunds, Miller, Kelley, & White, 1979; Foreit & Foreit, 1978), possibly because they have more accurate expectations regarding future coitus and the need for contraception. Finally, it seems clear that previously experienced sexual behaviors often form the basis for sexual fantasy. For example, Sue (1979) reported that about 43% of the males and 41% of the females in a college student sample had fantasized, during coitus, about a former lover, and there is also some evidence that prior experience with a sexual act is linked with heightened arousal responses to imagery that depicts that act (Griffitt, 1975). Thus, it is proposed that personal experience may be a teacher that, together with direct instruction and observational learning, shapes informational, expectative, and fantasy responses to sex.

Cognitive Responses and Sexual Behavior

In this section, we consider some empirical evidence that links cognitive responses and preparatory and actual sexual behavior. We consider information and expectancies as determinants of preparatory and actual sexual behavior, and then consider fantasy–behavior links separately.

Information, Expectancy, and Preparatory Sexual Behavior.   Preparatory sexual behaviors are instrumental in facilitating the occurrence of overt sexual acts. Some preparatory sexual behaviors are rather covert (e.g., "sizing up" a potential sexual partner) whereas others are more overt (e.g., visiting a singles bar). Unfortunately, however, such preparatory sexual acts tend to be under-researched, particularly in relation to belief and expectancy determinants of preparatory sexual behavior.

One notable exception to this rule involves contraceptive behavior, a preparatory act that may be undertaken to facilitate the occurrence of sexual relations. Beginning in the early 1970s, Fishbein (1972) and his colleagues (i.e., Fishbein & Jaccard, 1973; Jaccard & Davidson, 1972) proposed that the theory of reasoned action (Ajzen & Fishbein, 1980; Fishbein & Ajzen, 1975)—which is based in part on informational and expectancy variables—might be a useful predictor of contraceptive behavior. In particular, the theory of reasoned action states that the basic determinants of behavior involve a person's beliefs about the consequences of a behavior (and evaluations of these consequences) and a person's expectancies that reference persons approve of the behavior in question (and the person's motivation to comply with these reference persons; see Ajzen & Fishbein, 1980, Davidson & Jaccard, 1975, 1979, and Fisher, 1984, for a fuller discussion of the theory and its application to contraceptive behavior). Thus, research on the theory of reasoned action and contraceptive behavior is conceptually relevant to the proposed link between information, expectancies, and preparatory sexual behavior. As it turns out, this research is quite supportive of the proposed links. For example, in a study concerning oral contraception, Davidson and Jaccard (1975) found strong correlations (in the .69 - .74 range) between beliefs and evaluations, expectancies and motivation to comply, and women's intentions to use oral contraceptives. A 2-year follow-up study (Davidson & Jaccard, 1979) found that these intentions were strongly predictive of future contraceptive behavior. In a related study of condom use, Fisher (1984) found that condom-relevant beliefs and evaluations, and expectancies and motivation to comply, were predictive of intentions to use condoms during the following month, and these intentions were predictive of reported condom use per se. Table 6.1 presents beliefs and expectancies that differed for those who intended to use condoms and those who did not. Moreover, this research also established that belief- and expectancy-based factors had effects on contraceptive behavior that were independent of the effects of emotions (erotophobia–erot-

Table 6.1
Mean Beliefs and Expectancies[a]

	Those Who Intended to Use Condoms	Those Who Did Not Intend to Use Condoms
Beliefs about Consequences of Condom Use		
Using condoms prevents pregnancy	1.54	2.74**
Using condoms prevents venereal disease	1.89	2.98**
Expectancies That Referents Approve or Disapprove Condom Use		
Doctor thinks I should use condoms	3.11	4.06**
Girlfriend (sex partner) thinks I should use condoms	2.30	5.17**
Friends think I should use condoms	2.86	4.35**

** = $p < .01$ for simultaneous confidence interval.

[a]Beliefs and expectancy scores range from 1 (likely) to 7 (unlikely). These specific beliefs and evaluations were selected from a larger set of contrasts. The overall multivariate pattern of intender-nonintender differences was significant in the larger set of contrasts, and these specific intender-nonintender differences were selected because they emerged as significant on the univariate level as well (see Fisher, 1978, for the complete set of contrasts).

ophilia) on this behavior. A second line of research, incidentally, has linked women's expectancies that they cannot become pregnant and their failure to utilize contraceptives in premarital coitus (E. R. Allgeier, 1983; Kantner & Zelnik, 1973; Sorensen, 1973). Hence, research in the contraceptive domain is consistent with the Sexual Behavior Sequence's assumptions concerning beliefs and expectancies as determinants of preparatory sexual behavior.

Information, Expectancy, and Overt Sexual Behavior. According to the present model, an individual's sex-related cognitions will guide, in part, his or her overt sexual behavior. Perhaps the most comprehensive research evidence in this regard comes from investigations of beliefs about the personal acceptability of sexual behavior, and reported sexual behavior. For example, Reiss (1967) surveyed university students' beliefs about the acceptability of premarital sexual acts (kissing, petting, and coitus), and found that 64%–78% of respondents reported current sexual behavior that matched their beliefs about the acceptability of such behavior. Although it is not possible to infer that beliefs caused the sexual behavior in question, it is instructive to note that when behavior was more extreme than that accepted by a person's beliefs, guilt reactions were often reported, and the more extreme the belief-behavior discrepancy, the more likely, in general, a guilt reaction was. Moreover, findings for belief-behavior concordances have been found in cross-generational and cross-cultural studies as well

(Christensen & Gregg, 1970). These investigators reported a high degree of belief–behavior concordance for premarital coitus across cultures (two U.S. and one Danish group were sampled) and generations (testing was done in both 1958 and 1968). Belief-behavior agreement was greater in 1968 than in 1958, and behavior-evoked guilt was less common in 1968, perhaps owing to the greater belief-behavior consistency. The power of the association of belief and overt sexual behavior is such that Kaats and Davis (1972) have noted that standards of belief were "the most powerful predictor of the extent of sexual experience" (p. 565), and the link between beliefs about the acceptability of sexual behavior and reported behavior has been confirmed in research through the late 1970s and early 1980s (Cvetkovich & Grote, 1983; DeLamater & MacCorquodale, 1979). Although these data do not preclude the possibility of reciprocal behavior–belief links (which, as noted earlier, likely do exist), the correlational findings quite consistently support the proposed link between relevant beliefs and overt sexual behavior.[1]

A second body of research that bears on the link between informational responses and behavior has investigated the relation of sexual knowledge and reported sexual behavior. On one hand, research has linked relatively high levels of sexual knowledge with a degree of sexual restraint. A. R. Allgeier (1978), for example, found that students who scored highest on a test of sexual knowledge had a later average age of onset of masturbation and premarital coitus, and Kantner and Zelnik (1973) found that children whose parents had discussed sex with them tended to delay intercourse and to utilize contraception when they did have coitus. On the other hand, studies by Zuckerman, Tushup, and Finner (1976) and West (1976) found that exposure to sex education in college or high school resulted in increases in a variety of sexual behaviors, although the increases were not always large. Moreoever, A. R. Allgeier (1978) found that although sexually knowledgeable students delayed onset of coitus, once they began to have intercourse they did so with more partners than did less knowledgeable students. Although it is tempting to conclude, tongue in cheek, that sexual knowledge leads to both sexual restraint and promiscuity, perhaps the relevant overarching concept may be that sexual knowledge permits self-directed, personally constructive sexual behavior. Knowledgeable individuals delayed coitus (avoiding potential for misadventure at this stage) and enjoyed a

---

[1]In this section, beliefs about the acceptability of sexual behavior were linked with performance of the behavior in question. It is noted that beliefs about the acceptability of sexual behavior may be construed as evaluations, which are part of the affective–evaluative subsystem of the Sexual Behavior Sequence. Nonetheless, these beliefs conform to definitions of beliefs (notions about the attributes of a sexual phenomenon; cf. Fishbein & Ajzen, 1975) and seem subjectively to be more "cognitive than visceral" (cf. Clore & Byrne, 1974, p. 151). Moreover, it is difficult to imagine a belief statement that lacks potential evaluative significance. The distinction between affect and cognition in psychology is an old and unresolved one (see Titchener, 1897); for a recent discussion of this issue, see Clore and Byrne, 1974.

number of coital partners, in protected intercourse, at an age more appropriate for such behavior. This speculation regarding a knowledge-adaptive sexual behavior link is quite tentative, of course, and must become the subject of future research (see A. R. Allgeier, 1983, for a discussion of correlates of sexual knowledge, and Kilmann, Wanlass, Sabalis, & Sullivan, 1981, for a review of sex education outcome research).

A third body of research deals with the relation of expectative responses and sexual behavior. Mosher (1966, 1968), for example, has investigated the behavioral consequences of sex guilt—"a generalized expectancy for self-mediated punishment for violating or anticipating violating standards of proper sexual conduct" (Mosher & Cross, 1971, p. 27). Such expectancies for self-mediated punishment (i.e., high levels of sex guilt) have been linked with behaviors as diverse as inability to produce sexual associations to double entendre words (Gailbraith & Mosher, 1968), avoidance of erotica (Mosher, 1973; Schill & Chapin, 1972), difficulty in learning sex education material (Schwartz, 1973), endorsing sex myths (Mosher, 1979), and expressing moral condemnation of other's sexual activity (Mendelsohn & Mosher, 1979). In the context of the present discussion, it is particularly interesting to note that high sex guilt individuals, who expect self-mediated punishment for violating sexual standards, report lower levels of overall sexual experience (Mosher & Abramson, 1977; Mosher & Cross, 1971), fewer premarital coital partners, and less frequent sexual intercourse (Mosher, 1973) compared to persons who are low in sex guilt.

A final line of research may be interpreted as supporting a link between expectancies and sex-related behavior. As mentioned earlier, Malamuth and Donnerstein (1982) have reported on a series of studies in which rape depictions were presented to subjects and subjects' reactions were assessed. The rape stimuli differed such that some depicted a "positive" outcome (the victim experienced involuntary sexual arousal) and some depicted a rape with a negative outcome (the victim abhorred her plight). These stimuli appear to manipulate subjects' expectancies that antifemale aggression has "positive" or negative consequences (cf., Malamuth & Check, 1981a, 1981b). With respect to behavior as a function of these expectancies, under circumstances where males had been exposed to rape/positive outcome stimuli (and presumably altered their expectancies to favor antifemale aggression) increased antifemale aggression was observed (Donnerstein & Berkowitz, 1981). Thus, across a number of subareas of sexual behavior, research has confirmed the proposed link between information, expectancies, and sexual behavior.

Fantasy, Preparatory, and Overt Sexual Behavior.   According to the Sexual Behavior Sequence and related theory (Byrne, 1977a, 1977b, 1983) internally produced sexual imagery may involve the recreation of past events, or the recombination of familiar elements into novel scenarios that the individual may—or may not—wish to experience. Fantasy is thought to have motivating properties (it may involve events that the individual wishes to approach or avoid) and it may also provide information concerning how to execute or avoid specific sexual behaviors. Through its motivational and informational properties, sexual fantasy should influence preparatory and overt sexual behavior. Thus, internal sexual imagery may depict an aversive situation (say, a "Summer of '42" type fantasy involving embarrassment at the purchase of contraceptives), and the motivational and informational value of this imagery should prompt avoidance of the preparatory sexual behavior in question. By the same token, fantasy involving overt sexual behavior (e.g., a covert replay of last night's lovemaking) ought to involve motivational and informational elements that prompt execution (or avoidance) of related overt sexual acts.

Although the postulated links between sexual fantasy and behavior seem reasonably straightforward, there is in fact a paucity of research on such associations, although research on imagery—behavior links in other areas (e.g., achievement imagery; Horner, 1972; McClelland, 1965) is somewhat better developed and may be interpreted as consistent with speculation about imagery—behavior links in the sexual domain.

What, then, is known in the empirical literature with respect to sexual fantasy? First, it is apparent that external cues can trigger sexual fantasy, and that such fantasy is sexually arousing (Byrne & Lamberth, 1971; Heiman, 1977; Hoon, Wincze, & Hoon, 1977). Conversely, depriving individuals of the ability to fantasize about sexual stimuli results in decreased arousal (Geer & Fuhr, 1976). Second, it has been found that sexual fantasy is a very common activity for most men and women (Hariton & Singer, 1974; Hessellund, 1976; Hunt, 1974; Sue, 1979), that men and women fantasize about many of the same erotic themes (Sue, 1979; but see also Mednick, 1977; McCauley & Swann, 1978), and that to the extent it has been investigated, fantasizing about sex has not been linked with interpersonal or intrapsychic difficulties (Hariton & Singer, 1974, but see Offit, 1977).

With respect to links between fantasy and preparatory sexual behavior, research evidence is scarce. It has been reported (Gross & Bellew-Smtih, 1983) that males may avoid pre-sex discussion of contraception because men may imagine the negative consequences of such discussion in terms of botched seductions, and women may give in to sexual advances out of imagined (perhaps veridical) fears of losing the male's affection. In a field study of contraceptive practices of university women, sexually active females who were inconsistent users of contraception and who failed to use a campus birth control clinic reported imagined negative reactions on the part of clinic personnel that presumably inhibited their use of the clinic (Fisher et al., 1979). Beyond these fragmentary findings on fantasy–preparatory sexual behavior links, little data exist. Anecdotally, it is presumed that males and females have elaborate seduction fantasies that guide preparatory actions ranging from selecting just the right clothing to ascertaining when one's parents will return home, and clinicians have proposed that the lack of appropriate sexual fantasy may be linked with low sexual desire and lack of preparatory sexual behaviors. Such hypotheses must become the subject of future empirical research.

In relation to sexual fantasy–overt sexual behavior links, somewhat more is known. Specifically, sexual fantasy appears to help maintain and enhance patterns of overt sexual behavior. For example, sexually functional (vs. dysfunctional) men and women appear to have longer sexual fantasies, and more positive feelings about fantasy, than sexually dysfunctional individuals (Zimmer, Borchardt, & Fischele, 1983). Moreover, sex therapy programs (i.e., Heiman, LoPiccolo, & LoPiccolo, 1976) have found it useful to introduce fantasy as a prompt for sexual arousal and orgasm. In a related vein, it has been found that paraphilic fantasies act to maintain paraphilias even in the face of aversion therapy (Evans, 1968, 1970), whereas in other cases reconditioning orgasm to appropriate fantasy has been successful in redirecting paraphilic behavior (Marquis, 1970). Similarly, Storms (1981) has suggested that sexual arousal may be conditioned to hetero- or homosexual fantasies and may produce enduring heterosexual or homosexual dispositions, and has adduced some data that are consistent with this assumption in relation to homosexual males.

Sexual fantasy has been found to enhance as well as to maintain patterns of sexual behavior. It appears that many individuals quite purposefully engage in sexual fantasy to add arousal and interest to ongoing sexual activity (Hariton & Singer, 1974; Sue, 1979; Zimmer, Borchardt, & Fischele, 1983). For example, Sue (1979) found that many undergraduates utilize fantasy during coitus for the purpose of facilitating sexual arousal (38% of males, 46% of females), to increase their partner's attractiveness (30% of men, 22% of women), to imagine activities the individual does not do (18% of men, 13% of women), and to relieve boredom (3% of males, 5% of females). Thus, findings suggest that sexual fantasy may help motivate and accentuate overt sexual behavior.

Information, Expectancy, Fantasy, and the Outcome of Sexual Behavior.   According to the Sexual Behavior Sequence, overt sexual behaviors will ordinarily result in a drive-reducing orgasmic response. This response will generally be positively reinforcing and will increase the likelihood of the activities that led up to the orgasm. It is also assumed, however, that information, expectancies, and fantasy may influence how the outcome of a sexual behavior is perceived and consequently whether the outcome is positively or negatively reinforcing. For example, for individuals who have acquired unrealistically extravagent beliefs, expectancies, and fantasy about sexual performance—whether from perusing the *Penthouse Forum* or the lastest sexuality text (Szaz, 1980)—the occurrence of a single coital orgasm in a night of lovemaking may be perceived as disappointingly meagre and may constitute a negative outcome that eventually depresses sexual interest and functioning. For a person who has quite modest beliefs, expectancies, and fantasy, the same objective outcome—coital orgasm—may be perceived as the thrill of a lifetime, and this positive outcome should strengthen the responses that preceded it. Thus, cognitive factors are viewed as capable of altering completely the reinforcing properties of overt sexual behavior.

Research designed specifically to explore the relation of information, expectancies, fantasy, and the outcome of sexual behavior has yet to be undertaken, but we can examine related research literature for clues regarding this relationship. For example, dysfunctional sexual outcomes are often treated by altering relevant sexual beliefs, expectancies, and fantasy (cf. Chernick & Chernick, 1977; Heiman, LoPiccolo, & LoPiccolo, 1976; Kaplan, 1979; Masters & Johnson, 1970; Zilbergeld, 1978), and the success of such interventions supports the proposed link between cognitive factors and the positive or negative outcome of sexual behavior.

Beyond this clinical evidence, there is a line of survey research that is tantalizingly suggestive of important links between belief, expectancy, fantasy, and the outcome of sexual behavior. In particular, Hunt (1974) surveyed religious and nonreligious persons with respect to the outcomes they experienced from premarital coitus. Not surprisingly, the religious individuals reported that premarital coitus was less pleasurable, compared to nonreligious persons who found premarital coitus pleasurable. Presumably, religious beliefs, expectancies, and imagery are antithetical to the enjoyment of premarital sexual "sin."

A related study of religious and nonreligious women's outcomes in marital coitus (Tavris & Sadd, 1978) provides further support for a link between sex-related cognitions and outcomes. Specifically, for religious persons, marriage is *the* venue for sexual expression, whereas for nonreligious persons marital sex may be less of a sacrament. If this assumption is correct, then marital sex might have a more positive outcome for religious than for nonreligious women, and precisely such effects have been observed. Tavris and Sadd (1978) found that more religious (77%) than nonreligious (64%) women rate marital sex as good or very good, and religious women (72%) were also more likely than nonreligious women (62%) to report that they always or almost always were orgasmic. These findings are at least suggestive of links between sex-related cognitions and outcomes, although additional research that bears directly on this relationship is still needed.

INTERACTIONS AMONG CONSTRUCTS OF THE SEXUAL BEHAVIOR SEQUENCE

Thus far, we have considered separately affective and cognitive determinants of sexual behavior from the standpoint of the Sexual Behavior Sequence. At this juncture, however, it seems germane to consider how the components of the affective and cognitive subsystems may interact with one another, because the affective and cognitive determinants may separately or interactively influence preparatory and actual sexual behavior and outcomes.

Theoretically, any of the mediating components in the center of the Sexual Behavior Sequence (see Fig. 6.1) may interact and have a joint effect on behavior. For example, one's affective–evaluative responses to sexuality may affect one's beliefs, expectancies, or fantasy. Thus, an erotophobic person may have negative sex-related beliefs and expectancies and absent or abbreviated sexual fantasies. Conversely, an individual's beliefs, expectancies, or fantasies may influence his or her affective and evaluative responses. In addition, affective and cognitive factors may affect sexual arousal (and vice versa). Research that bears on several of these interactive relationships is discussed next.

Affective–Evaluative Responses and Information, Expectancy, and Fantasy

Research has focused on the relationship of erotophobia–erotophilia (a measure of the affective–evaluative subsystem) and sex-related information, expectancies, and fantasy. In one study, Fisher et al. (1983) examined the link between erotophobia–erotophilia and the acquisition of sexual knowledge. In a university human sexuality course, these investigators found that erotophobic students mid-term exam marks ($M = 71\%$) were significantly poorer than erotophilic students' midterm marks ($M = 79\%$) in the sexuality course. Controlling for students' general grade point average did not affect this difference; sex-related affect seemed specifically to inhibit the acquisition of sexual knowledge and this finding is consistent with the theorized interaction of affective and cognitive factors in the Sexual Behavior Sequence.

Additional research on erotophobia–erotophilia, beliefs, expectancies, and fantasy are pertinent to this discussion. With regard to affective–evaluative responses and beliefs and expectancies, Fisher et al. (1979) found that erotophobic (vs. erotophilic) females had negative beliefs regarding a contraception clinic (e.g., beliefs that clinic physicians disapprove of dispensing contraception to unmarried women), and negative expectancies regarding contraception (e.g., they expected that their parents, boyfriends, sisters, and significant others would be less likely to approve their use of birth control). A related study found that erotophobic (vs. erotophilic) persons expected a more negative audience response after the audience had ostensibly heard them deliver a sexual message. Finally, a study by Walker (1983) is pertinent to the link between affective–evaluative responses and sexual fantasy. Walker assessed the relation of erotophobia–erotophilia, tendency to fantasize during masturbation or coitus, and explicitness of students' written sexual fantasies. Findings showed that erotophobic (vs. erotophilic) women fantasized less frequently during masturbation and produced shorter and less explicit written sexual fantasies; for males, erotophobic subjects were found to generate less explicit written sexual fantasies.

Taken together, these findings are consistent with the Sexual Behavior Sequence's assumptions about links between affective–evaluative responses and sex-related beliefs, expectancies, and fantasy.

Information, Expectancy, and Affective–Evaluative Responses

Two studies are relevant to the possible effects of beliefs and expectancies on affective–evaluative responses. In the first study, Branscombe (1982) showed a single, silent erotic film, "Sunbrushed," to a number of female undergraduates. Branscombe manipulated subject's beliefs and expectancies by informing some of them that the couple in the film were in fact a brother and sister in an incestuous relationship, whereas other subjects were told that the couple in the film were merely very much in love and eager to please one another. Results showed that this manipulation of belief and expectancy resulted in significantly different affective responses to the stimulus film; those who viewed what they believed to be an incest film showed negative affective responses to the erotica, whereas those who viewed what they believed was a loving couple responded with positive affect. Related research (Jazwinski & Byrne, 1978) manipulated subjects' beliefs about whether a couple in an erotic film were using contraception. Subjects' evaluations of the couple were then assessed. Interestingly enough, female subjects who believed that the stimulus couple were using contraception rated the couple as caring most for one another, whereas male subjects who believed that the couple were using contraception evaluated the couple as caring least for one another. (Presumably, the beliefs about contraception × sex of subject interaction represents an interaction of the manipulated beliefs with existing gender-specific beliefs). These experimental studies, involving the manipulation of beliefs and expectancies and finding corresponding alterations in affective and evaluative responses, are consistent with the Sexual Behavior Sequence's assumptions about the relation of cognitive and affective determinants of behavior.

Information, Expectancy, and Sexual Arousal

In an effort to examine the impact of beliefs and expectancies on sexual arousal, Fisher and Byrne (1978b) conducted an experiment that manipulated married individual's information about the relationship of a couple that was depicted in silent erotic films. Some of the subjects were told that the couple in the films was married and very much in love, some were told that the couple was experiencing a casual sexual encounter, and some were told that the couple consisted of a female prostitute and her client. After viewing the erotica that was prefaced by one of these instructional sets, subjects' sexual arousal was assessed by self-report. Results showed that married men and women reported the highest levels of sexual arousal to the erotica when they believed that it involved a casual sexual encounter, compared to the situation in which subjects believed that the erotica involved a married couple or a prostitute and a client. Thus, experimental evidence has confirmed the assumption that beliefs and expectancies may affect sexual arousal responses. Incidentally, some evidence exists concerning the reversal of this relationship (i.e., the ability of sexual arousal to influence beliefs and expectancies). Griffitt (1973) found that the degree of men's arousal responses to erotica was associated with their expectancies for how aroused females would be by this erotica ($r = .67$, $p < .005$), although female's arousal levels were not significantly correlated with their expectancies for male's arousal responses ($r = .24$, n.s.).

Direct and Indirect Effects of Affective and Cognitive Factors

The research discussed earlier in this chapter documented a number of presumably direct links between arousal, affective, and cognitive responses and sexual behavior and outcomes. In addition, the findings just reviewed showed numerous interactions among the mediating processes identified in the Sexual Behavior Sequence. According to the theory, sexual behavior will be determined by both direct and indirect effects of arousal, affective, and cognitive processes.

Research evidence has pointed to the existence of both direct and indirect effects of affective and cognitive factors on sexual behavior. For example, in a study of male contraceptive behavior, Fisher (1984) found statistically independent effects of affective and cognitive factors on contraceptive behavior, whereas in related research on female contraceptive practices, Fisher et al. (1979) found that affect worked through cognitive factors indirectly to affect behavior. The many differences between these two studies (i.e., different genders, operationalizations, contraceptive behaviors, etc.) preclude a conceptualization of why the interrelation of affective and cognitive processes differed in the two studies. Theoretical and empirical work is needed to specify the circumstances under which the direct and indirect effects of affective and cognitive factors will occur, and such conceptualizations may contribute to the ongoing debate in social psychology regarding the relation of affect and cognition (see, for example, Clark & Fiske, 1982; Lazarus, 1984; Zajonc, 1980, 1984).

DEVELOPMENTAL ASPECTS OF THE SEXUAL BEHAVIOR SEQUENCE

Up to this point, we have considered the sexual functioning of the individual from the standpoint of the fully elaborated Sexual Behavior Sequence. It is clear, however, that different components of this system phase in at different developmental stages, and that specific components of the system may be more or less influential at various points during the life span (see Byrne & Kelley, 1981, for a full discussion of developmental aspects of a generalized version of the Sexual Behavior Sequence). For this reason, I consider briefly some possible developmental changes in the Sexual Behavior Sequence across five somewhat arbitrary periods in an individual's developmental history—infancy, childhood, adolescence, adulthood, and aging.

Infancy

During infancy (roughly from birth through the development of initial language) two processes—involving arousal and affective responses to sex—appear to be important developmental foci. It is known that infants are responsive to unconditioned erotic stimuli in the form of genital touch. Judging by observation of infantile masturbation, it appears that infants are aroused by such stimulation, they experience positive affective responses (e.g., joy) to this stimulation, and they appear to engage in preparatory sexual behavior (e.g., tugging off a diaper, rolling onto their pelvises, etc.) in order to self-stimulate (an overt sexual behavior). Given the persistence of such self-stimulatory activity in infants, it also appears that the outcome of this behavior is positively reinforcing during infancy.

In addition to responsiveness to unconditioned erotic stimuli, it also seems clear that infants have the ability to learn via classical conditioning processes. This has two implications at the level of infantile sexuality. First, by way of simple association of genital touch and other stimuli, previously neutral cues may become conditioned erotic stimuli that can elicit arousal and affective responses and preparatory and overt sexual behavior. Thus, an infant who holds a cloth bunny while engaging in genital self-stimulation may learn arousal, affective, and sexual behavior responses to this conditioned erotic cue.

The ability of the infant to learn by way of classical conditioning also paves the way for a second sort of sexual development at this time. Unconditioned or conditioned erotic cues can be and often are paired with emotion-producing punishments or rewards, and across repeated pairings erotic cues (or what will later be socially defined as such) may come to elicit the negative or positive emotions originally elicited by punishment or reward. Thus, an infant whose genitals are selectively ignored at bathtime or who is ignored or directly chastised during episodes of masturbation or nudity may develop negative affective responses to these activities that serve to attenuate arousal, preparatory, and overt sexual behavior and to make sexual outcomes negative during infancy. In this fashion, the infant who presumably is born with a disposition to enjoy sexual touch may develop the beginnings of erotophobia. It is also possible, of course, that infantile sexuality will be paired with positive emotional experiences (e.g., laughter, a hug) and such associations should reinforce a positive affective response disposition to sexuality in infancy.

Thus, it is proposed that an infant is arousable and is capable of learning conditioned arousal and affective responses to various sexual cues. Moreover, the ability of the infant to develop feelings about sexuality some time before he or she develops sophisticated cognitive abilities may be a critical developmental phenomenon. In particular, the fact that affective responses may precede development of complex cognitive abilities may mean that existing affective responses will direct cognitive activity with respect to sexuality when such cognitive activity phases in to the system (cf. Abramson, 1983; Byrne & Kelley, 1981). Thus, the infant who has conditioned negative emotional responses to sex may not seek out sexual information (e.g., learn sexually relevant language such as genital names) or may selectively seek out and process information that is consistent with his or her affective disposition (e.g., rapidly may learn rules concerning nudity, masturbation, etc.) in a fashion similar to that demonstrated for older individuals (cf. Fisher et al., 1983). The infant who has learned more positive emotional responses to sex may show similar affectively based cognitive biases but in the opposite direction. Hence, it is suspected that affect is developmentally primary in that it may direct the activity of later emerging cognitive abilities in the sexual domain.

Childhood

During childhood (from the emergence of language to puberty), sophisticated cognitive and linguistic abilities may have a profound influence on the development of sex-related evaluations, beliefs, expectancies, and fantasy. As a result of being able to seek out and assimilate sexual information it is believed that a child's evaluative responses to sexuality become increasingly well articulated. Evaluations of sexuality are motivated by the child's affective responses (which are themselves solidified by linguistically based learning) such that negative and positive affective responses begin to be justified or explained for the child by correspondingly negative or positive evaluations (cf. Byrne et al., 1974). Thus during childhood visceral affective responses may become linked with verbalizable evaluations (e.g., "that's dirty," or "that's not nice,") that "explain" to the child why sexuality makes him or her feel the way it does. By the same token, linguistically based learning during childhood initiates the development of informational responses to sexuality (e.g., sexual information, verbal labels) and related expectancies. Finally, information and expectative responses may join with emerging imagery ability to form the beginnings of sexual fantasy (e.g., imagined scenarios regarding where babies come from, what grown-ups do when they make love, etc.). As mentioned earlier, it is believed that early acquired affective responses to sexuality direct much of this emerging cognitive activity such that cognitive developments are consistent with original affective dispositions. Of course, cognitive learning also has the potential to alter affective responses, provided that the cognitive learning is sufficiently extensive. Together, affect and cognition are assumed by the Sexual Behavior Sequence to direct the preparatory and overt sexual behaviors of childhood (e.g., seeking privacy, self-stimulation, sexual play with age mates) and to determine the nature of the outcome of these behaviors.

Adolescence

It has been proposed that the development of affective components of the Sexual Behavior Sequence begins during infancy, and the development of the cognitive components begins during childhood. What then are the developmental tasks for the Sexual Behavior Sequence during adolescence, from the period of puberty to the formation of stable interpersonal relationships? Basically, it is proposed that the Sexual Behavior Sequence must grow to meet two challenges that occur during adolescence, challenges that involve physiological and social components. With respect to physiology, the adolescent becomes more sexually excitable, orgasmic response to genital stimulation becomes more likely, and reproductive ability begins. The adolescent must develop affective and cognitive responses that are specific to, and that help shape, these newly emergent processes. Feelings, evaluations, beliefs, and expectancies may be acquired in relation to masturbation, premarital sexual activity, and contraception, among other topics, and these responses will help shape the nature of adolescent sexual behavior and the quality of its outcome. It also seems likely that sexual fantasy comes into prominence during adolescence because cognitive and imagery abilities improve and because there is greater motivation to consider sexual possibilities in the safety of fantasy and to plan and rehearse in fantasy sexual behaviors that one is now motivated and able to execute.

Sexuality is not only a physiologically based entity during adolescence, but a socially based phenomenon as well, and the Sexual Behavior Sequence develops in relation to social stimuli during adolescence. An adolescent's feelings, evaluations, beliefs, expectancies, and fantasies will shape—and be shaped by—sociosexual interactions during adolescence. In this way, the Sexual Behavior Sequence first takes on a prominently interpersonal focus during adolescence, such that the individual must seek out and interact sexually with another human being who has in effect "another" Sexual Behavior Sequence of arousal, affective, and cognitive factors that must be dealt with. During adolescence, individuals likely seek out for interpersonal sexual behavior someone with similar arousal, affective, and cognitive responses to sex (cf. Byrne, 1971; Fisher & Byrne, 1981), but it is important to note that interpersonal sexual behavior likely also modifies the Sexual Behavior Sequences of the individuals involved as well. Thus, the Sexual Behavior Sequence develops during adolescence to meet the demands of an emerging physiologically based sexuality and the demands for interpersonal sexual behavior.

Adulthood

By adulthood (post-occupational entry), the basic processes of the Sexual Behavior Sequence are well developed but still need to respond to sexual events that are characteristic of adulthood, and still may be shaped by these events. For those who establish long-term heterosexual relationships, sex-related arousal, affective, and cognitive processes of two individuals must continue to interact successfully in the sexual-interpersonal field in the long term. This may involve growth toward convergence of the Sexual Behavior Sequences of two individuals, attempts to modify the sexually relevant responses of another, or both. For married individuals, learned affective and cognitive responses to sexuality may influence how one copes with such phenomenon as sexual behavior during pregnancy, sexual boredom, sexual fidelity, and sexuality in competition with other life demands (occupation, children, Monday night football, and the like). For those who remain unmarried or who choose alternative sexual lifestyles (e.g., homosexual individuals), learned affective and cognitive responses will also shape sexual adaptations and determine the quality of the outcomes of these adaptations. Moreover, the Sexual Behavior Sequence with which one confronts adult sexual demands will not only determine adult sexuality, but the nature of adult sexual demands should continue to modify an adult's arousal, affective, and cognitive sexual responses in a lifelong reciprocal relationship.

Aging

A final developmental stage of the Sexual Behavior Sequence occurs during the period of marked physiological decline in sexual capacity. It is known (Masters & Johnson, 1966) that although sexual capabilities persist throughout life, significant physiologically based changes do occur with aging. It is proposed that the nature of an individual's affective and cognitive responses will help determine how successfully he or she copes with such changes. For example, an individual with positive affective responses to sexuality, accurate information and expectancies about sexuality and aging, and fantasy that can serve as an adjunct to other sources of arousal may be much better able to continue with sexual enjoyment in later years than an individual who has negative emotional responses to sex, inaccurate beliefs about sexuality and aging, and limited fantasy ability. Once again, not only will the nature of one's Sexual Behavior Sequence determine sexual behavior and outcomes during aging, but the process of sexual aging itself ought to influence one's arousal, affective and cognitive responses in a continuing reciprocal relationship. Moreover, aging is a period of social as well as physiological changes, including leaving one's occupation for retirement, death of a spouse, and so on, and individuals' affective and cognitive responses to sexuality will both shape responses to these challenges and be shaped by them.

In summary, then, it has been proposed that various components of the Sexual Behavior Sequence phase in at different stages of development; affective processes are important in infancy, beliefs and expectancies during childhood, fantasy during adolescence. Beginning with adolescence, the Sexual Behavior Sequence becomes prominently an interpersonal process. In adulthood and aging, it is speculated that a mature Sexual Behavior Sequence both influences our responses to characteristic sexual challenges at these times and itself continues to be changed by these challenges. Hence, the Sexual Behavior Sequence is viewed as influencing sexual events and being influenced by them throughout the life of the individual.

MACRO-LEVEL VARIABLES, THE SEXUAL BEHAVIOR SEQUENCE, AND INDIVIDUAL SEXUAL BEHAVIOR

At the beginning of this chapter, it was proposed that the Sexual Behavior Sequence is one part of a macro- to micro-level chain of causation of individual sexual behavior. In terms of this model, evolutionary and cultural forces are viewed as distal variables that affect arousal, affective, and cognitive processes that I have argued are the immediate causes of sexual behavior. In this concluding section, I speculate about how macro-level evolutionary and cultural forces may affect the internal processes of the Sexual Behavior Sequence and hence shape individual sexual behavior.

Evolution, Culture, and Sexual Arousal

Evolution and Arousal.   Perhaps the most important effect of evolution on sexuality involves postulated male–female differences in arousal responses to erotic cues. In particular, it has long been taken for granted that natural selection has favored a relatively asexual female (who is inherently less aroused by unconditioned or conditioned erotic stimuli) and a relatively hypersexual male (who is inherently easily aroused by unconditioned or conditioned erotic stimuli; see Gallup, this volume for related discussion). Consider, for example, scientific and popular opinion, from 1903 to the present, on the issue of gender differences in sexual arousability:

> Man has beyond doubt the stronger sexual appetite of the two. From the period of pubescence he is instinctively drawn towards woman. His love is sensual, and his choice is strongly prejudiced in favor of physical attractiveness....Woman, however, if physically normal and properly educated, has but little sensual desire. If it were otherwise, marriage and family life would be empty words. (Krafft-Ebing, 1903/1939, p. 14)

> Professor Higgins was right—men wish that women's sexuality was like their's, which it isn't. Male sexual response is far brisker and more automatic: it is triggered easily by things, like putting a quarter in a vending machine. (Comfort, 1972, p. 71)

> A man is willing to expend a little time and a few sperm in any mating opportunity, and often courts indiscriminately. A female must be more selective, for a mismating can cost her much wasted nurture and reproductive potential. (Daly & Wilson, 1978, p. 79)

Evidence that is often marshalled in support of the conception of the inherently unarousable female/hyperarousable male includes findings that women less often engage in certain sexual behaviors (i.e., masturbation, extramarital coitus, etc.) than do men (Hunt, 1974; Kinsey, Pomeroy, & Martin, 1948; Kinsey, Pomeroy, Martin, & Gebhard, 1953), they do not seek out or purchase erotica as often as men do (Kinsey et al., 1953; Nawy, 1973; Wilson & Abelson, 1973), and women rarely develop fetishes or deviant patterns of sexual arousal.

Scientists are so confident about inherent gender differences in arousal responses that a number of conceptualizations have been developed to account for this presumed eternal truth. Thus, theories suggest that women are less sexually arousable than men because women's testosterone levels are only one-sixth those of men (Hyde, 1982; Salhanick & Margolis, 1968); other theories focus on women's obligation to nurture offspring as an explanation for their relative sexual disinterest (Daly & Wilson, 1978; Krafft-Ebing, 1903/1939); and still others point out that because women's genital anatomy is hidden from its owner, women are less likely to masturbate or to be aware of their physiological sexual responses and hence are less arousable than men are (Hyde, 1982).

I am not entirely prepared to accept the premise that evolution enters the system to favor inherently unarousable females and hyperarousable males, because the data do not seem entirely consistent with this position. First, I think that there is a good deal of evidence to show that women's sexuality may not be as exclusively based on reproductive imperatives as was once thought, and in fact large portions of female sexual arousal response may be more or less "gratuitous" and purely directed to the pursuit of hedonic pleasure. For example, women are continuously sexually responsive throughout the menstrual cycle (including possible peaks of sexual interest both at ovulation and premenstrually; Kinsey et al., 1953; Udry & Morris, 1968), and they are sexually active while lactating and postmenopausally. The persistence of sexual response through periods of diminished or absent fertility suggests the presence of sexual interest quite apart from that necessary to support reproduction per se. Moreoever, on a physiological and anatomical level, women's capacity for multiple orgasms (vs. men's refractory period pattern; Masters & Johnson, 1966), and the fact that the clitoris has no direct reproductive function (unlike the penis which is a conduit for sperm) seem to suggest the presence of sexual interest in women that is at least in part not limited to that needed for reporductive success.

A second set of observations suggests that there have been dramatic changes in women's sexual behavior during the past quarter century—changes that are highly inconsistent with the notion of naturally selected, inherent gender differences in arousability. For example, although it is true that the absolute incidence and frequency of masturbation is greater in men than in women (Kinsey et al., 1948, 1953) it is also true that in the last 20 or so years women have shown a sharp increase in masturbatory behavior such that "Today, both young single females and adult married females have moved closer to the male pattern of behavior" (Hunt, 1974, p. 56). Similarly, although it is generally found that only half as many women as men engage in extramarital coitus (Kinsey et al., 1948, 1953; Hunt, 1974), Tavris and Sadd (1978) discovered that among women whose social circumstances are similar to men's—those who are employed outside the home—extramarital coitus rates were virtually identical for women and men.

The existence of such variations in women's sexual behavior suggests that social factors, in addition to any inherent biological differences, are a major influence on sexual arousability and consequent behavior, and perhaps it has always been so. For example, it is easy to believe that women *learned* sexual reserve when contraception was nonexistent, pregnancy was physically dangerous, and nurturing offspring was an exclusively female occupation. Thus, the evolutionary notion of female sexuality as limited by reproductive contingencies may have been correct but may have worked not by the incredibly tedious process of natural selection but by the faster, vastly less costly, and characteristically human ability to adapt rapidly by learning. This assumption would of course explain the rapid changes in female sexual interest that have recently been observed: Increases in female sexual behavior may represent a similar learned adaptation to present circumstances that include effective contraception, medical advances in the management of pregnancy, formula for feeding babies, the existence of day care, professional opportunities for women and so on. Thus, I argue that learned arousal, affective, and cognitive responses to existing contingencies may contribute profoundly to gender differences in arousability. Consequently, evolution is seen as working through the Sexual Behavior Sequence not merely in terms of naturally selected response tendencies, but importantly, in terms of evolving social conditions that mediate evolving learned responses to sexuality along the dimensions identified in the Sexual Behavior Sequence.

Culture and Arousal.   It is proposed that cultural forces may enter the Sexual Behavior Sequence by blunting or facilitating unconditioned or conditioned sexual arousal. Our own culture, both historically and at present, is an excellent example of the cultural blunting of unlearned and learned sexual arousal. For example, Victorian era experts such as Sylvester Graham taught that loss of an

ounce of semen is equivalent to loss of 40 ounces of blood and therefore intercourse ought to be limited to 12 times a year so as not to debilitate a man or
shorten his life span; other experts strongly criticized female's practice of riding
bicycles for fear of calamitous accidental sexual arousal (Haller & Haller, 1977).
More recently, Dr. Spock's (1978) *Baby and Child Care* couselled, "I myself
don't recommend retraction [of the foreskin] and washing because it seems like
too much stimulation of the penis by the parent" (p. 191). With 28 million
copies sold, *Baby and Child Care* doubtlessly qualifies as a major cultural
influence—in this case a cultural influence that proscribes sexual arousal in
young children and which, together with many other such influences, may help
shape culture-specific patterns of sexual arousal and behavior.

Our culture's blunting of sexual arousal does not, incidentally, appear to be
particularly gender equalitarian, but rather seems to favor attenuation of female
(vs. male) arousal. There has been a traditional double standard that punishes
female's sexual experience but encourages males to explore sexually (Kinsey et
al., 1948, 1953; Pietropinto & Simenauer, 1977), and we tend to teach about the
normality of a vigorous male and weak female sexual response (Comfort, 1972).
Still another example of our culture's selective blunting of female arousal is
provided by Rindskopf (1981), who surveyed sex education books for children.
It was found that although 87% of children's sexuality texts described the penis,
only 16% described the clitoris, thus denying young female readers information
about the location or labeling of a major source of female sexual arousal.

Our own culture, of course, is not unique in patterning the attenuation of
sexual arousal (see Gregersen, this volume for a related discussion of human
sexuality in cross-cultural perspective). Anthropological evidence (Messenger,
1971) concerning the Irish island of Innis Beag is a case in point. In this
community, most girls are not prepared for the onset of menstruation and find it a
traumatic experience. Sexual relations are regarded as a duty for the wife, evidence suggests that female orgasm is unknown, and men regard coitus as de-
bilitating. Nudity is so repellent to Innis Beag men that they do not learn how to
swim (it would require the use of scanty clothing) and consequently some of the
men—who make their living fishing at sea—drown when their boats capsize.

In addition to blunting sexual arousal, culture may also act to facilitate its
expression. For example, although they are operating with a biological substrate
similar to our own, the Yolngu tribe of Australia's Northern Territory have
learned vastly differnt patterns of sexual expression than is true in our culture
(Money, Cawte, Bianchi, & Nurcombe, 1970). Yolngu children are permitted to
masturbate and to play at coital behavior, and at least until recently the kunapipi
ceremony permitted a free exchange of sexual partners. In Mangaia, in the South
Pacific, boys are given expert instruction in how to engage in foreplay and
coitus, and girls are permitted to seek out a number of sexual partners during
adolescence (Marshall, 1971). And, in our own culture, encouragement for
sexual expression—although not at Mangaian levels—seems to be increasing

(Fisher & Byrne, 1981; Hunt, 1974). Based on these culture-specific patterns, then, it appears that cultural forces may alter the learning and expression of sexual arousal responses.

Evolution, Culture, and Affective–Evaluative Responses. Although evolution and culture may affect sexual arousal, whether or not arousal eventuates sexual behavior, depends in part on an individual's affective–evaluative responses. An evolutionary perspective might lead us to expect differences in affective–evaluative responses that are suited to some conception of reproductive necessity, resulting, for instance, in emotionally antisex females and emotionally prosex males. I propose, however, that, in the main, evolving cultural circumstances (rather than natural selection per se) promote rapidly learned affective–evaluative adaptations to these changing circumstances. Hence, discussion focuses on links between cultural circumstances and affective–evaluative responses to sexuality.

Anthropological evidence surveyed thus far suggests that there are profound differences in affective–evaluative responses to sex, and in consequent behaviors, across cultures. Thus residents of Innis Beag appear to be highly erotophobic and to have extremely low levels of sexual behavior, Yolngus and Mangaians seem to be highly erotophilic and to have extremely high levels of sexual behavior, and North Americans appear to be somewhere in between with respect to sexual affect, evaluations, and behavior. Within our own culture, moreover, it is possible to identify subcultures that vary on the affective–evaluative dimension. Middle (vs. lower class) individuals, religiously nondevout (vs. devout) persons, and members of the present (vs. past) generations appear to have more erotophilic affective–evaluative dispositions and more permissive sexual behavior (cf. Fisher & Byrne, 1981; Gilbert & Gamache, 1984; Hunt, 1974; Kinsey et al., 1948, 1953; see also McKinney, this volume for related discussion). In terms of the Sexual Behavior Sequence, then, cultural effects may enter the system by influencing affective–evaluative responses and these responses may interact with other factors in the system to affect sexual behavior.

Evolution, Culture, and Cognitive Responses. At the level of information, expectancy, and fantasy, an evolutionary perspective might presuppose differences in cognitions that are based on reproductive necessity. Thus, for example, females would be expected to have more reserved and selective sexual beliefs, expectancies, and fantasy than males, although this is by no means always the case. There is evidence of recent shifts to male–female similarity in sex related beliefs (see Bauman & Wilson, 1976; Christensen & Gregg, 1970; King, Balswick, & Robinson, 1977) and sexual fantasy (see Sue, 1979) that suggests that sex-related cognitions may be influenced strongly by evolving cultural forces as well as by the residue of natural selection. For this reason, it seems useful to again consider links between macro-level cultural forces and individual's informational, expectative, and fantasy responses to sex. For example, Reiss (1967) has found that beliefs about the acceptability of premarital sexual behavior vary systematically as a function of cultural factors such as religiosity, social class, and generation of birth. Christensen and Gregg (1970) report differential beliefs about the acceptability of premarital sex as a function of membership in a restrictive Mormon subculture in the U.S., a moderately restrictive midwestern subculture in the U.S., or a nonrestrictive Danish subculture. In addition, cultures appear to differ in the extent to which they provide formal sex education and in the degree of sexual knowledge of children in these cultures (see A. R. Allgeier, 1983; Koch, 1978; Lemery, 1983). Some evidence exists to suggest that sexual fantasy behavior may differ across social classes, with upper (vs. lower) socioeconomic status males engaging in more fantasy behavior (Kinsey et al., 1948). Thus, research suggests that cultural influences may work through the Sexual Behavior Sequence by affecting informational, expectative, and fantasy responses and presumably by way of these effects, culture may influence overt sexual behavior.

Cultural Factors, Sexual Behavior, and the Outcome of Sexual Behavior. There is some evidence to suggest that cultural factors affect not only arousal, affective, and cognitive processes as discussed earlier, but also influence overt sexual behavior and the outcome of this behavior as well. For example, in reviewing research on cultural background and sexuality, Fisher and Byrne (1981) found systematic differences in sexual behavior as a function of an individual's socioeconomic status, religiosity, and generation of birth. These differences, as a function of cultural status, involved behaviors as diverse as petting and coitus, marital intercourse, and extramarital involvement. Moreover, differences in the outcome of sexual behavior were also found as a function of cultural background differences; higher socioeconomic status persons reported more satisfaction with marital sex; religious persons reported less satisfaction with premarital but more satisfaction with marital sex; and recent generation of birth individuals reported less guilt about premarital coitus. (For additional findings relating cultural factors such as religiosity, religion, and socioeconomic status with sexual behavior of female teenagers, see Zelnik, Kantner, & Ford, 1981).

Taken together, these data suggest that macro-level factors may influence the arousal, affective, and cognitive responses to sexuality specified by the Sexual Behavior Sequence. By way of such influences, macro-level factors may also affect overt sexual behavior and the outcome of this behavior, and research is needed to identify direct (i.e., macro-level effects on behavior) and indirect (i.e., macro-level factors work through the system to affect behavior) influences in this regard. Such research should help clarify the role of the Sexual Behavior Sequence as a bridge between macro-level influences and individual sexual behavior.

SUMMARY

In this chapter, I have discussed a psychological appraoch to human sexuality, the Sexual Behavior Sequence. This model proposes that learned and unlearned sexual cues elicit arousal, affective, and cognitive responses that determine the nature of sexual behavior and the quality of the outcome of such behavior. A developmental schematization of this model was introduced to suggest the prominence of affective processes during infancy, informational processes during childhood, and fantasy processes during adolescence; during adulthood and aging the Sexual Behavior Sequence is further modified to meet sexual challenges that are characteristic of these stages. Although interpersonal effects occur at each developmental stage, the demands for interpersonal sexuality are most prominent beginning with adolescence. A reciprocal relationship was proposed such that the Sexual Behavior Sequence both affects sexual behavior and is affected by it throughout the life span. Finally, it was proposed that the Sexual Behavior Sequence may provide a conceptual bridge between macro-level factors and individual sexual behavior such that macro-level forces work through the components of the Sexual Behavior Sequence to affect individual sexual expression.

ACKNOWLEDGMENTS

Work on this manuscript took place, in part, while the author was on sabbatical leave at the Institute for Sex Therapy, Education, and Research, Sheba Medical Center, Tel Hashomer, Israel, and the Faculty of Medicine, Technion—Israel Institute of Technology, Haifa, Israel. The author wishes to thank Dr. Ami Sha'ked (Sheba Medical Center) and Dr. Zwi Hoch (Technion Faculty of Medicine) for their assistance. The author would also like to acknowledge a sabbatical leave fellowship (451-84-2152) from the Social Sciences and Humanities Research Council of Canada that partially supported this work.

REFERENCES

Abelson, H., Cohen, R., Heaton, E., & Suder, C. (1971). *National survey of public attitudes toward and experience with erotic materials.* (Technical Reports of the Commission on Obscenity and Pornography, Vol.6, pp. 1–138). Washington, DC: U.S. Government Printing Office.

Abramson, P. R. (1983). Implications of the sexual system. In D. Byrne & W. A. Fisher, (Eds.), *Adolescents, sex, and contraception* (pp. 49–61). Hillsdale, NJ: Lawrence Erlbaum Associates.

Adorno, T. W., Frenkel-Brunswick, E., Levinson, D. J., & Sanford, R. N. (1950). *The authoritarian personality.* New York: Harper. .

Ajzen, I., & Fishbein, M. (1980). *Understanding attitudes and predicting social behavior.* Englewood Cliffs, NJ: Prentice-Hall.

Allgeier, A. R. (1978, May). *Attitudinal and behavioral correlates of sexual knowledge.* Paper presented at the meeting of the Midwestern Psychological Association, Chicago.

Allgeier, A. R. (1983). Informational barriers to contraception. In D. Byrne & W. A. Fisher (Eds.), *Adolescents, sex, and contraception* (pp. 143–169), Hillsdale, NJ: Lawrence Erlbaum Associates.

Allgeier, E. R. (1983). Ideological barriers to contraception. In D. Byrne & W. A. Fisher (Eds.), *Adolescents, sex, and contraception,* (pp. 171–205). Hillsdale, NJ: Lawrence Erlbaum Associates.

Athanasiou, R. Shaver, P., & Tavris, C. (1970). Sex. *Psychology Today, 4,* 37–51.

Bandura, A. (1971). *Social learning theory.* Morristown, NJ: General Learning Press.

Bauman, K. E., & Wilson, R. R. (1976). Premarital sexual attitudes of unmarried university students: 1968 vs. 1972. *Archives of Sexual Behavior, 5,* 29–37.

Bem, D. J. (1972). Self-perception theory. In L. Berkowitz (Ed.), *Advances in experimental social psychology* (Vol.6 pp.1–62). New York: Academic Press.

Bose, S., DasGupta, S. K., & Burman, A. K. (1978). *Socialization antecedents of erotophobia—erotophilia in traditional and liberal Indian students.* Paper presented at the Fourth World Congress of Sexology, Rome, Italy.

Branscombe, N. R. (1982). *Effects of hedonic valence and physiological arousal on a second emotional state.* Unpublished master's thesis, University of Western Ontario, London, Ontario, Canada.

Byrne, D., (1965). Parental antecedents of authoritarianism. *Journal of Personality and Social Psychology, 1,* 369–373.

Byrne, D. (1971). *The attraction paradigm.* New York: Academic Press.

Byrne, D. (1977a). Social psychology and the study of sexual behavior. *Personality and Social Psychology Bulletin, 3,* 3–30.

Byrne, D. (1977b). The imagery of sex. In J. Money & H. Musaph (Eds.), *Handbook of sexology* (pp. 327–350). Amsterdam: Excerpta Medica.

Byrne, D. (1983). Sex without contraception. In D. Byrne & W. A. Fisher (Eds.), *Adolescents, sex, and contraception,* (pp. 3–31). Hillsdale, NJ: Lawrence Erlbaum Associates.

Byrne, D., Becker, M. A. & Przybyla, D. P. J. (1984). *Erotophobia–erotophilia as a predictor of sexual functioning among married and unmarried individuals.* Manuscript submitted for publication.

Byrne, D., & Blaylock, B. (1963). Similarity and assumed similarity of attitudes between husbands and wives. *Journal of Abnormal and Social Psychology, 67,* 636–640.

Byrne, D., Cherry, F., Lamberth, J., & Mitchell, H. E. (1973). Husband–wife similarity in response to erotic stimuli. *Journal of Personality, 41,* 385–394.

Byrne, D., Fisher, J. D., Lamberth, J., & Mitchell, H. E. (1974). Evaluations of erotica: Facts or feelings? *Journal of Personality and Social Psychology, 29,* 111–116.

Byrne, D., & Kelley, K. (1981). *An introduction to personality* (3rd ed.). Englewood Cliffs, NJ: Prentice-Hall.

Byrne, D., & Lamberth, J. (1971). *The effect of erotic stimuli on sexual arousal, evaluative responses, and subsequent behavior.* (Technical Reports of the Commission on Obscenity and Pornography, Vol. 8, pp. 41–67). Washington DC: U.S. Government Printing Office.

Byrne, D., Przybyla, D. P. J., & Grasley, D. (1982, April). *Sexual dysfunctions among undergraduates as correlates of sexual attitudes.* Paper presented at the meeting of the Eastern Psychological Association, Baltimore.

Chernick, A. B., & Chernick, B. A. (1977). The role of ignorance in sexual dysfunction. In B. Schlesinger (Ed.), *Sexual behaviour in Canada: Patterns and problems,* (pp. 76–83). Toronto: University of Toronto Press.

Christensen, H. T., & Gregg, C. A. (1970). Changing sex norms in America and Scandinavia. *Journal of Marriage and the Family, 32,* 616–627.

Clark, M. S., & Fiske, S. T. (Eds.). (1982). *Affect and cognition. The seventeenth annual Carnegie symposium on cognition.* Hillsdale, NJ: Lawrence Erlbaum Associates.

Clore, G. L., & Byrne, D. (1974). A reinforcement-affect model of attraction. In T. L. Huston (Ed.), *Foundations of interpersonal attraction* (pp. 143–170). New York: Academic Press.

Comfort, A. (1971). Likelihood of human pheromones. *Nature, 230,* 432–433.

Comfort, A. (Ed.) (1972). *The joy of sex. A gourmet guide to love making.* New York: Simon & Schuster.

Cvetkovich, G., & Grote, B. (1983). Adolescent development and teenage fertility. In D. Byrne & W. A. Fisher (Eds.), *Adolescents, sex, and contraception* (pp.109–123). Hillsdale, NJ: Lawrence Erlbaum Associates.

Daly, M., & Wilson, M. (1978). *Sex, evolution, and behavior. Adaptations for reproduction.* North Scituate, MA: Duxbury Press.

Davidson, A. R., & Jaccard, J. J. (1975). Population psychology: A new look at an old problem. *Journal of Personality and Social Psychology, 31,* 1073–1082.

Davidson, A. R., & Jaccard, J. J. (1979). Variables that moderate the attitude-behavior relation: Results of a longitudinal survey. *Journal of Personality and Social Psychology, 37,* 1364–1376.

Davidson, J. M. (1980). The psychobiology of sexual experience. In J. M. Davidson & R. J. Davidson (Eds.), *Psychobiology of consciousness* (pp. 271–332). New York: Plenum.

DeLamater, J., & MacCorquodale, P. (1979). *Premarital sexuality. Attitudes, relationships, behavior.* Madison, WI: University of Wisconsin Press.

Donnerstein, E., & Berkowitz, L. (1981). Victim reactions in aggressive erotic films as a factor in violence against women. *Journal of Personality and Social Psychology, 41,* 710–724.

Doty, R. L., Ford, M., Preti, G., & Huggins, G. R. (1975). Changes in the intensity and pleasantness of human vaginal ordors during the menstrual cycle. *Science. 190,* 1316–1318.

Evans, D. R. (1968). Masturbatory fantasy and sexual deviation. *Behavior Research and Therapy, 6* 17–19.

Evans, D. R. (1970) Subjective variables and treatment effects in aversion therapy. *Behavior Research and Therapy, 8,* 147–152.

Fishbein, M. (1972). Toward an understanding of family planning behaviors. *Journal of Applied Social Psychology, 2,* 214–227.

Fishbein, M., & Ajzen, I. (1975). *Belief, attitude, intention, and behavior: An introduction to theory and research.* Reading, MA: Addison-Wesley.

Fishbein, M., & Jaccard, J. J. (1973). Theoretical and methodological considerations in the prediction of family planning intentions and behavior. *Representative Research in Social Psychology, 4,* 37–51.

Fisher, W. A. (1978). *Affective, attitudinal, and normative determinants of contraceptive behavior among university men.* Unpublished doctoral dissertation, Purdue University, West Lafayette, Indiana.

Fisher, W. A. (1980). *Survey of sexual knowledge among Canadian undergraduates.* Unpublished manuscript, University of Western Ontario, London, Ontario, Canada.

Fisher, W. A. (1984). Predicting contraceptive behavior among university men: The role of emotions and behavioral intentions. *Journal of Applied Social Psychology, 14,* 104–123.

Fisher, W. A., & Byrne, D. (1978a). Individual differences in affective, evaluative, and behavioral responses to an erotic film. *Journal of Applied Social Psychology, 8,* 355–365.

Fisher, W. A., & Byrne, D. (1978b). Sex differences in response to erotica? Love versus lust. *Journal of Personality and Social Psychology, 36,* 117–125.

Fisher, W. A., & Byrne, D. (1981). Social background, attitudes and sexual attraction. In M. Cook (Ed.), *The bases of human sexual attraction* (pp. 23–63). New York: Academic Press.

Fisher, W. A., Byrne, D., Edmunds, M., Miller, C. T., Kelley, K., & White, L. A. (1979). Psychological and situation-specific correlates of contraceptive behavior among university women. *Journal of Sex Research. 15,* 38–55.

Fisher, W. A., Byrne, D. & White, L. A. (1983). Emotional barriers to contraception. In D. Byrne & W. A. Fisher (Eds.), *Adolescents, sex, and contraception* (pp. 207–239). Hillsdale, NJ: Lawrence Erlbaum Associates.

Fisher, W. A., Byrne, D., White, L. A., & Kelley, K. (1984). *Erotophobia–erotophilia as a dimension of personality.* Manuscript submitted for publication.

Fisher, W. A., Fisher, J. D., & Byrne, D. (1977). Consumer reactions to contraceptive purchasing. *Personality and Social Psychology Bulletin, 3,* 293–296.

Fisher, W. A., & Gray, J. (1983, November). *Erotophobia–erotophilia and couples' sexual behavior during pregnancy and after childbirth.* Paper presented at the meeting of the Society for the Scientific Study of Sex, Chicago, Illinois.

Fisher, W. A., Miller, C. T., Byrne, D., & White, L. A. (1980). Talking dirty: Responses to communicating a sexual message as a function of situational and personality factors. *Basic and Applied Social Psychology, 1,* 115–126.

Foreit, K. G., & Foreit, J. R. (1978). Correlates of contraceptive behavior among unmarried U.S. college students. *Studies in Family Planning, 9,* 169–174.

Freud, S. (1959). *Collected papers* (Vol. 4). New York: Basic Books.

Gailbraith, G. G., & Mosher, D. L. (1968). Associative sexual response in relation to sexual arousal, guilt, and external approval tendencies. *Journal of Personality and Social Psychology, 10,* 142–147.

Gebhard, P. (1977). The acquisition of sex information. *Journal of Sex Research, 13,* 148–169.

Geer, J. H., & Fuhr, R. (1976). Cognitive factors in sexual arousal. The role of distraction. *Journal of Consulting and Clinical Psychology, 44,* 238–243.

Gilbert, F. S., & Gamache, M. P. (1984). The sexual opinion survey: Structure and use. *Journal of Sex Research, 20,* 293–309.

Gordon, S. (1977). *Community family life education program for parents.* Syracuse, NY: Institute for Family Research and Education.

Griffitt, W. (1973). Response to erotica and the projection of response to erotica in the opposite sex. *Journal of Experimental Research in Personality, 6,* 330–338.

Griffitt, W. (1975). Sexual experience and sexual responsiveness: Sex differences. *Archives of Sexual Behavior, 4,* 529–540.

Griffitt, W. (1979a). Sexual stimulation and sociosexual behaviors. In M. Cook & G. Wilson (Eds.), *Love and attraction: An international conference.* New York: Pergamon Press.

Griffitt, W. (1979b, May). *Sex and sexual attraction.* Paper presented at the meeting of the Midwestern Psychological Association, Chicago.

Griffitt, W., & Kaiser, D. L. (1978). Affect, sex guilt, gender, and the rewarding-punishing effects of erotic stimuli. *Journal of Personality and Social Psychology, 36,* 850–858.

Griffitt, W., May, J., & Veitch, R. (1974). Sexual stimulation and interpersonal behavior: Heterosexual evaluative responses, visual behavior, and physical proximity. *Journal of Personality and Social Psychology, 30,* 367–377.

Griffitt, W., & Veitch, R. (1971). Hot and crowded: Influence of population density and temperature on interpersonal affective behavior. *Journal of Personality and Social Psychology, 17,* 92–98.

Gross, A. E., & Bellew-Smith, M. (1983). A social psychological approach to reducing pregnancy risk in adolescence. In D. Byrne & W. A. Fisher (Eds.), *Adolescents, sex, and contraception* (pp. 263–272). Hillsdale, NJ: Lawrence Erlbaum Associates.

Haller, J. S., & Haller, R. M. (1977). *The physician and sexuality in Victorian America.* New York: Norton.

Hariton, E. B., & Singer, J. L. (1974). Women's fantasies during sexual intercourse: Normative and theoretical implications. *Journal of Consulting and Clinical Psychology, 42,* 313–322.

Heiman, J. R. (1977). A psychophysiological exploration of sexual arousal patterns in females and males. *Psychophysiology, 14,* 266–274.

Heiman, J., LoPiccolo, L., & LoPiccolo, J. (1976). *Becoming orgasmic: A sexual growth program for women.* Englewood Cliffs, NJ: Prentice Hall.

Hessellund, H. (1976). Masturbation and sexual fantasies in married couples. *Archives of Sexual Behavior, 5,* 133–147.

Hoon, P. W., Wincze, J. P., & Hoon, E. F. (1977). The effects of biofeedback and cognitive mediation upon vaginal blood volume. *Behavior Therapy, 8,* 694–702.

Horner, M. S., (1972). Toward understanding of achievement-related conflicts in women. *Journal of Social Issues, 28,* 157–175.

Hunt, M. (1974). *Sexual behavior in the 1970s.* Chicago: Playboy Press.

Hyde, J. S. (1982). *Understanding human sexuality* (2nd ed.). New York: McGraw-Hill.

Jaccard, J. J., & Davidson, A. R. (1972). Towards an understanding of family planning behaviors: An initial investigation. *Journal of Applied Social Psychology, 2,* 228–235.

Jazwinski, C., & Byrne, D. (1978). *The effect of a contraceptive theme on response to erotica.* Unpublished manuscript, State University of New York at Albany, Albany, New York.

Kaats, G., & Davis, K. (1972). The social psychology of sexual behavior. In L. Wrightsman (Ed.), *Social psychology in the seventies* (pp. 548–580). Monterey, CA: Brooks-Cole.

Kantner, J. F., & Zelnik, M. (1973). Contraception and pregnancy: Experience of young unmarried women in the United States. *Family Planning Perspectives, 5,* 21–35.

Kaplan, H. S. (1979). *Disorders of sexual desire.* New York: Simon & Schuster.

Kilmann, P. R., Wanlass, R. L., Sabalis, R. F., & Sullivan, B. (1981). Sex education: A review of its effects. *Archives of Sexual Behavior, 10,* 177–205.

King, K., Balswick, J. O., & Robinson, I. E. (1977). The continuing premarital sexual revolution among college females. *Journal of Marriage and the Family, 39,* 455–459.

Kinsey, A. C., Pomeroy, W. B., & Martin, C. E. (1948). *Sexual behavior in the human male.* Philiadelphia: Saunders.

Kinsey, A. C., Pomeroy, W. B. Martin, C. E., & Gebhard, P. H. (1953). *Sexual behavior in the human female.* Philadelphia: Saunders.

Koch, P. B. (1978, April). *A comparison of the sex education of primary school children as expressed in art in Sweden and the United States.* Paper presented at the Eastern Regional Meeting of the Society for the Scientific Study of Sex, Atlantic City, New Jersey.

Krafft-Ebing, R. von (1939). *Psychopathia sexualis. A medico-forensic study.* New York: Pioneer. (Translation of 12th edition, originally published 1903.)

Lazarus, R. S. (1984). On the primacy of cognition. *American Psychologist, 39,* 124–129.

Lemery, C. R. (1983). *Children's sexual knowledge as a function of parents' affective orientation to sexuality and parent-child communication about sex: A causal analysis.* Unpublished master's thesis, University of Western Ontario, London, Ontario, Canada.

Levinger, G., & Breedlove, J. (1966). Interpersonal attraction and agreement: A study of marriage partners. *Journal of Personality and Social Psychology, 3,* 367–372.

LoPiccolo, J. (1977). Direct treatment of sexual dysfunction in the couple. In J. Money & H. Musaph (Eds.), *Handbook of sexology* (pp. 1227–1244). Amsterdam: Excerpta Medica.

Malamuth, N. M. (1981). Rape fantasies as a function of exposure to violent sexual stimuli. *Archives of Sexual Behavior, 10,* 33–47.

Malamuth, N. M., & Check, J. V. P. (1981a). The effects of mass media exposure on acceptance of violence against women: A field experiment. *Journal of Research in Personality, 15,* 436–446.

Malamuth, N. M., & Check, J. V. P. (1981b, August). *The effects of exposure to aggressive-pornography: Rape proclivity, sexual arousal and beliefs in rape myths.* Paper presented at the meeting of the American Psychological Association, Los Angeles.

Malamuth, N. M., & Donnerstein, E. (1982). The effects of aggressive-pornographic mass media stimuli. In L. Berkowitz (Ed.), *Advances in Experimental Social Psychology* (Vol. 15, pp. 103–136). New York: Academic Press.

Marquis, J. N. (1970). Orgasmic reconditioning: Changing sexual object choice through controlling masturbation fantasies. *Journal of Behavior Therapy and Experimental Psychiatry*, *1*, 263–271.

Marshall, D. S. (1971). Sexual behavior on Mangaia. In D. S. Marshall & R. C. Suggs (Eds.), *Human sexual behavior* (pp. 103–162). Englewood Cliffs, NJ: Prentice-Hall.

Masters, W. H., & Johnson, V. E. (1966). *Human sexual response*. Boston: Little, Brown.

Masters, W. H., & Johnson, V. E. (1970). *Human sexual inadequacy*. Boston: Little, Brown.

McCauley, C., & Swann, C. P. (1978). Male-female differences in sexual fantasy. *Journal of Research in Personality*, *12*, 76–86.

McClelland, D. C. (1965). Toward a theory of motive acquisition. *American Psychologist*, *20*, 321–333.

Mednick, R. A. (1977). Gender-specific variables in sexual fantasy. *Journal of Personality Assessment*, *41*, 248–254.

Mendelsohn, M. J., & Mosher, D. L. (1979). Effects of sex guilt and premarital sexual permissiveness on role-played sex education and moral attitudes. *Journal of Sex Research*, *15*, 174–183.

Messenger, J. C. (1971). Sexual repression: Its manifestations. In D. S. Marshall & R. C. Suggs (Eds.), *Human sexual behavior* (pp. 14–20). Englewood Cliffs, NJ: Prentice-Hall.

Michael, R. P., Bonsall, R. W., & Warner, P. (1974). Human vaginal secretions: Volatile fatty acid content. *Science*, *186*, 1217–1219.

Money, J., Cawte, J. E., Bianchi, G. N., & Nurcombe, B. (1970). Sex training and traditions in Arnhem land. *British Journal of Medical Psychology*, *43*, 383–399.

Mosher, D. L. (1966). The development and multitrait-multimethod matrix analysis of three measures of three aspects of guilt. *Journal of Consulting Psychology*, *30*, 25–29.

Mosher, D. L. (1968). Measurement of guilt in females by self-report inventory. *Journal of Consulting and Clinical Psychology*, *32*, 690–695.

Mosher, D. L. (1973). Sex differences, sex experience, sex guilt, and sexually explicit films. *Journal of Social Issues*, *29*, 95–112.

Mosher, D. L. (1979). Sex guilt and sex myths in college men and women. *Journal of Sex Research*, *15*, 224–234.

Mosher, D. L., & Abramson, P. R. (1977). Subjective sexual arousal to films of masturbation. *Journal of Consulting and Clinical Psychology*, *45*, 796–807.

Mosher, D. L., & Cross, H. J. (1971). Sex guilt and premarital sexual experiences of college students. *Journal of Consulting and Clinical Psychology*, *36*, 27–32.

Nawy, H. (1973). In the pursuit of happiness? Consumers of erotica in San Francisco. *Journal of Social Issues*, *29*, 147–161.

Offit, A. (1977). *The sexual self*. New York: Ballantine.

Pietropinto, A., & Simenauer, J. (1977). *Beyond the male myth*. New York: Times Books.

Rachman, S. (1966). Sexual fetishism: An experimental analogue. *Psychological Record*, *16*, 293–296.

Reiss, I. L. (1967). *The social context of premarital sexual permissiveness*. New York: Holt, Rinehart & Winston.

Rindskopf, K. D. (1981, November). *Subtle signals: A content analysis of sex education books for children*. Paper presented at the meeting of the Society for the Scientific Study of Sex, New York.

Sachs, D. H., & Byrne, D. (1970). Differential conditioning of evaluative responses to neutral stimuli through association with attitude statements. *Journal of Experimental Research in Personality*, *4*, 181–185.

Salhanick, H. A., & Margolis, R. H. (1968). Hormonal physiology of the ovary. In J. J. Gold (Ed.), *Textbook of gynecologic endocrinology* (pp. 67–94). New York: Harper & Row.

Schill, T. R., & Chapin, J. (1972). Sex guilt and male's preference for reading erotic magazines. *Journal of Consulting and Clinical Psychology*, *39*, 516.

Schwartz, J. (1973). Effects of sex guilt and sexual arousal on the retention of birth control information. *Journal of Consulting and Clinical Psychology, 41,* 61–64.

Sorensen, R. C. (1973). *The Sorensen report. Adolescent sexuality in contemporary America. Personal values and sexual behavior ages thirteen to nineteen.* New York: World.

Spock, B. (1978). *Baby and child care.* New York: Pocket Books.

Storms, M. D. (1981). A theory of erotic orientation development. *Psychological Review, 88,* 340–353.

Sue, D. (1979). Erotic fantasies of college students during coitus. *Journal of Sex Research, 15,* 299–305.

Szaz, T. S. (1980). *Sex by prescription.* Garden City, NY: Anchor Press/Doubleday.

Tavris, C., & Sadd, S. (1978). *The Redbook report on female sexuality.* New York: Dell.

Titchener, E. B. (1897). *An outline of psychology.* New York: MacMillan.

Udry, J. R., & Morris, N. M. (1968). Distribution of coitus in the menstrual cycle. *Nature, 220,* 593–596.

Walker, J. (1983). *Sexual activities and fantasies of university students as a function of sex role orientation.* Unpublished honors thesis, University of Western Ontario, London, Ontario, Canada.

Watts, P. R. (1977). Comparison of three human sexuality teaching methods used in university health classes. *Research Quarterly, 48,* 187–190.

Weidner, G., Istvan, J., & Griffitt, W. (1979, May). *Beauty in the eye of the horny beholders: Evaluation of attractive, medium attractive and unattractive men, by sexually aroused women.* Paper presented at the meeting of the Midwestern Psychological Association, Chicago.

West, N. W. (1976). *The effect of instruction in family planning on knowledge attitudes and behavior of London (Ontario) senior secondary school students.* Unpublished doctoral dissertation, Ohio State University, Columbus, Ohio.

Wilson, W. L., & Abelson, H. I. (1973). Experience with and attitudes toward explicit sexual materials. *Journal of Social Issues, 29,* 19–39.

Yarber, W. L., & Whitehill, L. L. (1981). The relationship of parental affective orientation toward sexuality and responses to sex-related situations of preschool children. *Journal of Sex Education and Therapy, 7,* 36–39.

Zajonc, R. B. (1980). Feeling and thinking. Preferences need no inferences. *American Psychologist, 35,* 151–175.

Zajonc, R. B. (1984). On the primacy of affect. *American Psychologist, 39,* 117–123.

Zelnik, M., Kantner, J. F., & Ford, K. (1981). *Sex and pregnancy in adolescence.* Beverly Hills: Sage.

Zilbergeld, B. (1978). *Male sexuality.* New York: Bantam.

Zillmann, D. (1979). *Hostility and aggression.* Hillsdale, NJ: Lawrence Erlbaum Associates.

Zimmer, D., Borchardt, E., & Fischele, C. (1983). Sexual fantasies of sexually distressed and nondistressed men and women: An empirical comparison. *Journal of Sex and Marital Therapy, 9,* 38–50.

Zuckerman, M., Tushup, R., & Finner, S. (1976). Sexual attitudes and experience: Attitude and personality correlates and changes produced by a course in sexuality. *Journal of Consulting and Clinical Psychology, 44,* 7–19.

7

Coition As Emotion

Dolf Zillmann
Indiana University

Cannon (1929) has most convincingly promoted the view that acute emotional states are responses to environmental threats and that these responses are designed to aid the organism in coping with the threats. More specifically, in his so-called emergency theory of emotion he proposed that intense sympathetic activation provided the energy needed for vigorous action and that, evolutionarily speaking, energetic action is vital in dealing effectively with endangering conditions. Just two high-powered response tendencies are specified in his famous paradigm: fight or flight. Both are obviously adaptive in that they serve the preservation of the individual.

In terms of human emotions, the emergency-resolving behavior dichotomy of fight versus flight corresponds, of course, with the dichotomy of anger versus fear. Although often inferred post facto from overt behavior, anger and fear are generally held to be fight- or flight-motivating experiential states that are characterized by substantial to extreme sympathetic dominance in the autonomic nervous system (cf. Averill, 1982; Izard, 1977; Marks, 1969). Indeed, the excitatory component of acute anger and acute fear seems so pronounced and obtrusive that other emotions pale by comparison. So-called positive emotions, in particular, appear incapable of matching the intensity of sympathetic reactions to situations in which the individual's welfare or well-being is placed at risk. Reactions of delight and joy, for instance, rarely, if ever, have the excitatory intensity typical of Cannon's coping emotions (cf. Grings & Dawson, 1978). Moreover, positive emotions that have great excitatory intensity are often immediately subsequent to negative ones, and their extraordinary intensity may be due to this temporal arrangement. Joy, for instance, may come in the wake of the successful removal or avoidance of endangering conditions and owes its intensity to lingering sympathetic excitation from the preceding noxious experience (cf. Zillmann, 1983b). Additionally, joy often entails elements of excitation from apprehensions about the possibility that expected incentives might not be attained (cf. Malmo, 1965, 1975) or that other gratifying conditions might not materialize (Zillmann, 1980).

Acute anger and acute fear, especially in their extreme forms as rage and terror, stand out, then, as the basic emotions linked with sympathetic hyperactivity. This scheme of things seems to have been so convincing to those exploring the psychophysiology of human emotions that another experience associated with sympathetic hyperactivity has received little, if any, recognition as an emotion: namely, acute sexual arousal. Traditionally, sexual excitedness is simply not thought of as an emotion—certainly not as one comparable to the likes of anger and fear. There is not even a single, simple label for it. Yet, as we shall see that as an emotion, sexual excitedness fits the bill on all counts.

First of all, during the excitement and plateau phases (cf. Masters & Johnson, 1966), sexual arousal qualifies as a state characterized by sympathetic dominance in the autonomic nervous system, and thus as a state that prepares the organism for vigorous action. In this sense, sexual arousal is just as catabolic as Cannon's coping emotions. Fight, flight, and coition are all behaviors that rapidly deplete energy. The stimulus conditions for all these behaviors evoke reactions designed to furnish the needed energy. And all these behaviors are phasic or episodic in that the energy provided characteristically fuels just one behavioral engagement. The fact that sexual arousal involves some parasympathetically controlled response components (i.e., genital vasocongestion) does not invalidate this assessment. Second, anger, fear, and sexual arousal are all experiential states in which the individual is fully cognizant of both causal circumstances and appropriate goal responses. In all these states, furthermore, the level of sympathetic excitation tends to determine the intensity of the emotional experience (cf. Zillmann, 1978). Finally, although sexual arousal and preparedness for coition cannot readily be classified as coping emotions, these responses are also adaptive. However, rather than serving the preservation of self, they obviously serve the preservation of the species.

Cannon's fight-or-flight paradigm might thus understate the case of hypersympathetic, emergency-type emotions. Coition is a contender and should be recognized as a third primary emotion of this kind. But regardless of any formal classificatory inclusion of sexual arousal and coition as emotions, recognition of the fact that as both motivational, experiential conditions and consummatory behaviors, anger, fear and sexual arousal—the fight-flight-coition trichotomy—are comparable hypersympathetic states has intriguing theoretical and practical implications. Most significantly, the sympathetic commonality in this trichotomy should produce interdependencies capable of altering the precoital and coital behaviors and, perhaps most importantly, their experiential quality dependent on preceding and/or concurrent nonsexual but nonetheless arousing events.

We explore these possibilities more specifically now. First, we outline the physiological bases for sympathetic commonality in the fight-flight-coition tri-chotomy. We then document response commonalities. Thereafter, we look into the research that established specific dependencies of sexual behavior on the other hypersympathetic emotions, and we discuss their implications in terms of both theory and practice.

COMMONALITIES IN FIGHT, FLIGHT, AND COITION

Fight, flight, and coition are associated in numerous ways. The most fundamental connections, however, have been established in neurophysiology and endocrinology. These connections have been detailed elsewhere (Zillmann, 1983a). Suffice it here to point out the nature of the principal ones.

Central Connections

Research on the central representation of sexual responsiveness as well as of aggressive behaviors, including fear and flight reactions, has been pioneered by MacLean (e.g., 1962, 1968a, 1968b, 1973). In studies with male nonhuman primates (e.g., MacLean & Ploog, 1962) it was observed that electrical brain stimulation of loci in extreme proximity to areas that control erection produced responses associated with fight or flight. Likewise, stimulation of loci in extreme proximity to areas controlling fight or flight reactions was found to produce erection. More significantly, stimulation of fight-flight areas eventually produced sexual excitedness as well, and stimulation of sexual areas similarly co-instigated agonistic reactions. From this and related research (e.g., de Molina & Hunsperger, 1957) MacLean concluded that excitation in one region, owing to proximity and interconnectedness, tends to perfuse into the other, thereby producing the characteristically delayed co-elicitation effect. More specifically, he proposed that excitation of amygdaloid structures—those thought to control fight and flight—spills over into septal structures—those thought to control sexual behavior—and vice versa. And because both amygdaloid and septal structures are immediately linked to the anterior hypothalamus, he assumed that excitation originating in the amygdala recruits septal excitation along the way; he further assumed that excitation originating in the septum likewise recruits amygdaloid excitation on its path.

MacLean's theory and research not only lay the foundation for a close association between fight, flight, and coition as primary emotions, but also emphasizes their adaptive significance as a unit. As he considers amygdaloid functioning implicated with self-preservation (through fight and flight, among other things) and septal functioning with the sustenance of the species (through sexual action and reproductive activities in a broader sense), the neural-spillage hypothesis brings the two most basic, adaptive behavioral inclinations into joint operation.

Autonomic Connections

The strong sympathetic reactions associated with Cannon's coping emotions are produced by thoracolumbar outflow (cf. Crouch, 1978; Guyton, 1972). Particularly through the lesser and least splanchnic nerves from the lower thoracic plexus, impulses from higher brain centers impact the adrenal medullae. Direct innervation by sympathetic fibers thus prompts the release of the catecholamines that mediate the general reaction of sympathetic excitedness.

Essentially the same sympathetic innervation serves sexual excitedness. Specifically, through the last thoracic and first lumbar nerves impulses from higher centers reach the adrenal medullae, prompting catecholamine release. Most significantly, however, this outflow reaches the sexual organs as well (e.g., Crosby, Humphrey, & Lauer, 1962). The combined outflow function forms, in fact, what is called the *psychogenic* sexual center (e.g., Weiss, 1972). Figure 7.1 shows its operation schematically. Psychogenic sexual stimulation—which translates to exposure to distal (i.e., visual and/or auditory) sexual stimuli—is therefore capable of producing both sympathetic excitedness and genital tumescence (cf. Zillmann, 1983a).

The obvious and confusing discrepancy between Cannon's coping emotions and sexual arousal concerns the alternative, yet primary control of genital tumescence. Parasympathetic sacral outflow, known as the *reflexogenic* sexual center, produces genital vasocongestion. This control, organized in highly robust spinal sexual reflexes (cf. Bard, 1940; Beach, 1967), is also schematized in Fig. 7.1. For later reference (in Behavioral Connections section) it should be mentioned that the parasympathetic innervation of the reflexogenic sexual center also exerts a degree of control over micturition and defecation (e.g., Bors & Comarr, 1971).

Mainly from research with men and women who suffered spinal cord injuries (cf. Weiss, 1972), the two autonomic systems controlling sexual arousal are known to be capable of rather autonomous functioning. The impairment or loss of either thoracolumbar or sacral outflow alone does not result in the loss of genital functioning. The capacity for genital tumescence is largely maintained. Intact sacral structures ensure tumescence in response to appropriate tactile stimulation. Concomitant sympathetic arousal may suffer, however. Intact thoracolumbar structures, on the other hand, upon distal sexual stimulation leave the sympathetic response component unimpaired, while tumescence may suffer somewhat. The functional autonomy is immaterial, however, for individuals with unimpaired spinal and autonomic functioning. The systems simply operate in an interrelated fashion. Specifically, sympathetic outflow from the thoracolumbar cord acts *synergistically* with parasympathetic outflow from the sacral cord in producing both genital vasocongestion and sympathetic excitation in the peripheral structures.

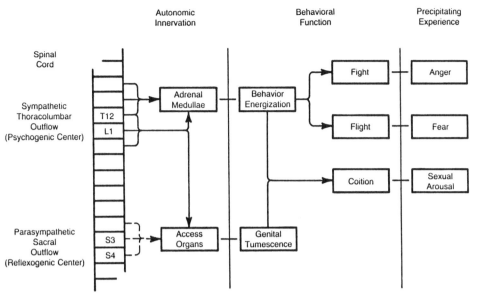

FIG. 7.1.   Scheme of the spinal outflow in fight, flight, and coition. The sexual access organs are innervated by parasympathetic fibers from the sacral nerves. The nerves constituting the reflexogenic sexual center are numbered S3 and S4 (S=sacral). The access organs are also innervated by sympathetic fibers from the thoracolumbar nerves. The nerves constituting the psychogenic sexual center are numbered T12 and L1 (T=thoracic, L=lumbar). The adrenal medullae are innervated by sympathetic fibers of the same origin: the lower thoracic nerves, especially the least splanchnic nerve from T12. Genital tumescence is thus linked to increased sympathetic excitation in the peripheral structures. Comparable sympathetic excitedness is characteristic of agonistic behaviors. Strong excitedness of this kind is capable of effecting sacral outflow that produces genital tumescence and related responses under sacral control.

Obviously, the joint operation of sympathetic and parasympathetic outflow differs for fight and flight, on the one hand, and sexual behavior, on the other. Whereas sympathetic activity seems equally involved in these behaviors, parasympathetic, sacral outflow seems specific to precoital and coital action. We see later (in Behavioral Connections section) that this separation is less clear-cut than it may appear to be.

Endocrine Connections

Adrenal functioning affects both sexual and aggressive behaviors in numerous ways. The adrenal cortex, for instance, secretes adrenal sex hormones that resemble the gonadal sex hormones, and these androgens have been found capable of potentiating both sexual and aggressive behaviors in either gender (cf. Leshner, 1978; Zillmann, 1983a). The influence of androgens is tonic rather than phasic, however, and pertains to emergency situations only in the sense that it creates favorable physical preconditions for fight, flight, and coition as episodic emergency behaviors. Whalen's (1966) concept of "arousability" is based on these preconditions. For sexual behavior, androgenization may create preconditions favorable to coital engagements by fostering penile or clitoral hypertrophy (e.g., Luttge, 1971), among other things (cf. MacLusky & Naftolin, 1981); and for fight-and-flight behavior, but especially the former, favorable preconditions are created through the virilization of the skeletal musculature at large (e.g., Ehrhardt, 1977). The adrenal cortex, furthermore, supplies glucocorticoids that provide energy for extended periods of time. The effect is again tonic and aids in furnishing the backdrop, so to speak, for behavioral emergencies such as fight, flight, or coition.

As our concern is with phasic behavior, we can ignore the influence of adrenocortical hormones and concentrate on the action of the adrenal medullae. The medullae release the sympathomimetic catecholamines epinephrine and nor-epinephrine. Especially through the hyperglycemic effect of epinephrine, this release quasi-instantaneously provides the energy for vigorous action. The burst of energy to the skeletal muscles is comparatively short-lived, however. The extreme level of energy supply cannot be maintained for any length of time. The supply is readily exhausted by emergency action. If not, homeostatic regulation will normalize autonomic activity after some time (cf. Adolph, 1968).

As the analysis of autonomic innervation (see Autonomic Connections section) suggests, catecholamine release should be equally involved in fight, flight, and coition or in the precipitating emotions of these behaviors—namely, anger, fear, and sexual arousal. Endocrinological research has firmly established that this is indeed the case (e.g., Levi, 1965, 1969, 1972).

Behavioral Connections

The strength of the sympathetic component of sexual arousal and of coital engagements has been assessed in peripheral manifestations. Masters and Johnson (1966) recorded heart rates ranging from 110 to more than 180 bpm for both males and females during coital activities. Hyperventilation was evident in both genders, with respiration rates above 40 per minute. Blood pressure underwent substantial changes, too. Compared against basal levels, systolic pressure increased between 40 and 100 mm Hg in males and between 30 and 80 mm Hg in females. Diastolic pressure also increased, but not as strongly: between 20 and 50 mm Hg in males and between 20 and 40 mm Hg in females. These and similar findings (e.g., Bartlett, 1956; Fox & Fox, 1969) are somewhat compromised, however, in that the skeletal-motor activity involved contributed to the excitatory reaction. This is obviously the case for data from coition, but it also applies to the automanipulative techniques that have been employed in the research. Nonetheless, the contention by Masters and Johnson that the physical exertion associated with coition is not sufficient to produce the observed cardiorespiratory concomitant of sexual activities seems well supported by findings concerning the impact of exposure to explicit portrayals of precoital and coital behaviors on sympathetic excitation. Exposure to graphic erotica is devoid of exertion, yet produces sympathetic reactions that are, though somewhat weaker overall, quite comparable to those during precoital and coital behaviors (cf. Stern, Farr, & Ray, 1975; Zillmann, Bryant, Comisky, & Medoff, 1981). On systolic blood pressure, for example, exposure to erotica has been found to produce average increases as high as 20 mm Hg (e.g., Zillmann, 1971).

Anger and fear, not to mention fight and flight, are much more difficult to produce in laboratory situations. Some of the procedures that could be used proved effective, however, in producing acute anger and acute fear. Although, compared to anger and fear outside the laboratory, the created emotional states were probably far from extreme, their sympathetic component was pronounced and is generally comparable to that of sexual excitedness (cf. Marks, 1969; Zillmann, 1979). During acute anger, for instance, systolic blood pressure was found to be elevated by about 20 mm Hg on the average (e.g., Zillmann & Sapolsky, 1977); and during acute fear, it was found to be elevated by the very same amount (e.g., Ax, 1960).

Granted that patterned differences may exist in the sympathetic accompaniment of anger, fear, and sexual arousal, it should be clear that the emergency emotions fight, flight, and coition are all relying on a strong sympathetic reaction that furnishes the energy for an episode of action.

In view of such sympathetic commonality among the emergency emotions, the parasympathetic discrepancy between anger/fear and sexual arousal seems most obtrusive. But as indicated in the section on Autonomic Connections, this appearance is somewhat deceiving. First of all, the parasympathetic outflow that makes for the reflexogenic sexual center also reaches the detrusor muscle of the urinary bladder and the distal colon and rectum (cf. Zillmann, 1983a). This innervation not only plays a specific part in sexual functioning (cf. Masters & Johnson, 1966), but it is linked to intense sympathetic excitedness and, presumably because of this, is involved in the nonsexual emergency emotions as well. It is common knowledge that extreme sympathetic excitation carries with it the parasympathetically controlled inclination to empty bladder and bowels. This inclination is so closely allied with fear (and with aggression to the extent that defensive fighting is characteristically precipitated by fear) that in the research with rodents and other mammals, nonhuman primates included, fear is measured through micturition and defecation (cf. Nevin, 1973). The parasympathetic oddity attached to sympathetic dominance in the autonomic nervous system has even been granted survival value in that both fight and flight are facilitated by the prompt reduction of excess weight (e.g., Cannon, 1929).

But the fact that in emergency emotions the strong sympathetic response tends to carry with it particular parasympathetic responses, all linked to sacral outflow, seems most obtrusively documented in anthropological research. Gajdusek (1970) reported that uncovered men exhibited some degree of erection during more or less all sympathetic emotions. Anger and fear especially seem to be associated with genital blood flooding. The utility of such reactions is not immediately apparent. It can only be speculated that the combination of thoracolumbar sympathetic outflow and sacral parasympathetic outflow (see Fig. 7.1) forms a patterned response. Although this patterned response is appropriate only for sexual engagements, its interconnections are apparently so strong that the sexual component is pulled along in nonsexual emergencies as well. However, regardless of the specific mechanics involved, the sympathetic/parasympathetic response commonalities in the emergency emotions show that it is incorrect to view sexual arousal as a sympathetic/parasympathetic state and, in contrast, anger and fear as purely sympathetic emotions. These commonalities further suggest that the sacral control of parasympathetic sexual and nonsexual responses is less specific than generally believed and far from superbly differentiated.

INTERDEPENDENCIES IN FIGHT, FLIGHT, AND COITION

Numerous interdependencies between the emergency emotions can be expected on the basis of the described sympathetic and parasympathetic connections. Specifically, it can be expected that within the fight-flight-coition trichotomy— or within the precipitating emotions anger, fear, and sexual arousal, respectively—arousal from a prior emotion will facilitate the subsequent emotion, and simultaneous arousal from a nondominant emotion will facilitate the dominant emotion.

Predictions of behavioral facilitation due to sympathetic commonality can be derived from the excitation-transfer paradigm (cf. Zillmann, 1978, 1983a). This paradigm is based on the following principal assumptions: (a) owing to slack humoral mediation, sympathetic excitation dissipates sluggishly, and excitatory residues are likely to enter into subsequent behaviors and experiences; (b) individuals generally do not partition confounded sympathetic excitation nor trace it to different contributing sources; (c) regardless of its specific sources, sympathetic excitation energizes the behavior enacted in response to prevailing stimuli; (d) arousal states tend to be attributed in toto to the most obtrusive inducers at hand; and (e) the perceived intensity of an arousal state tends to determine the intensity of an emotional experience. These assumptions and the research evidence backing them have been more fully discussed elsewhere (Zillmann, 1983b). Suffice it here to project their implications.

For emotional behaviors in succession, the transfer paradigm predicts that residual sympathetic excitation from fight/flight or anger/fear, respectively, will

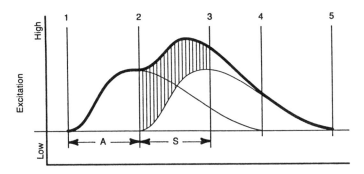

Time of Activity

FIG. 7.2.   A model of excitation transfer in which residual excitation from a preceding excitatory reaction combines additively with the excitatory reaction to current stimulation. An antecedent stimulus condition (A), persisting from time 1 to time 2, is assumed to produce excitatory activity that has entirely decayed only at time 4. Similarly, a subsequent stimulus condition (S), persisting from time 2 to time 3, is assumed to produce excitatory activity that has entirely decayed only at time 5. Residual excitation from condition A and excitation specific to condition S combine from time 2 to time 4. The extent to which the transfer of residues from condition A increases the excitatory activity associated with condition S is shown in the shaded area (reprinted, with permission, from D. Zillmann, *Hostility and aggression.* Hillsdale, NJ: Lawrence Erlbaum Associates, 1979).

inseparably combine with sympathetic excitation from sexual stimulation and thereby facilitate the subsequent sexual arousal and coital activities. Analogously, it predicts that residual excitation from sexual arousal will combine with excitation from the instigation of anger or fear or from overt agonistic behaviors, respectively. Figure 7.2 presents a graph model of this behavioral facilitation.

For concurrently evoked emotional behaviors it is predicted that sympathetic excitation deriving from secondary sources will inseparably combine with excitation produced by the behavior- and/or experience-determining, primary stimulation and facilitate that behavior and/or experience. If fear/flight or anger/fight constitutes the primary emotion and sexual arousal is secondary, the portion of sympathetic excitation from sexual arousal will intensify these agonistic emotions. If, on the other hand, agonistic emotions are secondary and sexual arousal is primary, the portion of excitation from fear/flight or anger/fight, respectively, will facilitate sexual arousal. Figure 7.3 presents a graph model of this type of behavioral facilitation.

In contrast to the situation concerning sympathetic excitation, no particular paradigm exists from which the consequences of parasympathetic commonalities in the emergency emotions could be projected. Despite anatomical intertwinement, the pathways of sacral control are abviously not identical, and the involvement of some connections (e.g., from S2) has remained somewhat uncertain (cf.

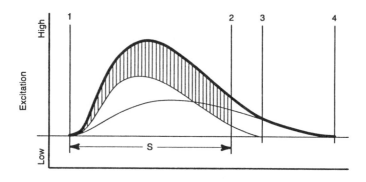

Time of Activity

FIG. 7.3.   A model of excitation transfer in which excitation from a secondary excitatory reaction combines additively with the excitatory reaction to the primary, behavior-directing stimulation. The stimuli for the primary (PR) and secondary reaction (SR) concur from time 1 to time 2. It is assumed that the excitatory activity of PR has entirely decayed at time 3 and that decay of the activity of SR is complete at time 4. Behavior directed by the primary stimulation (S) is associated with the combined excitatory activity of PR and SR. The extent to which the transfer of secondary excitation increases excitation specific to the primary stimulation is shown in the shaded area (reprinted, with permission, from D. Zillmann, *Connections between sex and aggression.* Hillsdale, NJ: Lawrence Erlbaum Associates, 1983a).

Pick, 1970). Specific predictions are not feasible as a result. However, as sacral outflow is linked to extreme states of sympathetic excitedness, it is conceivable that this patterned autonomic reaction is favored in such states. In other words, extreme sympathetic excitedness might produce a readiness for sacrally controlled responses and thereby facilitate their occurrence and, if they occur, their strength. This readiness, moreover, might not be highly specific, and response specificity might depend on extended sexual or nonsexual stimulation. If so, it could be expected that genital vasocongestion is facilitated by preceding anger or fear and fight or flight, respectively. And likewise it could be expected that, when agonistic emotions come about in the wake of sexual excitedness, both micturition and defecation are facilitated.

Facilitation of Agonistic Emotions

The capacity of sexual arousal—or more accurately, of the sympathetic component of sexual arousal—to facilitate agonistic behaviors is not in doubt. Numerous investigations have shown that feelings of irritation and annoyance as well as hostile and aggressive actions can be intensified by sexual prearousal (cf. Zillmann, 1983a). As our interest here is more with effects on (rather than of) sexual arousal, we only briefly summarize the pertinent research.

In the initial study exploring excitation transfer from sexual arousal to ago-nistic behavior (Zillmann, 1971), male subjects were aggressively instigated, sexually stimulated or not, and then provided with an opportunity to retaliate against their annoyer. Sexual arousal was accomplished by exposure to an erotic film featuring a heterosexual couple engaged in precoital behavior. In two non-sexual conditions, subjects were exposed to an aggressive film or to a film devoid of hostile action. All films were identical in length to assure equal time separation between provocation and retaliation.

The excitatory capacity of the neutral, aggressive, and sexual materials was determined by pretesting. Sympathetic reactions were assessed in peripheral manifestations. Among other things, systolic and diastolic blood pressures were measured before and after exposure. The analysis of such measures showed the excitatory potential of the sexual stimulus to be above that of the aggressive stimulus and, in turn, that of the aggressive stimulus to be above that of the neutral stimulus. On the basis of this information it was expected that residues of sympathetic excitation should be the strongest following exposure to the sexual film, intermediate after the aggressive film, and weakest after the neutral film. The intensity of aggressive actions taken during this period, owing to the com-bination of excitation in response to the renewed interaction with the annoyer and the residues from film exposure, should vary accordingly. The findings, present-ed in Fig. 7.4, fully confirmed these expectations.

The aggression-facilitating effect of sexual prearousal was obtained in several subsequent studies as well (e.g., Donnerstein & Hallam, 1978; Meyer, 1972;

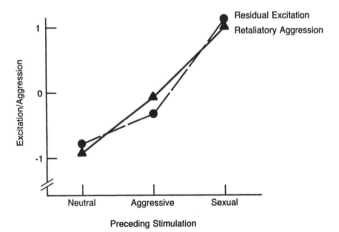

FIG. 7.4. Facilitation of aggressive behavior by excitation transfer from sexual stimulation. Residual excitation from exposure to communication was assessed in a composite measure, sympathetic activation, involving systolic and diastolic blood pressures and heart rate (circles, broken line). Retaliatory aggression was assessed in the intensity of electric shock delivered to the annoyer (triangles, solid line). Residual excitation and aggression are expressed in z scores for ease of comparison (adapted from Zillmann, 1971).

Zillmann, Hoyt, & Day, 1974). Additionally, it was observed under conceptually and procedurally different conditions. Donnerstein, Donnerstein, and Evans (1975) and Cantor, Zillmann, and Einsiedel (1978), for instance, reported aggression-facilitation from sexual excitedness prior to provocation (rather than prior to retaliation). Sympathetic residues from sexual arousal apparently are capable of intensifying experiences of annoyance and anger, and this intensification can have a somewhat delayed impact on overt aggression. The facilitating effect of sexual prearousal on the experience of anger and on noninjurious hostile actions specifically was also ascertained (e.g., Ramirez, Bryant, & Zillmann, 1982). Finally, the findings, which were initially limited to males, were eventually extended to females (e.g., Baron, 1979; Cantor, Zillmann, & Einsiedel, 1978).

To what extent can the sympathetic component of sexual arousal be considered implicated with such facilitation of agonistic emotions? Could it not be that exposure to erotica is disturbing—sexually frustrating, at best, and repulsive, at worst—and this disturbance adds to annoyance from the instigation to aggression? Various findings rule out the latter account. First of all, with few exceptions (cf. Zillmann, Bryant, Comisky, & Medoff, 1981) erotica evoke hedonically positive reactions. And the fact that these materials enjoy the great commercial popularity that they do is hardly consistent with the idea that exposure induces frustrations. Second, erotica that have only a negligible impact on sympathetic excitation either do not facilitate agonistic behaviors (e.g., Zillmann, Bryant, & Carveth, 1981; Zillmann & Sapolsky, 1977) or, owing to their hedonic quality and its incompatibility with aggression, actually diminish their intensity (e.g., Baron, 1974; Ramirez, Bryant, & Zillmann, 1982). Third, and most importantly, when the strength of the sympathetic response of erotica and nonerotica (i.e., stimuli devoid of sexual denotations or connotations) is matched, both stimulus types, if sufficiently potent excitationally, facilitate agonistic behaviors to similar degrees (Zillmann, Bryant, Comisky, & Medoff, 1981). Equally damaging to any explanation based on sexual frustration, and further supportive of the proposal that the aggression-facilitating effect of sexual arousal is mediated by its sympathetic component, is evidence from research on physical exercise. When exertion is employed to produce excitation for transfer into agonistic behaviors, aggression facilitation is commensurate with that from comparable amounts of excitation deriving from sexual stimulation (e.g., Zillmann, Katcher, & Milavsky, 1972).

Facilitation of Sexual Emotions

Some time ago, Ovid (1947, *Artis amatoriae*) furnished detailed descriptions of the extraordinary male delight of coition with a maiden "struck dumb" by fear. And he thought precoital fighting capable of enhancing the female's pleasures, too. Men of science have occasionally entertained comparable views. Russell

(1969), for example, attributed the great passion of an extramarital affair to the anxieties experienced during a war night—bombardment, flaming skies, and the like. Freud (e.g., 1938/1958, 1940), in his discussions of sadism and masochism, thought—essentially—that male sexuality benefits from aggression (i.e., anger and fight) and female sexuality from fear (linked to forced submission). In more general terms he contended (e.g., 1912/1943) that aversive experiences associated with denial, frustration, and repression are prerequisites to sexual passions: "It takes an obstacle to drive the libido to great height [p. 88; author's translation]." Freud asserted that whenever in human history the thwarting of sexual satisfaction by natural barriers was insufficient, cultural barriers were erected in order for love to become enjoyable again. He went so far as to claim that, without such barriers, love becomes worthless and life empty! More recent discussions of sexuality (e.g., Janda & Klenke-Hamel, 1980; Luria & Rose, 1979) echo much of the ancient folklore and of early psychology in treating it as a truism that coition "is never sweeter" than right after an argument or a fight, if not during extended struggle.

The wealth of speculation contrasts sharply with the paucity of pertinent research findings. Rigorous experimentation on behavioral fight-flight-coition interdependencies is obviously limited to infrahuman species. In the research with humans, the coping emotions of anger and fear are difficult to create as required; and the exploration of sexual activities has been severely restricted until recently. Nonetheless, pertinent research does exist, and we briefly inspect it. We first describe some highly suggestive studies with lower mammals and then address the scarce work with human subjects on the facilitation of sexual excitedness. Finally, we discuss research on sexual attraction; in so doing, we selectively draw from numerous existing studies in this particular area.

Facilitation of Coition.   Research with rodents has produced dramatic demonstrations of sex facilitation by agonistic prearousal. Barfield and Sachs (1968), for instance, conducted an investigation in which male rats in the presence of an estrous female received mildly painful electric shock. Compared against a no-shock control, reception of shock led to greatly enhanced sexual activity. Caggiula and Eibergen (1969) employed sexually naive male rats in a similar investigation. Shock prompted copulatory behavior in about four times as many animals as in the control condition. The additional finding that the same shock treatment produced aggressive reactions in males that confronted another male rather than the estrous female attests to the behavior-guiding function of environmental cues and the energizing function of arousal—arousal that can be assumed to have been produced by the shock. Further evidence for such an interpretation comes from an investigation by Crowley, Popolow, and Ward (1973). These investigators conditioned sexually inactive male rats (so-called noncopulators) to associate tones with electric shock and then presented the tones when the males were in the presence of an estrous female. The tones induced copulation with great regularity. The investigators attributed this extraordinary effect to an arousal augmentation by the anticipation of pain—that is, to fear. Both the infliction of pain in an attack-like situation and fear thereof can thus be viewed as coition enhancers in rodents.

Suggestive as these demonstrations may be, owing to a multitude of non-homologous conditions in human sexuality and coping emotions (cf. Zillmann, 1983a), they prove little, if anything, about fight/flight-coition interdependencies at the human level. In these matters, there is no substitute for research with human subjects. However, because drastic demonstrations—such as those with lower mammals—are not feasible, the interdependencies under consideration can only be established through the eventual integration of demonstrations of particular facets or subprocesses of the presumed grand process.

Facilitation of Sexual Arousal. Perhaps the closest approximation to a direct demonstration of the enhancing effect of agonistic emotions on sexual arousal in humans to date has been accomplished in an investigation by Hoon, Wincze, and Hoon (1977). These investigators induced or did not induce fearlike distress in female subjects and immediately thereafter exposed them to sexually arousing stimuli. Vaginal blood-volume changes were monitored throughout these treatments, volume increases serving as a measure of sexual excitedness. The findings, summarized in Fig. 7.5, revealed that distressed females become more rapidly and more intensely sexually aroused than females in a nondistressed, affectively neutral state. A fear-like experience, then, apparently produced con-

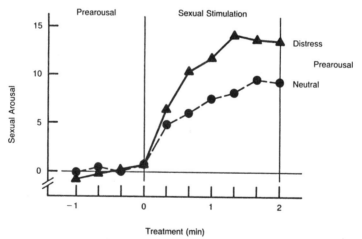

FIG. 7.5.   Genital vasocongestion after sympathetic prearousal. Female subjects were placed in distress or not and then exposed to erotic materials. Vaginal blood-volume changes were measured in mm as deviations from basal levels. The reported measures are averaged over 20 second periods (adapted from Hoon, Wincze, & Hoon, 1977).

ditions favorable to sacrally controlled parasympathetic responses in addition to characteristic sympathetic reactions (cf. Grings & Dawson, 1978).

The finding that distress can facilitate capillary engorgement in the vagina during subsequent sexual stimulation is of considerable importance. First, it seems to confirm the popular beliefs concerning sexual enhancement after fright, quarrel, or fight. They can, in fact, be taken as suggesting that rape may create superior conditions for coition and sexual experience. And to the extent that the infliction of pain can be assumed to produce parasympathetic and sympathetic reactions similar to those associated with distress generally, and there is reason to expect that (cf. Sternbach, 1968), the findings point up the possibility of exploiting aversion for sexual pleasure. Second, the findings are consistent with our proposals concerning the facilitation of parasympathetic sacral outflow through sympathetic excitation deriving from agonistic emotions. The findings thus shed light on the mechanisms of the aversion–pleasure conversion that characterize the still mystery-shrouded sadomasochistic sexual behaviors.

Given the gravity of the findings, a closer examination of the study by Hoon et al. (1977) is indicated. As much rests on the distressing experience that was created (actually, anxiety was the intended state), the operationalization of this experience seems crucial. Unfortunately, it can be questioned on several counts. Exposure to films was the means by which emotions were induced. Sexual stimulation was accomplished by a film featuring a couple engaged in precoital behavior. A travelogue served as a no-affect control stimulus. The critical distress-inducing materials detailed tragic automobile accidents, including the occupants' death cries. Subjects thus witnessed the victimization of others, but neither experienced pain themselves nor did they anticipate suffering pain. The type of emotional experience produced by such stimulation is usually classified as *empathetic distress* (cf. Zillmann, 1980). Empathetic distress is characteristically less intense than distress from actual pain or fear of painful stimulation (cf. Sternbach, 1968), and it could be argued that effects of empathetic distress are not representative of effects of distress from immediate threats to a person's own well-being or welfare. On the other hand, these effects may be comparable. In fact, generalizations might be conservative rather than exaggerated. This is to say that the distress facilitation of sexual arousal that Hoon et al. (1977) recorded might have been stronger, had distress been more convincingly manipulated. Still, the created distressing experience might be deemed too remote from the infliction and suffering of pain, or from associated apprehensions, to allow responsible generalizations about the effect of pain and fear of pain on sexual arousal.

Generalization of the distress facilitation of females' sexual arousal, as observed by Hoon et al. (1977), is further mitigated by the findings of a related study conducted by Wolchik, Beggs, Wincze, Sakheim, Barlow, and Mavissakalian (1980). This investigation attempted to extend the findings by Hoon et al. to males, and it succeeded only in part. The procedures employed were essentially those of the earlier study, except that penile tumescence was measured and a somewhat different type of distressing film was used in addition to the types of materials used previously. Again, a travelogue served as the control stimulus, and an erotic film was employed to induce sexual arousal. One prearousal film showed fatal and near fatal car accidents as in the earlier study. The other, additional prearousal film featured the anxieties of persons threatened with amputation of limbs. A pretest showed this second film to elicit stronger anxiety reactions than the accidents film.

Wolchik et al. (1980) observed that all three nonerotic films had negligible effects on erection. Subsequent exposure to the erotic film produced significantly different levels of penile tumescence, however. Preexposure to the most distressing (i.e., anxiety-inducing) film, presumably because it evoked the most intense sympathetic excitedness, resulted in greater tumescence than preexposure to the control film. The findings, up to this point, are supportive of the view that prearousal, especially noxious prearousal, is capable of facilitating sexual excitedness. Fear-like reactions thus appear to enhance sexual arousal in men just as well as in women. Such an interpretation is challenged, however, by the related finding that preexposure to the accidents film produced less erection than preexposure to the presumably less arousing control film.

As pretesting had shown the accidents film to be depressing rather than anxiety-inducing, Wolchik et al. (1980) considered the quality of prearousal emotions implicated in the mediation of the facilitation of sexual arousal. They thought anxiety capable of facilitating erection, but depression likely to inhibit it. This interpretation is consistent with their observations. At the same time, however, it raises the question why, in the earlier study by Hoon et al. (1977), women responded so differently to so similar a film. Why should men be depressed and women be scared by films depicting violent car accidents? Additionally, why should men be depressed by such depictions and respond with high anxiety to seeing others threatened with amputation of limbs? On the other hand, if the pretest findings concerning anxiety versus depression are accepted at face value, it can be speculated that depression may have had a suppressing effect on subsequent erection because of especially low levels of sympathetic excitation commonly associated with that state. Only the direct assessment of excitatory activity during these stimulus transitions will eventually clarify the mechanisms involved. Until such clarification, it would seem prudent to acknowledge that qualitatively different affective states may differently affect subsequent sexual arousal, and that only distress that respondents construe as anxiety has been shown to facilitate subsequent genital vasocongestion in both men and women.

The focus on genital vasocongestion in the studies by Hoon et al. (1977) and Wolchik et al. (1980) can be seen as narrow and taken to challenge further the claim that this research establishes the facilitation of sexual behavior and/or sexual experience through noxious prearousal. Although pronounced genital vasocongestion is an essential part of sexual activity and for men virtually indispensable, it does not, in and of itself, assure superior intensity or quality of sexual behavior and, in particular, sexual experience. It can be argued that such behavior and experience will be enhanced only to the extent that genital vasocongestion is accompanied by strong sympathetic activity. Can it be assumed that noxious prearousal furnished strong sympathetic reactions for transfer into sexual arousal and thus secured this type of accompaniment? Such transfer is strongly suggested by various related studies. Hare, Wood, Britain, and Frazelle (1971), for instance, exposed subjects to materials very similar to the accident films employed by Hoon et al. and by Wolchik et al. and observed distress responses associated with intense sympathetic reactions in both males and females. A similar investigation by Craig and Wood (1971) with male subjects corroborated these findings. It also showed that the peripheral manifestations of autonomic arousal associated with distress were virtually indistinguishable from those associated with sexual excitedness. It can be considered likely, then, that genital vasocongestion that is facilitated by distressing pretreatments will be accompanied by energizing excitatory responses that favor vigorous sexual action and that foster intense emotional experience.

The studies by Hoon et al. (1977), Wolchik et al. (1980), Hare et al. (1971), and Craig and Wood (1971), when considered together, may be viewed as highly suggestive of the involvement of sympathetic residues from preceding states in the enhancement of sexual excitedness, but they still do not establish it. The presumed involvement was directly demonstrated, however, in an investigation by Cantor, Zillmann, and Bryant (1975).

Affectively neutral strenuous exercise was employed to produce sympathetic excitation for transfer into males' responses to sexual stimulation. Prearousal enhancement of sexual excitedness was expected under conditions in which subjects were unlikely to recognize the source of prevailing residual excitation. Or alternatively, enhancement was not expected under conditions in which subjects either could correctly identify the source of residual excitation (as immediately after exertion, when heavy breathing and trembling hands were obtrusive reminders of the fact that they were still excited from exercise) or residues had become negligible. Three critical phases were determined by pretest: a first period in which subjects were still aroused from exercise (as measured in peripheral manifestations of sympathetic excitation) and perceived themselves as being still aroused from exertion; a second period in which subjects perceived themselves as having recovered but actually were still aroused from exertion; and a third period in which subjects perceived themselves as having recovered and actually had recovered. In the first phase, transfer is jeopardized by the person's inability to misconstrue residual excitation from exercise; the second phase constitutes the ideal transfer period; and the third phase serves as a control condition, as it is devoid of transferable residues.

Subjects in the main experiment again performed strenuous exercise and then were placed into one of the three predetermined phases for sexual stimulation. A

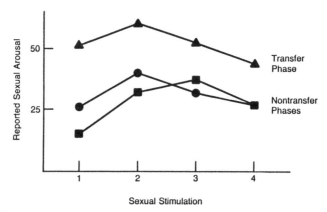

Sexual Stimulation

FIG. 7.6.   Facilitation of sexual excitedness by excitation transfer from exertion. Sexual stimulation occurred immediately following strenuous physical exercise when subjects perceived themselves as being aroused from the exercise (squares), in the transfer phase when subjects were still aroused from exercise but failed to recognize it (triangles), or after further delay when subjects had actually recovered and believed themselves to have recovered (circles). Only residual excitation that was not correctly attributed to its inducing condition facilitated sexual excitedness (adapted from Cantor, Zillmann, & Bryant, 1975).

film featuring coition served as the stimulus. It was halted at different times to allow subjects to record the degree to which they perceived themselves to be sexually excited. As can be seen from Fig. 7.6, the findings were fully consistent with the predictions. Sexual excitedness, compared against the control, was significantly enhanced during the transfer period only. Despite higher levels of residual excitation, it was particularly low during the first phase.

The findings lend strong support to the excitation-transfer explanation of the facilitation of sexual excitedness; and in so doing, they refocus attention on the implications of sympathetic commonality in the emergency emotions and on the significance of sympathetic excitedness for emotional experience. In practical terms, the findings project great generality for the enhancement of sexual experience and sexual behavior through prearousal. This is because they show the hedonic quality of prearousal to be immaterial. Nonetheless, because noxious experiences tend to instigate sympathetic reactions of greater intensity than do pleasant experiences, the agonistic emotions should outdo all others as pre-arousers of great potency. Arguing, quarreling, fighting, being threatened, being scared, and being beaten should all qualify as noxious, agonistic experiences that entail heightened sympathetic activity and that, hence, hold promise of enhancing sexual experiences that develop in the aftermath or materialize concurrently.

Facilitation of Sexual Attraction.   Excitation transfer is obviously not limited to the facilitation of sexual emotions in the immediate context of coition (i.e., precoital and coital behaviors associated with acute sexual excitedness), but should occur in sexual emotions that ultimately serve coition. Sexual attraction is a case in point. If such attraction is considered an experiential state that motivates sexual access and that is characterized by increased sympathetic activity, it should be subject to transfer facilitation just as any other sympathetic emotion.

A considerable amount of research has addressed this issue, usually under the headings *romantic* or *passionate love* (e.g., Walster, 1971). As this work is discussed at length elsewhere (Zillmann, 1983a), we review only the essentials here.

Dutton and Aron (1974) explored the relationship between fear and sexual attraction in a most imaginative series of field and laboratory experiments. Men who had just been frightened and men who had not were approached by an attractive female interviewer. In a Thematic Apperception Test (TAT) that she administered, the frightened men exhibited stronger sexual imagery than the nonfrightened. The frightened men also detected more sex appeal in the female interviewer. No such differences were observed when the interviewer was male. Additionally, the difference in sexual imagery and sexual attraction was observed only in men who were recently frightened, not after a delay (10 minutes) during which any fear-related excitedness presumably had dissipated. The findings are consistent with the view that residual excitation from fear can transfer into subsequently evoked sexual attraction and intensify it. As excitatory developments were not directly measured, the findings are open to alternative explanation, however.

Kenrick and Cialdini (1977) proposed such an explanation, arguing that the dissipation of noxious arousal—rather than surviving portions of affectively ambivalent excitation—promoted sexual attraction. Dutton and Aron's (1974) frightened men, in this view, may have experienced relief in the female's presence, and their feelings of comfort may have found expression in increased sexual attraction. Love, then, is seen as growing on the termination of turmoil, quarreling, and fighting—not on exploiting excitation from these aversive experiences.

In efforts to clarify what really happened in the earlier research, Kenrick, Cialdini, and Linder (1979) conducted a series of studies that closely followed the procedures of Dutton and Aron's (1974) laboratory experiment. Inexplicably, all these studies failed to replicate the earlier findings, and there seemed nothing left that needed explaining.

Not all research efforts resulted in failures to replicate, however. Dienstbier (1979) devised a new procedure and succeeded, for the most part, in demonstrating that residues from aversive arousal can enhance heterosexual liking. Essentially, he aroused men through startle and then assessed attraction to a female who had been present. The prearoused men were found to be more attracted to the female than were the nonaroused counterparts in the control condition. This finding is consistent with both the transfer and the relief explanation. Interestingly, replacement of the female by a male bystander reversed the results:

Prearoused men found this man less attractive than did their nonaroused counter-parts. This outcome accords with transfer predictions only if it is assumed that the affective response to the male bystander was one of dislike. It does not accord with the relief explanation, however, as relief was just as much a factor with the male as with the female target of attraction. Dienstbier was also able to replicate the earlier demonstration by Dutton and Aron (1974) that showed the prearousal enhancement of sexual attraction to be short-lived and to vanish with the dissipa-tion of residual excitation. Lastly, he showed that prearousal enhancement ap-plies to females' attraction to males as well as to males' attraction to females.

Recent research by White, Fishbein, and Rutstein (1981) provides further evidence against the relief explanation and in support of transfer projections concerning sexual attraction. These investigators confronted prearoused or non-aroused males with an attractive or an unattractive female and assessed the female's appeal under the various circumstances. In a first investigation, pre-arousal was accomplished by affectively neutral strenuous exercise. Compared with their not prearoused counterparts, prearoused males reported greater attrac-tion to the attractive female and less attraction to the unattractive female. Pre-arousal thus intensified the immediate affective reaction to the target person, making it better when good and worse when bad. This is exactly as predicted from the excitation-transfer paradigm. In a follow-up investigation, prearousal was accomplished by exposure to either a grisly account of mob killings or popular humor. Both treatments were found to be more arousing than an in-nocuous medical exposé used as a control stimulus. The findings fully replicated the first study in that both prearousal treatments produced the described divergent interaction. Hedonically opposite arousal treatments (i.e., horror, comedy) thus had perfectly parallel effects. Such an outcome is most damaging to the relief reasoning. It cannot be assumed that the measured positive affective reactions that were induced by exposure to comedy were followed by appreciable relief that could have fostered increased attraction. All things considered, the findings concerning the facilitation of sexual attraction through prearousal are entirely consistent with the transfer explanation. The transfer paradigm, then, deals with romantic inclinations just as effectively as with emotions of greater urgency— namely, acute sexual excitedness, precoital efforts, and coital activities.

SEXUAL BOREDOM AND INCIDENTAL REMEDIES

There can be little doubt that after considerable juvenile exuberance and some more mature indulgence with sex (cf. Kinsey, Pomeroy, & Martin, 1948; Kinsey, Pomeroy, Martin, & Gebhard, 1953), libidinal urges fade, and both men and women become less active sexually. The successive loss of sexual interest is most evident during the 40s, 50s, and 60s (e.g., Pfeiffer, Verwoerdt, & Davis,

1972). Interestingly, diminished interest often predates physical impairments that may come with age and that might explain the loss of libido. Robust reflexogenic control of coital preparedness is likely to be fully operative when psychogenic control starts to show symptoms of sluggishness and failure and renders potential potency just that: potential.

The treatment of coital readiness and coition as emergency emotions sheds lights on such developments. On the premise that (a) sympathetic excitedness is a vital part of sexual arousal, particularly its experiential quality, and that (b) psychogenically controlled sympathetic excitedness is subject to habituation, it can be proposed that loss of libido is often nothing less and nothing more than excitatory habituation to sexual stimuli (cf. Zillmann, 1983a). The characteristic comment of sexually dissatisfied intimates who are breaking up—namely, that "the excitement has gone" out of their relationship—epitomizes the suggested mechanics. Despite potentially unimpaired genital functioning, and frequently because of it, unexcited sexual activities are deemed drab and unfulfilling. Reliance on the reflexogenic control of sexual arousal through genital manipulation (i.e., through tactile stimulation) apparently is generally unappealing; and intimates would rather sense pulsating, sexual eagerness before the bodies make contact.

Nonetheless, sex-related excitatory habituation can be considered a fact of life. Excitatory reactions to essentially all stimulus conditions diminish with repeated exposure (cf. Buck, 1976; Grings & Dawson, 1978). Rigorous demonstrations of excitatory habituation in a strictly coital context with humans do not exist, however; and that for obvious reasons. But there are numerous investigations that pertain to the issue, and that consistently project habituation (cf. Zillmann, 1983a).

One of the most suggestive studies has been conducted by Michael and Zumpe (1978) with nonhuman primates. These investigators simulated the continual sexual receptivity of the human female by placing female rhesus monkeys into continual estrus. The treated females were joined with males in daily test sessions over a period of 4 years, and sexual activities were recorded during these sessions. The experiment's crucial variation was the replacement of the females with which the males were familiar by identically treated novel females at the beginning of the fourth year and the restoration of the initial situation after a month with the novel females. The findings show dramatic habituation of the sexual response to familiar females. After 3 year's time, sexual activity was a fraction of that during the first year. The introduction of novel females prompted libido and sexual activity to jump back to initial heights. The elevated activity levels were not sustained, however, when the familiar females were reintroduced. Despite maintenance of potency, there was no indication of any carryover from the resurgence of sexual action in the interim.

Demonstrations of the habituation of sexual excitedness in humans are limited to erotic materials. Repeated and potentially massive exposure to coital scenes has been found to diminish sympathetic reactions considerably, both in men and in women (Zillmann & Bryant, 1984). Genital vasocongestion in men has been found to diminish correspondingly (Reifler, Howard, Lipton, Liptzin, & Widmann, 1971). If the portrayal of eager bodies and sexual actions in living color thus fosters a loss of sexual excitedness, can it be assumed that exposure to usually less enticing and fewer bodies in the bedroom does not?

If findings such as these are any indication, one should expect loss of libido—especially through visual stimulation—among intimates who share their relationship for extended periods of time. The secure, frictionless relationship that provides great comfort to the parties involved would seem to be the most vulnerable. But regardless of who it might be whose "excitement has gone," the question arises as to what people do to restore the juvenile sexual urges they so treasure?

Humankind's oldest and probably most frequently called upon remedy for excitatory, sexual habituation is the change of sexual partners. Daring liaisons are antithetical to sexual boredom—because of sympathetic excitement to the brim that fuels sexual eagerness and coital experience; and not because greater swelling of phallus and clitoris, although such reactions may be part of the facilitated experience. According to the transfer model, acute guilt feelings should do just as well as a sense of danger in enhancing the passions.

And speaking of sexual passions, especially at extreme levels where they tend to be characterized as ecstasy, the delivery and/or reception of bodily pain has served as an enhancer for ages and across cultures (cf. Ford & Beach, 1951). The sympathetic accompaniment of acute pain is strong and effectively resists habituation. This has lead to the characterization of pain as the sex enhancer par excellence (cf. Zillmann, 1983a). It should not be a surprise, then, to find that painful stimulation—in the form of scratching and biting—is a rather popular ingredient of sexual engagements in contemporary society (e.g., Gebhard & Johnson, 1979; Hunt, 1974). To be sure, in its common utilization, pain is at low intensities and dominated by sexual sensations.

Excitatory habituation to sexual enticers such as the female body has also long been recognized intuitively and been fought accordingly. Lingerie and similar adornments of the body provide some degree of habituation-retarding stimulus variation (cf. Michael & Zumpe, 1978), and their contemporary mass consumption would seem to suggest that problems with excitatory habituation are widespread.

Technically, sexual adornments can be viewed as fetishes to which excitatory reactions are conditioned (cf. Rachman, 1966; Simon & Gagnon, 1969). The mechanisms through which these stimuli acquire the power to elicit sexual excitedness are essentially those of fetishes whose use, because of the extraordinary nature of the stimuli involved, tends to be classified as deviant practice (cf. McGuire, Carlisle, & Young, 1965). Through masturbatory or coital conditioning, potentially all initially neutral stimuli can become sexual stimuli—although some lend themselves better to that than others (cf. Zillmann, 1983a). But whatever their particulars, fetishes can be considered the most innocuous sex enhancers available. They are, essentially, arousers whose largely incidental ontogenesis is a private matter between stimulus and respondent and whose use does not demean or victimize anybody.

The so-called "pure theater" of sadomasochism, bondage and its kin, cannot make such claims. The arousing stimuli—whether considered to induce fright, triumph of domination, or joy of submission—seem too close to coercion and violence for an unqualified endorsement. And in its nontheatrical forms, sadism and masochism (i.e., flagellation, strangulation, etc.) are unlikely to be deemed wholesome—if only because of the occasional accidental mutilation or death of a devotee (cf. Zillmann, 1983a). Still, in theory, sadomasochism is a simple extension of the common scratching and biting that accompanies precoital and coital behavior. Both are mostly noncoercive forms of exploiting the sympathetic component of pain for increased sexual excitement.

Also in theory, the coercive attainment of sexual access, rape, should enhance sexual excitedness for the person who is callous enough to the welfare of others to commit such an atrocity. As we have seen earlier, the victim's terror is likely to foster superior conditions for coition; and the violator's hostile actions, together with fear of detection, can only add excitement to the sexual inclinations and actions. Rape obviously gives sexual access to those who have difficulties attaining it by noncoercive means (e.g., Groth, 1979). But the temptation might also exist in those who are both aggressively callous and blasé about sex. If there is any basis to Freud's earlier cited contention (see Section on Facilitation of Sexual Emotions) that libido thrives on obstacles and that they are created if necessary, we have cause for concern indeed. Sexual access has become a matter of convenience in contemporary western societies, and sexual coercion offers itself as a high-excitement, mania-promising solution to the tedium of habitual recreational sex.

But extreme solutions aside, there are clear indications in crosscultural research (cf. Ford & Beach, 1951) that in promiscuous societies—that is, in societies in which sexual access can be readily attained by noncoercive means— the deliberate involvement of pain in coition is far more popular than in non-promiscuous ones. Similar differences have been observed in contemporary western societies (cf. Hunt, 1974; Zillmann, 1983a). The promiscuous single person stands out as the type of person who is inclined to involve the infliction and/or reception of pain in precoital and coital activities. Is it callousness due to the fact that the relationships in question have no tomorrow, and the persons involved need not be concerned about the welfare of their mates? Or is it a selfish effort at maximizing sexual pleasure? Or is it both? At present, we cannot claim to know. But in exploring the peculiar mixtures of sexual and agonistic inclinations—inclinations that seem to gain popularity—the treatment of fight, flight, and coition as highly related emergency emotions appears to hold promise.

REFERENCES

Adolph, E. G. (1968). *Origins of physiological regulations.* New York: Academic Press.
Averill, J. R. (1982). *Anger and aggression: An essay on emotion.* New York: Springer-Verlag.
Ax, A. F. (1960). Psychophysiology of fear and anger. In L. J. West & M. Greenblatt (Eds.), *Explorations in the physiology of emotions* (Psychiatric Research Reports No. 12, pp. 167–175). Washington, DC: American Psychiatric Association.
Bard, P. (1940). The hypothalamus and sexual behavior. *Research Publications of the Association for Research in Nervous and Mental Diseases, 20,* 551–579.
Barfield, R. J., & Sachs, B. D. (1968). Sexual behavior: Stimulation by painful electrical shock to skin in male rats. *Science, 161,* 392–393.
Baron, R. A. (1974). The aggression-inhibiting influence of heightened sexual arousal. *Journal of Personality and Social Psychology, 30,* 318–322.
Baron, R. A. (1979). Heightened sexual arousal and physical aggression: An extension to females. *Journal of Research in Personality, 13,* 91–102.
Bartlett, F. (1956). Physiologic responses during coitus. *Journal of Applied Physiology, 9,* 469–472.
Beach, F. (1967). Cerebral and hormonal control of reflexive mechanisms involved in copulatory behavior. *Physiological Reviews, 47,* 289–316.
Bors, E., & Comarr, A. E. (1971). *Neurological urology.* Baltimore: University Park Press.
Buck, R. (1976). *Human motivation and emotion.* New York: Wiley.
Caggiula, A. R., & Eibergen, R. (1969). Copulation of virgin male rats evoked by painful peripheral stimulation. *Journal of Comparative and Physiological Psychology, 69,* 414–419.
Cannon, W. B. (1929). *Bodily changes in pain, hunger, fear and rage: An account of researches into the function of emotional excitement* (2nd ed.). New York: Appleton-Century-Crofts.
Cantor, J. R., Zillmann, D., & Bryant, J. (1975). Enhancement of experienced sexual arousal in response to erotic stimuli through misattribution of unrelated residual excitation. *Journal of Personality and Social Psychology, 32,* 69–75.
Cantor, J. R., Zillmann, D., & Einsiedel, E. F. (1978). Female responses to provocation after exposure to aggressive and erotic films. *Communication Research, 5,* 395–411.
Craig, K. D., & Wood, K. (1971). Autonomic components of observers' responses to pictures of homicide victims and nude females. *Journal of Experimental Research in Personality, 5,* 304–309.
Crosby, E. C., Humphrey, T., & Lauer, E. W. (1962). *Correlative anatomy of the nervous system.* New York: Macmillan.
Crouch, J. E. (1978). *Functional human anatomy* (3rd ed.). Philadelphia: Lea & Febiger.
Crowley, W. R., Popolow, H. B., & Ward, O. B., Jr. (1973). From dud to stud: Copulatory behavior elicited through conditioned arousal in sexually inactive male rats. *Physiology and Behavior, 10,* 391–394.
de Molina, F., & Hunsperger, R. W. (1957). Affective reactions obtained by electrical stimulation of the amygdala. *Journal of Physiology* (Proceedings of the Physiological Society), *138,* 29–30.
Dienstbier, R. A. (1979). Emotion-attribution theory: Establishing roots and exploring future perspectives. In H. E. Howe & R. A. Dienstbier (Eds.), *Nebraska Symposium on Motivation* (Vol. 26, pp. 237–306). Lincoln: University of Nebraska Press.
Donnerstein, E., Donnerstein, M., & Evans, R. (1975). Erotic stimuli and aggression: Facilitation or inhibition. *Journal of Personality and Social Psychology, 32,* 237–244.
Donnerstein, E., & Hallam, J. (1978). Facilitating effects of erotica on aggression against women. *Journal of Personality and Social Psychology, 36,* 1270–1277.
Dutton, D. G., & Aron, A. P. (1974). Some evidence for heightened sexual attraction under conditions of high anxiety. *Journal of Personality and Social Psychology, 30,* 510–517.
Ehrhardt, A. A. (1977). Prenatal androgenization and human psychosexual behavior. In J. Money & H. Musaph (Eds.), *Handbook of sexology* (Vol. 1, pp. 245–257). Amsterdam: Excerpta Medica.

Ford, C. S., & Beach, F. A. (1951). *Patterns of sexual behavior.* New York: Harper.

Fox, C. A., & Fox, B. (1969). Blood pressure and respiratory patterns during human coitus. *Journal of Reproduction and Fertility, 19,* 405–415.

Freud, S. (1940). Das Ökonomische Problem des Masochismus. In *Gesammelte Werke* (Vol. 13, pp. 369–383). London: Imago.

Freud, S. (1943). Beiträge zur Psychologie des Liebeslebens. In *Gesammelte Werke* (Vol. 8, pp. 65–91). London: Imago. (Original work published 1912)

Freud, S. (1958). *Abriss der Psychoanalyse.* Frankfurt: Fischer Bücherei (Original work published 1938)

Gajdusek, D. C. (1970, March). Physiological and psychological characteristics of Stone Age man. In *Engineering and Science* (pp. 26–33; 56–62). Symposium on Biological Bases of Human Behavior. Pasadena: California Institute of Technology.

Gebhard, P. H., & Johnson, A. B. (1979). *The Kinsey data: Marginal tabulations of the 1938–1963 interviews conducted by the Institute for Sex Research.* Philadelphia: Saunders.

Grings, W. W., & Dawson, M. E. (1978). *Emotions and bodily responses: A psychophysiological approach.* New York: Academic Press.

Groth, A. N. (1979). *Men who rape: The psychology of the offender.* New York: Plenum.

Guyton, A. C. (1972). *Structure and function of the nervous system.* Philadelphia: Saunders.

Hare, R., Wood, K., Britain, S., & Frazelle, J. (1971). Autonomic responses to affective visual stimulation: Sex differences. *Journal of Experimental Research in Personality, 5,* 14–22.

Hoon, P. W., Wincze, J. P., & Hoon, E. F. (1977). A test of reciprocal inhibition: Are anxiety and sexual arousal in women mutually inhibitory? *Journal of Abnormal Psychology, 86,* 65–74.

Hunt, M. (1974). *Sexual behavior in the 1970s.* New York: Dell Books.

Izard, C. E. (1977). *Human emotions.* New York: Plenum.

Janda, L. H., & Klenke-Hamel, K. E. (1980). *Human sexuality.* New York: Van Nostrand.

Kenrick, D. T., & Cialdini, R. B. (1977). Romantic attraction: Misattribution versus reinforcement explanations. *Journal of Personality and Social Psychology, 35,* 381–391.

Kenrick, D. T., Cialdini, R. B., & Linder, D. E. (1979). Misattribution under fear-producing circumstances: Four failures to replicate. *Personality and Social Psychology Bulletin, 5,* 329–334.

Kinsey, A. C., Pomeroy, W. B., & Martin, C. E. (1948). *Sexual behavior in the human male.* Philadelphia: Saunders.

Kinsey, A. C., Pomeroy, W. B., Martin, C. E., & Gebhard, P. H. (1953). *Sexual behavior in the human female.* Philadelphia: Saunders.

Leshner, A. I. (1978). *An introduction to behavioral endocrinology.* New York: Oxford University Press.

Levi, L. (1965). The urinary output of adrenalin and noradrenalin during pleasant and unpleasant emotional states: A preliminary report. *Psychosomatic Medicine, 27,* 80–85.

Levi, L. (1969). Sympatho-adrenomedullary activity, diuresis, and emotional reactions during visual sexual stimulation in human females and males. *Psychosomatic Medicine, 31,* 251–268.

Levi, L. (1972). Stress and distress in response to psychosocial stimuli: Laboratory and real life studies on sympathoadrenomedullary and related reactions. *Acta Medica Scandinavica* (Suppl. 528).

Luria, Z., & Rose, M. D. (1979). *Psychology of human sexuality.* New York: Wiley.

Luttge, W. G. (1971). The role of gonadal hormones in the sexual behavior of the rhesus monkey and human: A literature survey. *Archives of Sexual Behavior, 1,* 61–68.

MacLean, P. D. (1962). New findings relevant to the evolution of psychosexual functions of the brain. *Journal of Nervous and Mental Disease, 135,* 289–301.

MacLean, P. D. (1968a). Alternative neural pathways to violence. In L. Ng (Ed.), *Alternatives to violence: A stimulus to dialogue* (pp. 24–34). New York: Time-Life Books.

MacLean, P. D. (1968b). Contrasting functions of limbic and neocortical systems of the brain and their relevance to psychophysiological aspects of medicine. In E. Gellhorn (Ed.), *Biological foundations of emotion* (pp. 73–106). Glenview, IL: Scott, Foresman.

MacLean, P. D. (1973). Special Award Lecture: New findings on brain function and sociosexual behavior. In J. Zubin & J. Money (Eds.), *Contemporary sexual behavior: Critical issues in the 1970s* (pp. 53–74). Baltimore: Johns Hopkins University Press.

MacLean, P. D., & Ploog, D. W. (1962). Cerebral representation of penile erection. *Journal of Neurophysiology, 25,* 29–55.

MacLusky, N. J., & Naftolin, F. (1981). Sexual differentiation of the central nervous system. *Science, 211,* 1294–1303.

Malmo, R. B. (1965). Finger-sweat prints in the differentiation of low and high incentive. *Psychophysiology, 1,* 231–240.

Malmo, R. B. (1975). *On emotions, needs, and our archaic brain.* New York: Holt, Rinehart & Winston.

Marks, I. M. (1969). *Fears and phobias.* New York: Academic Press.

Masters, W. H., & Johnson, V. (1966). *Human sexual response.* Boston: Little, Brown.

McGuire, R. J., Carlisle, J. M., & Young, B. G. (1965). Sexual deviations as conditioned behaviour: A hypothesis. *Behaviour Research and Therapy, 2,* 185–190.

Meyer, T. P. (1972). The effects of sexually arousing and violent films on aggressive behavior. *Journal of Sex Research, 8,* 324–333.

Michael, R. P., & Zumpe, D. (1978). Potency in male rhesus monkeys: Effects of continuously receptive females. *Science, 200,* 451–453.

Nevin, J. A. (Ed.). (1973). *The study of behavior: Learning, motivation, emotion, and instinct.* Glenview, IL: Scott, Foresman.

Ovid. (1947). *[The art of love, and other poems]* (J. H. Mozley, trans.). Cambridge, MA: Harvard University Press.

Pfeiffer, E., Verwoerdt, A., & Davis, G. (1972). Sexual behavior of middle life. *American Journal of Psychiatry, 128,* 1262–1267.

Pick, J. (1970). *The autonomic nervous system.* Philadelphia: Lippincott.

Rachman, S. (1966). Sexual fetishism: An experimental analogue. *Psychological Record, 16,* 293–296.

Ramirez, J., Bryant, J., & Zillmann, D. (1982). Effects of erotica on retaliatory behavior as a function of level of prior provocation. *Journal of Personality and Social Psychology, 43,* 971–978.

Reifler, C. B., Howard, J., Lipton, M. A., Liptzin, M. B., & Widmann, D. E. (1971). Pornography: An experimental study of effects. *American Journal of Psychiatry, 128,* 575–582.

Russell, B. (1969). *The autobiography of Bertrand Russell: The middle years 1914–1944.* New York: Bantam.

Simon, W., & Gagnon, J. H. (1969). On psychosexual development. In D. A. Goslin (Ed.), *Handbook of socialization theory and research* (pp. 733–752). Chicago: Rand McNally.

Stern, R. M., Farr, J. H., & Ray, W. J. (1975). Pleasure. In P. H. Venables & M. J. Christie (Eds.), *Research in psychophysiology* (pp. 208–233). London: Wiley.

Sternbach, R. A. (1968). *Pain: A psychophysiological analysis.* New York: Academic Press.

Walster, E. (1971). Passionate love. In B. I. Murstein (Ed.), *Theories of attraction and love* (pp. 85–99). New York: Springer-Verlag.

Weiss, H. D. (1972). The physiology of human penile erection. *Annals of Internal Medicine, 76,* 793–799.

Whalen, R. E. (1966). Sexual motivation. *Psychological Review, 73,* 151–163.

White, G. L., Fishbein, S., & Rutstein, J. (1981). Passionate love and the misattribution of arousal. *Journal of Personality and Social Psychology, 41,* 56–62.

Wolchik, S. A., Beggs, V. E., Wincze, J. P., Sakheim, D. K., Barlow, D. H., & Mavissakalian, M. (1980). The effect of emotional arousal on subsequent sexual arousal in men. *Journal of Abnormal Psychology, 89,* 595–598.

Zillmann, D. (1971). Excitation transfer in communication-mediated aggressive behavior. *Journal of Experimental Social Psychology, 7,* 419–434.

Zillmann, D. (1978). Attribution and misattribution of excitatory reactions. In J. H. Harvey, W. Ickes, & R. F. Kidd (Eds.), *New directions in attribution research* (Vol. 2, pp. 335–368). Hillsdale, NJ: Lawrence Erlbaum Associates.

Zillmann, D. (1979). *Hostility and Aggression.* Hillsdale, NJ: Lawrence Erlbaum Associates.

Zillmann, D. (1980). Anatomy of suspense. In P. H. Tannenbaum (Ed.), *The entertainment functions of television* (pp. 133–163). Hillsdale, NJ: Lawrence Erlbaum Associates.

Zillmann, D. (1983a). *Connections between sex and aggression.* Hillsdale, NJ: Lawrence Erlbaum Associates.

Zillmann, D. (1983b). Transfer of excitation in emotional behavior. In J. T. Cacioppo & R. E. Petty (Eds.), *Social psychophysiology: A sourcebook* (pp. 215–240). New York: Guilford Press.

Zillmann, D., & Bryant, J. (1984). Effects of massive exposure to pornography. In N. M. Malamuth & E. Donnerstein (Eds.), *Pornography and sexual aggression* (pp. 115–138). New York: Academic Press.

Zillmann, D., Bryant, J., & Carveth, R. A. (1981). The effect of erotica featuring sadomasochism and bestiality on motivated intermale aggression. *Personality and Social Psychology Bulletin, 7,* 153–159.

Zillmann, D., Bryant, J., Comisky, P. W., & Medoff, N. J. (1981). Excitation and hedonic valence in the effect of erotica on motivated intermale aggression. *European Journal of Social Psychology, 11,* 233–252.

Zillmann, D., Hoyt, J. L., & Day, K. D. (1974). Strength and duration of the effect of aggressive, violent, and erotic communications on subsequent aggressive behavior. *Communication Research, 1,* 286–306.

Zillmann, D., Katcher, A. H., & Milavsky, B. (1972). Excitation transfer from physical exercise to subsequent aggressive behavior. *Journal of Experimental Social Psychology, 8,* 247–259.

Zillmann, D., & Sapolsky, B. S. (1977). What mediates the effect of mild erotica on annoyance and hostile behavior in males? *Journal of Personality and Social Psychology, 35,* 587–596.

8

Integrating Sex Research

Kathryn Kelley
State University of New York at Albany

The preceding chapters have presented a variety of approaches to the study of human sexual behavior. Using Byrne's metaphor introduced in chapter 1, the image of the elephant has been made clearer and more available to our scientific understanding through the authors' visions of the field. The utility of their approaches will, of course, depend on the ultimate criteria of scientific relevance—testability and success at prediction and explanation. With increasing professional respectability, the field of sexology will need to accept the responsibility for being scientifically accountable. Without that, even the elephant's image begins to fade, and we can retreat into our private fantasies of what a scientific understanding of sexuality could provide for us.

THEORETICAL BENEFITS OF SEXOLOGICAL RESEARCH

Among the benefits of sexological research is a potential for theoretical understanding of the wide variety of topics that are under investigation. Rather than assume that a given perspective is totally correct, we can be reminded that scientific advances rarely occur on the basis of only one perspective. They often progress by standing on the collective shoulders of previously accumulated empiricism and theory. Two points can be offered about the current state of sexology in this regard. First, integrative attempts at theorizing about sexuality now exist. These await the efforts and imaginations of both seasoned and novice sex researchers. From the conservative end of the political spectrum, the term *pornology* may be considered more appropriate to describe our endeavors. For sexologists, however, the challenge lies in the possibility of advancing the private experience of sexuality to a communicable level. Second, a great need exists for basic research on human sexuality—and resultant reports of studies that eschew the newsy empiricism of low-level fact-finding activities in favor of well-grounded methodology that can eventually provide better answers to questions raised by the sexual experience. Application of this knowledge toward the solution of problems can alleviate the vacuum found to occur when basic research is missing.

METHODOLOGICAL IMPROVEMENTS
IN SEXOLOGICAL RESEARCH

Besides the advantages of theoretical emphasis, scientific perspectives can give us an additional guide to better methodology. Research on sexuality has been no exception to the general trend toward improvements in methods found in the social sciences. Self-report instruments and the related surveys are, of course, subject to the difficulties of social desirability, reporting bias, omission, and simple forgetting, and have been subject to refinement as well. The problem of volunteer bias occurs in our studies as well as in other fields, and this known element results, in part, from the ethical needs for informed individuals participating in a sensitive research area. Also part of our methodology are ways to increase the use of informed consent techniques, although in this field it sometimes becomes unnecessary to inform our participants of deceptions so widely used in other parts of the social sciences. The reason for this is that deception appears to be used fairly infrequently. Our stimuli can have comparatively great impact on participants, thus making deception a superfluous technique.

Methodological and ethical concerns like these can be cited unfairly in order to cast doubt on controversial or disagreeable research findings. Among college undergraduates taking our human sexuality courses, for example, students sometimes object to findings because of confounds due to volunteer bias, and so on. The temptation appears to be great to dismiss findings or theories because they disagree with our own experiences or authority's dictates.

Purely methodological research can give us more effective vehicles for uncovering knowledge about sexuality. Some better methods are an end in themselves; for other methodological research a goal seems to be not improvement, but an antiscientific bias designed to stop research because it is viewed as having so many related difficulties as to make it meaningless. This negative activity of discouraging scientific activity may convince some to adopt that position. The danger is that repeated attacks due to antisexual and antiscientific bias may stem the promising tide of new knowledge; we can continue to anticipate that detractors will contribute to the field in the ways they apparently deem appropriate.

COMPARISON OF METHODS

A more positive tack would be to illustrate some productive techniques for arriving at these findings. Because this volume's contributors outline several facets to sexuality, it should be possible to describe ways to capitalize on the different approaches. Let us examine the different routes implied by these perspectives, by introducing a particular finding based in the psychosexual tradition and consider the effect of varying the conceptual emphasis. In my laboratory, college students volunteered to view brief erotic films at 24-hour intervals across a 1-week span. The purpose of the study was to determine whether both sexes' affective responses and sexual arousal responses would become more negative and less intense, respectively, with repeated exposure to the same explicit film of heterosexual intercourse. The results confirmed this hypothesis. A second hypothesis concerned the effects of the content of the film shown at the fifth experimental session. Some subjects viewed a film of the same actors performing oral-genital acts, while others saw a new set of actors engaging in heterosexual intercourse. Thus, it was possible to compare the effects of changing to the different activity or to different actors. A sex difference emerged, such that males indicated greater arousal in response to new actors, whereas for females, the greater excitatory stimulus was the change to oral–genital acts by the same actors. On a psychological level, participants expressed concern about the stimulus in the same pattern found for self-reported sexual arousal. Thus, females indicated greater concern about the new acts, whereas males did so with respect to new actors.

An important point to make about the results of this study concerns possible overlap with the predictions of other approaches to sexuality. A tenet of one biosexual perspective includes sex differences, in which males respond more favorably to variety in partners than females. This prediction, supported by some animal findings, was partially supported by these results. Whether the sex difference represents a learned response bias only on a psychological level could be revealed by physiological recordings, also discussed in this volume. If the physiological response patterns mirror the self-report data on sexual arousal and concern, we would have additional evidence for the validity of the biological hypothesis.

The sociological and cross-cultural perspective could be integrated into this research as well. The demographic backgrounds of the actors could be varied along with that of the respondents. How do individuals respond to erotic acts performed by those similar to and different from themselves in social class, age, race, and so on? Similarity could be hypothesized to have more positive effects than dissimilarity, for example. For erotic actors performing acts disapproved by the viewers, such as oral-genital activity for those with negative sexual attitudes, the interaction of background and sexual attitudes might occur. The few studies of repeated exposure to erotica have only been undertaken in the United States, yet the phenomenon of erotic satiation and renewed interest undoubtedly occurs worldwide and perhaps takes different forms in a variety of cultures. In addition, what is the effect of viewing others who violate our norms, follow scripts different from our own, or play roles that are not part of our repertoire?

The social psychological theory advanced by Zillmann also has relevance to this study. What, for example, would be the behavioral and attitudinal outcome of the different film effects demonstrated here? Would different audiences respond less antisocially following repeated erotic exposure, if a follow-up film could circumvent the subsequent antisocial behavior? The combinative effects of compounded sources of arousal might also occur, perhaps by incorporating positive emotional components such as humor or love into the erotic theme.

Possibilities abound for the design and execution of studies related to this one finding, if the implications are drawn from the different perspectives. The approaches may even be combined in an integrative attempt at demonstrating their utility. The possibility therefore exists for examining a given sexual phenomenon in its different aspects, all of which can contribute new and potential useful knowledge about sexuality as a component of human responding.

DIMENSIONS USED TO COMPARE APPROACHES

The alternative approaches presented in this volume can be examined with respect to a number of dimensions, presented in Table 8.1. These dimensions were chosen on the basis of themes, similarities, and differences recurring in the authors' summaries. Therefore, these dimensions grew out of the specific approaches and may not apply to a different set of viewpoints. The theoretical considerations, content differences, and mechanisms may provide a reasonable vehicle for analyzing their contributions.

With respect to theoretical considerations, the focus may be comprehensive or specific. A specific focus would delineate a relatively limited area for examination, whereas a comprehensive one would attempt to examine the major portion of phenomena of interest. Kenneth Spence's comparison of the theory of the pendulum with that of relativity probably applies here. Second, the theoretical presentation itself may have varying goals, either to propose or support a theory or to describe a general approach. Having an axe to grind, as it is sometimes phrased, may be one outcome of the initial, descriptive work. A third dimension consists of the degree of novelty and controversy embodied within the framework, compared to the traditional, generally accepted nature of its tenets.

Content differences occurred repeatedly in these presentations, including whether individual development was a primary focus. Some approaches identified socialization as a primary determinant, whereas others adopted a basic

Table 8.1
Comparisons Made Among Chapters
in Regard to Theoretical Considerations,
Content Differences, and Mechanisms

Theoretical Focus:	Comprehensive vs. Specific
Theoretical Presentation:	Proposed or Supported vs. Descriptive
Theoretical Viewpoint:	Novel, Controversial vs. Traditional, Generally Accepted

Content Differences

Individual Development:	Life-Span Developmental vs. Nondevelopmental
Primary Determinant:	Socialization vs. Biological Input
Cultural Centrality:	Culture-Subculture Central vs. Noncentral

Mechanisms

Range of Phenomena:	Wide vs. Narrow
Resolution:	Predictions Offered vs. Conclusions Drawn
Base of Empirical Support:	Strong vs. Suggestive

biological input. A third source of variation in content, cultural centrality, also appeared.

The viewpoints seemed to function on the basis of different mechanisms as well. In order to support their analyses, some used a wide range of phenomena as examples. Others selected only a few for intensive examination. Their resolution of the possibilities and opportunities thus raised also varied, some offering fairly specific sets of predictions and others drawing conclusions from which predictions may originate. They also sought different degrees of empirical support.

COMPARISONS AMONG THE METHODS

The outline in Table 8.2 describes the alternative approaches on the basis of these dimensions. With respect to theoretical focus, McKinney outlined a fairly comprehensive picture of different sociological perspectives. The other authors tended to restrict their foci: Fisher on affective-psychological theory; Gallup on evolutionary theory; Gregerson on anthropological data; Rosen and Beck on physiological measurement; and Zillmann on emotion and coition. Fisher, Gallup, and Zillmann proposed or supported specific theories, whereas the remaining three sets of authors gave descriptive accounts of their and others' work. By proposing that individuals compete for sexual and reproductive success, Gallup proposed a novel viewpoint that may evoke considerable controversy. Zillmann's application of excitation transfer theory to sexual arousal and behavior

Table 8.2
Comparisons Applied to Chapters

Author and Topic	Theoretical Considerations	Content Differences	Mechanisms
Fisher on Affective-Psychological Theory	Specific Focus Supported Theory Traditional View	Life-span Developmental Socialization Culture Not Central	Strong Empirical Base Specific Predictions Offered Wide Range of Phenomena
Gallup on Evolutionary Theory	Specific Focus Proposed Theory Novel, Controversial View	Developmental Biological Input Culture Not Central	Suggestive Empirical Base Conclusions Drawn Wide Range of Phenomena
Gregerson on Anthropological Theory	Specific Focus Descriptive Traditional View	Nondevelopmental Socialization Culture Central	Strong Empirical Base Specific Predictions Offered Wide Range of Phenomena
McKinney on Sociological Theory	Comprehensive Focus Descriptive Traditional View	Developmental Socialization Culture-subculture Central	Strong Empirical Base Conclusions Drawn Wide Range of Phenomena
Rosen and Beck on Physiological Measurement	Specific Focus Descriptive Traditional View	Nondevelopmental Biological Input Culture Not Central	Strong Empirical Base Conclusions Drawn Narrow Range of Phenomena
Zillmann on Emotion and Coition	Specific Focus Proposed Theory Novel, Controversial View	Nondevelopmental Biological Input Culture Not Central	Strong Empirical Base Specific Predictions Offered Narrow Range of Phenomena

also qualifies it for the novel, controversial category. The remaining perspectives described more traditional, generally accepted positions. The ubiquitous characterizations of sexuality as having sociological, affective-psychological, culturally based, and potentially measurable substrates are examined in detail by the other authors.

The analyses vary with respect to content. Some posited that the stage of individual development affected the sexual outcomes, although not in the maturational terms indicated by developmental psychologists. The evolutionary (Gallup) and sociological (McKinney) chapters described this factor, whereas Fisher's contribution on affect and psychology additionally mentioned aging in a life-span approach. The primary determinant was variously identified either as primarily socialization in the affective psychological, sociological, and anthropological contributions. In contrast, the evolutionary (Gallup), measurement (Rosen and Beck), and emotional (Zillmann) viewpoints adopted biological input as the primary determinant. Cultural and/or subcultural variation appeared as the central focus in the anthropological and sociological chapters, although Fisher did mention this source of influence.

The mechanisms used by the contributors to support their cases also varied, ranging from the examination of many phenomena as examples and applications in the evolutionary, sociological, affective-psychological, and anthropological views. Rosen and Beck on measurement, and Zillmann on emotion-coition, differed from the others by focusing on only a few phenomena in some depth. Some, such as Gregerson on anthropology, Zillmann on emotion, and Fisher on affect, regularly offered specific predictions. Gallup's evolutionary view suggested two areas of prediction on sexual attraction and homosexuality. Others preferred to draw more general conclusions, leaving it mainly to the fertile imaginations of their readers to develop hypotheses about sociological and measurement issues. For the base of empirical support, the authors presented generally strong empirical work on humans, although evolutionary theory gave a number of illustrations from animal data.

The approaches varied with respect to the dimensions developed in Table 8.1. They differed to the extent that it appears no particular pattern of theoretical analysis was adopted among any subgroup of authors. Thus, for example, the descriptive technique was associated with socialization as a primary determinant in two out of the three cases. A majority of the contributions was characterized by strong empirical support, specific theoretical focus, a traditional viewpoint, and a wide range of phenomena used to support their position. Their variations in strategy suggest a richness and promise that may stimulate greater efforts to uncover the empirical foundations of human sexuality. The prospects for understanding are impressive, as revealed in these authors' contributions.

Author Index

Italics denote pages with bibliographic information.

Subject Index

A

Aboriginal America, 100–101
Aboriginal Australia, 99
Adultery, 97
Agonistic emotions, 181–184
  facilitation of, 182–184
America, 101
Anal intercourse, *see* Foration
Anovulation, 27, 29, 31
Anthropological theory (of sexuality), 87–101,
  206
Arousal, *see* Sexual response cycle or Sexual
  pleasure
  physiological components of,
  see sex, physiology of
  psychological components of, 45, 46, 55–
    57, 60, 67–68, 74, 76, 131–165
  see *also sex,* and cognitions; sex, and emo-
    tions; sex and expectancies; sex, and
    fantasies; sex, and attitudes
  subjective estimates of, see Arousal, psy-
    chological components of
Attraction
  facilitation of, 190–192

B

Bestiality, *see* Zoophilia
Black Africa, 97–98

Biosexology, 4–5, 7
Bipedalism, 33–36
Birth control, 9, 16, 44, 101, 105, 113, 144,
  145, 146
Bisexuality, 16
Breasts, 28–33
Bystander apathy, 18

C

Cancer, 15–16
Case studies, 114
Causal relationships, 112–123, 124, 114
Cervix, 57
Chastity, 97, 98
  see also Virginity
Chastity belts, 20
Child molestation, *see* Pedophilia
Circular reasoning, 13
Circumcision, 92, 07
Cisvestism, 95
Classical conditioning, 134–135, 155
Clitoridectomy, 92, 97
Clitoris, 57, 92
Conception, 27, 28, 31, 44
Concubines, 98
Conflict theory, 111–112, 117
Contraception, *see* Birth control
Control groups, 114
Copulation, *see* Sex